AWAKE!
FOR THE SAKE OF THE FUTURE

RUDOLF STEINER (1923)

AWAKE!
FOR THE SAKE OF THE FUTURE

12 Lectures given in Dornach, January 5 through 28, 1923

Translated by Jann W. Gates

RUDOLF STEINER

SteinerBooks

CW 220

SteinerBooks
Anthroposophic Press

610 Main Street
Great Barrington, Massachusetts 01230
www.steinerbooks.org

Translated by Jann W. Gates.

This book is volume 220 in the Collected Works (CW) of Rudolf Steiner, published by SteinerBooks, 2014. It is a translation of the German (GA 220) *Lebendiges Naturerkennen Intellektueller Sündenfall und spirituelle Sündenerhebung,* published by Verlag der Rudolf Steiner-Nachlassverwaltung, Dornach, Switzerland 1982.

Library of Congress Cataloging-in-Publication Data is available on request.

Print ISBN: 978-1-62148-105-8
eBook ISBN: 978-1-62148-106-5

CONTENTS

INTRODUCTION

My dear friends: you have come together this Christmas, some of you from distant places, to work in the Goetheanum... in the field of spiritual science. At the outset of our considerations I would like to extend to you—especially the friends who have come from afar—our heartiest Christmas greetings. Indications offered in my lectures, and in those of others, will, we hope, result in a harmony of feeling and thinking among those gathered together here in the Goetheanum. It is also my hope that those friends who are associated with the Goetheanum and more or less permanently reside here will warmly welcome those who have come from elsewhere. Through our working, thinking and feeling together, there will develop what must be the very soul of all endeavors at the Goetheanum, namely, our perceiving and working out of the spiritual life and essence of the world.

—Rudolf Steiner's opening remarks at the beginning of the course, *The Origins of Natural Science* (CW 326), December 24, 1922.

As participants gathered in the Great Hall of the first Goetheanum for Rudolf Steiner's opening address at the Christmas conference in 1922, it was clear that the anthroposophic nucleus in Dornach would be enhanced and enlivened by the presence of anthroposophists and visitors who lived and worked elsewhere. Just as the Goetheanum had been built by workers and volunteers from seventeen nations in the midst of World War I, the 1922 Christmas conference also drew participants from a broad geographic area. From Steiner's point of view this would be an opportunity for people to experience shared interests and goals regardless of differences in language and their individual commitments to anthroposophic initiatives. No one could have imagined that on Christmas Eve 1922 they soon would forge a bond for having witnessed together the destruction by fire of the Goetheanum on the night of December 31, 1922, to the morning of January 1, 1923.

During January 1923 Rudolf Steiner gave the twelve lectures published in this volume. The common thread in these talks is Steiner's affirmation that human beings have the capacity to fulfill the intertwined destinies of humanity and the planet Earth. There is an unusually strong interplay between the themes and examples Steiner selected and their immediate application to the needs of the anthroposophic movement in 1923. The magnitude of the loss of the first anthroposophic center hovered over the second week of the Christmas conference. When the lectures in this volume began on Friday, January 5, 1923 (they were held on Friday, Saturday, and Sunday for each of the four weekends that month), they attracted an influx of participants whose interest and sympathy had been heightened by the loss of the Goetheanum. One senses that Rudolf Steiner responded to spoken and unspoken questions being raised by the participants in the course; and that he chose examples that shed light on the tragic event, the consequences of which were not yet clear. Suddenly the question of one's personal relationship to anthroposophy seemed to be at stake. If, as Rudolf Steiner proposed, individuals should pursue all aspects of their lives from an anthroposophic perspective, what would that imply? If indeed an anthroposophic viewpoint could transform the way human beings understand the nature and cultivation of human capacities, acquire knowledge of the natural world, nurture human relations, and try to grasp the cosmos in the fullness of its spiritual realities, how would that shed light on human history and the future of modern societies?

The tone of individual lectures varied. Sometimes Steiner gently inspired and encouraged his listeners. On other occasions, he spoke with heightened intensity about persistent misconceptions, and candidly acknowledged the shortcomings of anthroposophists themselves. Again and again, in utter seriousness, his concern for the future of anthroposophy resounded in the crowded carpentry workshop: "Wake up." At every turn a question flickered in the silence: "Now what must we do?"

In the opening lecture of January 5, 1923, Rudolf Steiner struck a positive note. He spoke of the present day as "a time of the first light of a new day" in which human beings can generate through their own powers and capacities a living knowledge of Christ. The inner light, that is, the thought-generating capacity of the I was no longer an empty figure of speech. "The I has become the supporting essence and core of the strengthened soul." An anthroposophic perspective that acknowledged the spiritual nature of the cosmos also allowed individuals to experience the contemporary longing for the living Christ. "We must replace the Christ of oral and written tradition with a living Christ.... The revelation of Christ [now] speaks out of the spiritual world and into our thinking striving for illumination, into our feeling hearts, and into our will-filled humanity." Rudolf Steiner issued a bold challenge as he opened one of the first courses of 1923.

It is not certain that Rudolf Steiner had planned to speak further on the theme of "Meeting Humanity's New Need for Christ" on January 6. It seems more likely that he decided in the moment to respond to the empathy streaming from the entire audience, and to address the urgent need to bridge differences between older generations of anthroposophists and the recent infusion of young people who were being drawn to anthroposophy in post-World War I societies buffeted by political, economic, and cultural crises. Steiner was moved by the soul poignancy and will forces of the younger generation, and he paused to welcome specifically the university students and young professionals who were present. This younger generation was looking for approaches to science, the humanities, the arts, and the professions that were more substantive, more ethical, and more practical than what they found in the universities where they had studied. They wanted to know if and how anthroposophy could redirect entire fields of knowledge into more fruitful paths, and they longed to nurture a meaningful life within their souls.

Steiner asked the older members in the audience to imagine themselves within the experience of the younger generation. He described how the shortcomings in contemporary education affected the soul life of young people, yet left unaddressed their yearning to enter into their academic disciplines in a way that touched their hearts and their humanity. Members of the audience could experience inwardly what the students and young professionals faced in their lives and could grasp the deeper reasons why young people wanted to understand the nature of the human being and discover insights that would help them to transform practical aspects of modern civilization. Steiner concluded his remarks with an appeal for all generations to join forces on behalf of anthroposophy.

> May the younger people bring their very best; may the older people understand the best offered by the younger people; may understanding be extended from one to the other. Let us move beyond the solemn days we have just experienced, beyond the grief that still hovers over us. Let decisions be more than wishes or accolades. Let our decisions penetrate our hearts and reside so deeply within our souls that they become deeds.
>
> The deeds of the young, when they are achieved in the right way, will be cosmically significant deeds. The greatest beauty that will be created by an older person will be working together with human beings who are still capable of accomplishing "youthful" deeds. If you grasp this, you will be able to meet the younger generation with understanding. Through the beautiful examples offered by the older people to compensate for our loss, the young people will be able to see what will benefit the future and what also will satisfy their own inner well-being. Let each one of us see in the other what is just and imbued with strength. Let strength generate and empower strength. Only then shall we move forward together.

On the third evening, January 7, 1923, Steiner created a vivid imagination of the human being supported by the subtle imaginative impressions rising from the metals deep within the earth, on the one hand, and the rays of inspiration descending from the stars to human beings, on the other hand. Thus on the first weekend, those present were given encouragement about the potential of their human capacities, challenged to work together with good will and generosity on behalf of anthroposophy, and placed imaginatively within a cosmos that extended from the center of the earth to the furthest expanse of the universe.

In lectures four and five during the second weekend of the course, January 12 and 13, 1923, Steiner explored the biographies of three contemporaries of the sixteenth and seventeenth centuries who represented very different ways of understanding the human being in relation to the cosmos, and the relation of the cosmos to the human being. Anthroposophic insight illuminated the efforts of Jacob Boehme (1575–1624), Giordano Bruno (1548–1600), and Francis Bacon (1561–1626), to reach an understanding of a fundamental question; and he revealed what had escaped the grasp of each one. Steiner also pointed out the individual legacies of the three men for the modern era. The importance of appreciating different viewpoints held by contemporaries could not have been lost upon Steiner's audience in which a variety of anthroposophic perspectives were represented.

On January 14, 1923, the culminating lecture of the second weekend, Steiner spoke about "The Sleep of Civilization in the Present Era." Since the nineteenth century, popular culture has assumed that human history unfolds in a predictable, positive, linear progression. But, Steiner pointed out, there are times when destructive forces take the upper hand and simply erase a cultural legacy. This occurred in the late Hellenistic era; that is, in the fourth and fifth centuries of the Common Era (c.e.), when classical Greek temples, treasures and libraries were intentionally destroyed. The bitterest blow was the closing of the School of Philosophy in Athens in 529 c.e. Thereafter some efforts to preserve classical culture took place, but "whatever had a connection with the [classical Greek] past had to disappear and indeed these traces *did* disappear." Is it possible to destroy the fruits of human creativity in modern times, just as it occurred in ancient times? No one walking past the bare foundation that once supported the Goetheanum doubted the potential of a determined and destructive act of will.

Typically when human beings describe the consciousness of humanity in other epochs, they are under the influence of their own era and culture. The ancient Greek experienced as a vivid reality the soul-spiritual nature of the human being and sought to express the beauty of this hidden reality in artistic forms. Moderns may admire the "ideal" beauty that the ancient Greeks incorporated in their architecture, sculpture, and painting, but often lament that classical Greek art ignored the beautiful mosaic of individuality in the "real" world of human beings. If we imagine an ancient Greek who could look into the future and perceive the fundamental differences between classical Greece and our modern focus on sense perception, we would hear a different point of view. The ancient Greek would argue that the ancient Greeks were awake, and materialistic modern human beings are the ones who are asleep, because moderns are narrow-minded and have lost sight of the search for the essential, the true nature of the human being.

Steiner recognized the widespread symptoms of a sleeping civilization in the twentieth century. Anthroposophists would have to awaken through their energetic grasp of thinking, "for this awakened thinking leads you into everything else." Moreover, if the Anthroposophical Society wanted to be a reality, the living, streaming experience of love would have to be the foundation of mutual trust. He concluded the sixth address at the end of the second weekend of the course with the following expectation: "Think! Feel! Meditate on being awake! The esoteric task within the Anthroposophical Society today is the will to awaken. An awakened Anthroposophical Society will be the ray of light that shall ignite the will to awaken our entire present-day civilization."

During the third weekend of the course, Steiner began with an exploration of truth, beauty, and goodness. This lecture has been translated into various languages and frequently is published as a single lecture. In the twenty-first century a reader initially may be skeptical about the title "Truth, Beauty, Goodness." What can a philosopher, or any other writer for that matter, say that would be new on the subject of human ideals? And if the text is published without the third and fourth lectures in this volume (in which Steiner speaks about Jacob Boehme, Giordano Bruno, and Francis Bacon in relation to pre-earthly existence, the present, and post-earthly existence respectively), it may be a shock to see correspondences between truth, human physicality, and pre-earthly existence; threads linking beauty, etheric forces within the human being, and the present; and the idea that goodness expressed in moral deeds sows seeds for the future on behalf of the spiritual world. On the other hand, a reader may become engrossed in this refreshing approach to truth, beauty, and goodness.

In the eighth lecture, given on January 20, 1923, Rudolf Steiner touches upon the relationship between human beings and the elemental beings in nature, and then gives two specific examples of cultivating a living knowledge of nature. He encourages scientists, rather than to dissect the corpse of a fish to grasp its essential nature, to observe carefully and accurately the living fish in relation to the flow of water in which it is swimming, and the effects of the warmth and light from the sun. Another example follows: one observes closely how a bird receives its form in response to the air and sunlight in which it lives and moves. This, Steiner proposed, is the appropriate path leading to a living knowledge of animal physiology.

In the second half of that lecture Rudolf Steiner gives the anthroposophic movement direct responsibility for changing conventional modes of thinking and forming a new consensus of reality. He returns to the ideals of truth, beauty, and goodness presented on the previous day and places the ideals in relation to individual human beings and then in juxtaposition to nature and society.

Cultivating truth is the duty of the individual—a daunting task in the present age in which prejudice and indifference to careful observation abound. A sharpened awareness of truth allows us to enter the reality and experience of living creatures in nature, and to cultivate a feeling-imbued thinking about nature. Applying our enlivened powers of observation and thinking in the social realm, we can experience everything that is of interest or concern to the human beings around us.

> We cannot fulfill our true humanity if we are concerned only with self-knowledge. Today we must be linked to common universal humanity, our only relevant reality for human beings. We can live as human beings only by living in our social life. We must experience who others really are, what they experience with others. We must feel what others are feeling within themselves.

In the course of the ninth, tenth, and eleventh lectures, January 21, 26, and 27, 1923, Rudolf Steiner gives a memorable account of how, under medieval Scholasticism, an "intellectual fall" was incorporated into the much older tradition of the moral fall of the human being. The Fall of Humanity (what religions call a fall from divine grace or a loss of innocence through the knowledge of evil) marks the beginning of the historical development of humanity.

A consciousness of moral sinfulness typified the entire medieval Christian era; however, under the influence of Scholasticism in the twelfth and thirteenth centuries, the intellect was assimilated into the descriptions of moral sinfulness. The intellect is a powerful human capacity; but because of its human origin, it also bore the taint of human baseness. When, under Scholasticism, the intellect was declared fit only to examine the sense world, by implication the intellect was disqualified from investigating spiritual reality. Indeed knowledge of religious truth was assigned to the power of revelation and the transmission of divine guidance recorded in sacred records. Today human beings have forgotten that the exclusion of the intellect from spiritual investigations is a direct legacy of the medieval understanding of the moral Fall of Humanity.

In the fifteenth century the awareness of human freedom and independence emerged alongside the knowledge of the Fall. This opened a preparatory stage in humanity's struggle to develop self-generated discernment and decision-making, rather than to depend on the direct guidance of divine power. The Scholastic endorsement of the intellect to investigate nothing other than the material world passed directly into the modern natural-scientific perspective. The tenant of human baseness was put aside, but modern natural scientists are no less adamant that "limits" to human knowledge exist, and they declare just as dogmatically as the Scholastics that human beings can investigate only the sense world.

Rudolf Steiner acknowledged that the Scholastics still were connected to an earlier feeling-imbued thinking, and could imagine that a living spirituality flowed into their concepts. They also experienced the archetypal world as "real." However, they assumed the origin of human thoughts came from without rather than being generated in the depths of the soul.

Rudolf Steiner approached knowledge in light of a different goal, one that takes into account the human potential in our day, which draws thinking, feeling, and willing into a common alliance. It is possible for human beings to cultivate pure thinking out of their own inner activity. This will-generated thinking can be linked to a moral impulse and made manifest in deeds.

In our era humanity is capable of moving beyond the Fall. Human beings can acquire knowledge of the spiritual world when the intellect has been filtered through pure thinking. The moral and intellectual Fall can be overcome through self-generated human capacities. A new path can lead us to the spiritualization of knowledge and to a renewal of our recognition of the spiritual nature of the cosmos.

> In *The Philosophy of Freedom* I wanted to say: look into the depths of your soul. There you will find the remnant of a genuine and energetic thinking arising out of the inner self; a pure thinking that is more than ordinary thinking, a thinking that can generate a feeling-imbued knowledge, a thinking that lives in the human will. And this enlivened, pure thinking, working together with the will, can become the impulse for moral actions. In this context I have spoken about a moral intuition that is inspired by and permeated with moral imagination. But this can become a living reality only if the path you choose (even in the face of the increasing separation of the human being and human intellect from the divine-spiritual) is the path that leads you once more to the divine-spiritual. If you can discover spirituality in nature, then you also shall find the spirit in the human being.

In spite of (or partly because of) the sober reality of the first Goetheanum's being utterly consumed by fire, the lectures in this volume intentionally apply an anthroposophic perspective to biographies, theories of knowledge, scientific methods and discoveries, aesthetics, theology and philosophy, and the changing capacities of the human being and societies over the course of history. The present era with its possibilities for expanding the knowledge of nature and the cosmos, developing new human capacities and beneficial initiatives, contrasts sharply with the potential to endanger the future through indifference and devastating error. Every day we witness compassionate, generous deeds and pioneering innovations in support of nature and healthy societies as well as terrifying waves of willful exploitation of natural resources and indifference toward human deprivation and suffering. These lectures given in January 1923 clarify and confirm ways in which the destinies of humanity and the planet Earth can be fulfilled. Parallels exist between the world of 1923 and the planet Earth in the twenty-first century. The importance of these insights is clear even as we read them nearly a century after they were presented in 1923.

Let me conclude by bringing to you the words spoken by Rudolf Steiner on the first anniversary of the Goetheanum fire. The vision and the task still ring true:

> My dear friends, yesterday was the anniversary of the day on which we saw the tongues of flame devouring our old Goetheanum. Today we may hope—since a year ago we did not allow even the flames to distract us from continuing with our work—today we may hope that when the physical Goetheanum stands here once more, we shall have worked in such a way that the physical Goetheanum is only the external symbol for our spiritual Goetheanum, which we want to take with us as an idea as we now go out into the world.

— Rudolf Steiner, "The Responsibility Incumbent on Us," Final lecture given during the Christmas Conference, January 1, 1924. *The Christmas Conference...* 1923/1924. USA: Anthroposophic Press, 1990, p. 269.

Jann W. Gates,
Mexico City, October 2013

Selected lectures by Rudolf Steiner on modern science and the relationship of anthroposophy to fields of knowledge are listed in chronological order:

Rudolf Steiner, "Anthroposophy among the Sciences," April 8, 1922, and "Anthroposophy and the Arts," April 9, 1922, in *Damit der Mensch ganz Mensch werde: Die Bedeutung der Anthroposophie im Geistesleben der Gegenwart* (6 lectures, [Haager Hochschulkurs],The Hague, April 7-12, 1922, GA 82). Basel: Rudolf Steiner Verlag, 1994.

_____, *Anthroposophy Has Something to Add to Modern Sciences* (8 lectures, Zurich, November 5-14, 1917; October 8-17, 1918, CW 73). United Kingdom: Rudolf Steiner Press, 2005.

_____, *Anthroposophy and Science: Observation, Experiment, Mathematics* (8 lectures, [Freien anthroposophischen Hochschulkurs] Stuttgart, March 16-23, 1921, CW 324) Spring Valley: Mercury Press, 1991.

————, *Die Aufgabe der Anthroposophie gegenueber Wissenschaft und Leben* (Darmstaedt, [Darmstaedter Hochschulkurs], July 27-31, 1921, GA 77a). Dornach: Rudolf Steiner Verlag, 1997.

————, *The Origins of Natural Science* (9 lectures, Dornach, December 24, 1922-January 6, 1923, CW 326). Great Barrington, MA: SteinerBooks, 1996.

————, *Reimagining Academic Studies: Science, Education, Social Science, Theology, Linguistics,* (7 lectures, [Berliner Hochschulkurs], Berlin, March 6-11, 1922, CW 81). Great Barrington, MA: SteinerBooks, 2014.

Selected lectures by Rudolf Steiner on the practice of anthroposophy prepared especially for the younger generation or a mixed generation audience:

————, *Becoming the Archangel Michael's Companions: Rudolf Steiner's Challenge to the Younger Generation* (13 lectures, Stuttgart, October 3-15, 1922, CW 217). Great Barrington, MA: SteinerBooks, 2007.

————, *Earthly Knowledge and Heavenly Wisdom.* (9 lectures, Dornach, February 2-18, 1923, CW 221.) New York: Anthroposophic Press, 1991. These lectures were held on the three successive weekends following the lectures in this volume, CW 220.

————, "Looking back to the Burning of the Goetheanum on New Year's Eve 1922/23." (Dornach, December 31, 1923, CW 260) in *The Christmas Conference for the Foundation of the General Anthroposophical Society 1923/24* (trans. Johanna Collis). New York: Anthroposophic Press, 1990.

————, "Meditation for the Esoteric Youth Circle," in Part III, *Esoteric Lessons 1913-1923* (trans., Marsha Post; introduction, Christopher Bamford; CW 266/3). Great Barrington, MA: SteinerBooks, 2012. Accounts of the founding of the circle by its participants precede two esoteric lessons (Stuttgart, July 13, 1923, and Dornach, December 30, 1923) and this remarkable meditation.

————, "On the Reality of Higher Worlds" and "Paths to the Knowledge of Higher Worlds" (English translations of lectures 1 and 2 in *Die Wirklichkeit der hoeheren Welten*, Oslo, Norway, November 25 and 26, 1921, CW 79) United Kingdom: Anthroposophical Press, 1947. These two lectures were specifically requested by students, who arranged for their presentation in Oslo's largest auditorium.

————, "What was the Purpose of the Goetheanum and What is the Task of Anthroposophy?" (Basel, April 9, 1923, CW 84).

AWAKE!

FOR THE SAKE OF THE FUTURE

Rudolf Steiner

1

Meeting Humanity's New Need for Christ through a New Knowledge of Christ

Dornach, January 5, 1923

In the days just before the Goetheanum was destroyed by fire,[†] I presented lectures[†] about the relationship of the human being to the course of the year and other matters related to this theme. Today I would like to go back to an earlier time, one we have often considered and must understand well, if we are going to grasp the course of human development in the right way in our day. Processes that occur in the human being can be observed in the recurring phenomena of the changing seasons as well.[†] Over the course of time, knowledge from the ancient mysteries and schools of initiation was brought to those human beings who could grasp it and wished to spread this knowledge further. With this knowledge human beings strengthened their capacities for thinking, feeling, and willing and were able to see themselves in relation to the entire universe.

Now we can ask ourselves: How is it that in ancient times, human beings had an understanding of the relationship of the human being to the universe; that is, the relationship of the microcosm to the macrocosm, and knew how this was expressed in the unfolding seasons of the year? In the past, humanity had such an understanding, for the inner soul of the human being at one time was more closely bound to the formative forces of the etheric body than it is now. During the course I gave last year about philosophy, cosmology, and religion,[†] I spoke about the origin of the etheric element in human beings. After a person has passed through suprasensory life between death and a new birth, and already has sent the spirit-seed of the physical body to the earth, the individual draws together the powers of the cosmic ether from which the individual's etheric body is formed. Only afterward is the individual etheric body joined to the physical body that belongs to the human being during earthly life. The human being descends from the spiritual realms in such a way that the soul-spiritual nature becomes enfolded within the etheric body. Then the individual joins together the soul-spiritual and etheric elements with the physical inheritance one receives through father and mother.

In earlier times of humanity's development, an individual formed a bond with the etheric body before earthly life began; a bond that was more intimate than a person was able make during later ages, including our present time. This earlier intimate bond with the etheric body allowed the human being to understand knowledge stemming from the ancient mystery traditions. Looking at the physical sun, a human being knew that the sun was the physical expression of something spiritual. Knowing this, people understood what was meant when someone spoke about the Sun Spirit. Recognizing the sun as the physical expression of spiritual reality was possible because people had experienced the intimate bond between the soul-spiritual nature of the human being and the etheric body, or the body's formative forces. It would have seemed ridiculous to them if they had been expected to believe that the sun was a physical globe of gas floating in cosmic space, in the manner portrayed today by the astrophysicist. It was self-evident to human beings in an earlier time that the spiritual was inherent in the physical. And in all of the ancient mysteries, this spiritual aspect was identified and revered as the Sun Spirit.

By the fourth century of the Common Era (c.e.), the human being no longer experienced a close bond with the etheric body during the descent out of the spiritual realm into earthly existence. (Of course matters of time are approximate, but they are more or less accurate.) The bond had been loosened. Increasingly during earthly existence, the human being used only the physical body when gazing up toward the heavens. In ancient times, when people looked up to the sky, they saw the sun; but inwardly there arose the impression that beyond its physicality, something soul-spiritual was incorporated within it.

In the fourth century of the Common Era, the human being began to use only the physical body, the physical eye, to perceive the sun. A glance outward into the universe was no longer supported by the power of the etheric body or its formative forces. Increasingly, a person saw only the physical sun. The existence of the Sun Spirit, however, still could be learned as something that once was known and still could be described as traditional wisdom. Thus Julian the Apostate [331–363 c.e.]† learned from his teachers about the existence of such a Sun Spirit. (I have spoken about this on another occasion.†) We know that this Sun Spirit descended to the earth through the Mystery of Golgotha. The Sun Spirit exchanged his life in heaven for an earthly life, so that his influence after the Mystery of Golgotha would place humanity's development in harmony with the earth's planetary destiny.

You will note that the two points of time do not occur simultaneously. How does the point in time when the Mystery of Golgotha occurred, appear as we look back upon it today? We have to say that at the moment in which the Christ, the Sun Being, passed through the Mystery of Golgotha, he united himself with the existence of the earth. If we express this in everyday language we would say that since that point in time, Christ is on earth. However, the capacity to see the Sun Spirit existed for human beings up until the fourth century of the Common Era, because until that time they were still inwardly united with their etheric body or formative forces.

Just as it was possible to see Christ himself when he was physically present on the earth, it was also possible up until the fourth century of the Common Era to see in the sun an afterimage of Christ through one's etheric body. When you look intently at something and then close your eyes, you see an afterimage of the object. Likewise, until the fourth century, individuals who had a close connection to the etheric body could look at the sun and perceive an afterimage of the Sun Spirit as they looked out into the cosmos. Those who still were connected with their etheric body in this way (and this was the case mainly in areas of southern Europe, North Africa, and western Asia) could say out of direct experience that the Sun Spirit is visible if one looks out into the heavens. And these individuals did not understand what it meant when the teachers and leaders of other mysteries said, "The Christ is on earth." This I spoke about in the course entitled *Philosophy, Cosmology and Religion* in September 1922.

Remember that during the four hundred years after the Mystery of Golgotha, a great number of people could not grasp what was meant by the statement "Christ has appeared on earth." For them what happened in Palestine was an insignificant event, just as it seemed to be for various Roman writers,[†] who recorded it in an offhand way. For them, the man referred to as Christ was an insignificant personality who encountered death under unusual circumstances. These people would not have understood the profound Mystery of Golgotha. We can say that these individuals did not need to think of Christ on earth, for they still thought of him in the old way as being in heaven. For them, Christ was still the Spirit of the Cosmic All, who worked through Light. For them, he was the all-inclusive Light of Humanity. For them, there was no need to look within and to search for Christ within the human I.

There was a person who could not grasp why you would need to search for Christ on earth, and who instead understood that Christ is found in heaven, lives in the light, shines daily upon the earth after the sun rises, and no longer shines after the sun sets; such an individual was Julian the Apostate. For him, what occurred in Palestine was like other historical events. And it was an ordinary, even an insignificant, historical event because human beings living at that time did not yet experience a need or yearning for Christ. Today we wish to find out when and how this yearning to understand Christ in earthly manifestation first arose.

If we want to grasp the successive stages in the development of humanity and the earth after the Atlantean catastrophe, we must keep the following in mind. The Atlantean catastrophe, which I have often described, takes us back to the eighth and the ninth millennia before the Common Era. You may read about the first post-Atlantean period, the Ancient Indian cultural epoch, in my book *An Outline of Esoteric Science.*[†] In the Ancient Indian period, the human being lived primarily in the etheric body or the formative forces. The bond with the etheric body was so intense that you could say that the human being lived within or *inside* the etheric body or formative forces. It was as if the physical body was merely a garment; it was something external. The human being looked out into the cosmos more fully with the etheric eye than with the physical eye. During the Ancient Persian, or the second post-Atlantean era, human beings looked into their surroundings with the help of the Sentient Body. In the third or Egypto-Chaldean period, humanity viewed the world with the help of the Sentient Soul. During the Graeco-Latin or fourth post-Atlantean age, the human being saw the world through the Intellectual or Mind Soul.

In our own era, the fifth post-Atlantean age (that is, the historical present since the fifteenth century of the Common Era), humanity looks into the world through the Consciousness Soul. And this capacity to perceive with the Consciousness Soul brought about everything that I presented in my recent lectures about the origins of modern natural science[†] in their historical context. The Atlantean Catastrophe preceded, you recall, the Ancient Indian Period with its development of the *Etheric Body*; which preceded the Egypto-Chaldean Period with its development of the *Sentient Soul*, then came the Graeco-Latin Period and the ripening of the *Intellectual or Mind Soul*. Today our development as human beings is concerned with the *Consciousness Soul*.

Now let us clarify what all this actually means. If we wished to represent this reality schematically, we would have to show the physical body next to and separate from the etheric body. The soul first became active while the human being was still living entirely in the etheric body. That occurred in the first post-Atlantean or Ancient Indian epoch. When the soul asserted itself in the Sentient Body, it was still entirely within the etheric body. That took place during the second post-Atlantean or Ancient Persian epoch. During the Egypto-Chaldean or third post-Atlantean epoch, the human being initially continued to experience the soul within the etheric body. During this era the human being began to experience the soul inwardly as well. To the extent that human beings experienced the soul inwardly, they felt as if the soul extended partially or halfway beyond the etheric body.

During the Graeco-Latin cultural epoch (or the fourth post-Atlantean period), the soul element of the human being grew beyond the etheric body. Up until about the year 333 C.E. the human being still experienced the soul within the etheric element. By that time, however, a person also had grown beyond an awareness of the etheric body. The soul remained only loosely connected with the etheric body and had lost an inner connection to it.

The soul felt abandoned. It was obliged to go out into the world without the support of the etheric body. The need for Christ arose out of this process. When the soul was no longer inwardly connected to the etheric body, the human being could no longer gaze out into the heavens and see the Sun Spirit, not even as an afterimage. But in the course of cosmic development, the process of change extended over long periods of time. Only since the fourth century of the Common Era has the soul been inwardly emancipated from the etheric body. At first, however, the soul was inwardly weak and lacked sufficient strength to find the Christ Being in a new way. Moving from the fifth, sixth, and seventh centuries of the Common Era up until the fourteenth, fifteenth, and sixteenth centuries, and even into our era (although for the time being we will go only as far as the fifteenth century), we find that the inwardly emancipated (but still weak) soul felt something of the need for Christ. Because the soul was no longer connected to the etheric body, it could not seek Christ in the sun as it previously had been able to do. But it was not yet strong enough to search for Christ in the Mystery of Golgotha. That is to say, instead of seeking Christ in space, the emancipated soul needed to find the Christ Being within the course of time. The soul had to be strengthened inwardly in order to cultivate these capacities within itself. Up until the fifteenth century the human being was not strong enough to cultivate inner capacities sufficiently in order to receive knowledge of the cosmos through the soul. Therefore humanity restricted itself to searching for the knowledge of Christ and the cosmos from the books or teachings that the ancients had left behind. They accepted as an authentic source of their own knowledge what had been historically preserved.

We must acknowledge that the soul had to be inwardly strengthened. By the fifteenth century of the Common Era, mathematics, which had once been experienced through the etheric body or through the physical body by way of the etheric body, began to be expressed in abstractions. Furthermore, the abstraction was experienced as one's own. For example, we began to understand space as an abstract thought. This experience, in and of itself, did not bring human beings very far along. You can see, however, that it is a different kind of experience than a person could have had at an earlier point in time. This powerful impulse to draw something out of the depths of one's own soul arose because the connection between the soul and the etheric body that existed in ancient times was no longer at the service of humanity. Human beings had to inwardly strengthen themselves so that they could come to the Christ in the context of time, rather than space. In ancient times the etheric body had made it possible for humanity to see the Christ descending from the sun, to see the Christ in space. And so, up until the fourth century, civilized human beings could not really begin to understand the reports about the Christ and the Mystery of Golgotha, for this perspective is embedded in time.

We can see the irony in the fact that neither Emperor Constantine's[†] testimony of the Christ, nor the denial of the Christ by Emperor Julian the Apostate is based on a firm foundation. The historian Zosimus[†] explained that Emperor Constantine was converted to Christianity for personal reasons. He had committed so many crimes against members of his family that the priests of the old cults would no longer grant him forgiveness. He left the pagan gods and their priests because the Christian priests had promised him that they could absolve him of his guilt. Constantine's conversion to Christianity for personal reasons was less significant than it would have been if his allegiance to the Christ had arisen out of an inner soul necessity.

Initiation into the Eleusian Mysteries, even though they had already become very superficial, was all that Emperor Julian needed to become inspired by the Sun Spirit of ancient tradition. For Julian the Apostate, just as it was with Constantine, his allegiance did not rest on a deep foundation, even though he received extraordinarily important knowledge during his initiation in the Eleusinian Mysteries. In any case, neither a testimony in defense of the Christ nor a denial of the Christ was very important at that time, for humanity did not understand what was meant by the assertion that the Christ should be sought in a human form that lived within human history.

At the beginning of the fourth century of the Common Era, the only ways that the human being could find the way to the Christ or to an understanding of the cosmos was through historical tradition and the written accounts of oral tradition. The human soul was inwardly emancipated but still lacking in sufficient strength to find the way on its own to the Christ or to an understanding of the nature of the cosmos. An explanation of the cosmos as well as the Christ had to be built up again from a new foundation. The historical tradition also needed to be built up again. It existed partly in written form and partly as oral tradition. The oral transmission was complicated further, because only a relatively few human beings had access to the written transmissions, and these individuals would pass along to their listeners an oral interpretation of what they had read.

The situation I have just described remained unchanged for many centuries; and with regard to an understanding of the Christ, it remains so even today. But it was very significant in the fourth century that the soul had become inwardly free. Although there are precursors and subsequent contributors to a new direction in human development, we can still point to the year 333 c.e. as the point at which the emancipation of the soul occurred for individuals who were at the forefront of their time, even though we know that the emancipated souls were not yet strong enough to produce new knowledge out of their own powers. It was already true that a person who was aware of authentic accounts from earlier times, and thought deeply about these traditions, could say: "Not long ago, there were still human beings who could see something divinely spiritual in the sun. I no longer am able to see in that way. But now human beings who have the capacity to see something divinely spiritual have discovered that they can create other knowledge that lies deeply within them; for example, mathematical knowledge. My soul is now so constituted that it feels itself as an autonomous Being, but it is not yet able to summon knowledge out of itself; it cannot draw up powers from within in order to express new knowledge."

Beginning to draw mathematical and mechanical concepts out of human souls was the most significant accomplishment of the fifteenth and sixteenth centuries. Copernicus† was the first person who applied to the structure of the vault of heaven what he had experienced in his emancipated soul. The earlier astronomical systems of the universe were achieved through the help of persons who lived during the epoch of the Intellectual Soul. Those souls were not yet emancipated from the etheric body, and because the Intellectual Soul still had a measure of the power of the etheric body, they were able to see out into the cosmos. Up until the fifteenth century the Intellectual Soul was still present; but from that point forward, as humanity moved increasingly into the Consciousness Soul era, human beings could use only the physical body and the physical eye to see out into the cosmos. These are the reasons why, during all these centuries and even up until now, the knowledge of the Christ and the Mystery of Golgotha could be transmitted only through written texts or oral traditions.

What have we gained through the strengthening of the soul since the fourth and fifth centuries? Outwardly it is merely mechanistic knowledge, an understanding of the physical aspect. You will see that I have described examples of this in the natural-scientific course. But now the time has come in which the soul must be strengthened even further, so that what the soul, with the help of the etheric body, formerly could see by looking into the heavens (the Spirit Sun together with the physical sun) can be transformed. Now the human soul, casting its gaze inward, can develop the capacity to look into the I, to experience and feel the I; and to perceive, behind the I, the Christ.

Let us imagine the following, not just schematically, but very concretely. We know that during an earlier period of time, using one's physical sight, human beings could see the sun; and with the help of the etheric body, they could look behind the sun and see the Sun Spirit, that is, the Christ. Today if we look within, we encounter the I. We perceive the I and experience the feeling of its presence. But what we perceive is very dark. The feeling of the I first arises in the emancipated soul. At an earlier time the human being used to gaze out into the cosmos; now we must look within ourselves. Gazing out into the cosmos brought the human being together with the sun and the Christ. At first, gazing within merely allowed the human being to be brought together with the I. Now we must develop the capacity to discover behind the I what we used to experience out of the physical sun. The human being once was able to experience the Christ while watching the sun's light between sunrise and sunset. Now we experience the Christ as the illuminator of the knowledge streaming out of our I. Thus we now shall find in the Christ the strong support for our own I. Thus we can say that, in earlier times, the human being looked out at the sun and found the Christ-permeated Light. Now, as we sink deeply into the self, we learn to recognize the Christ-permeated I.

We stand at the beginning of such a possibility. Anthroposophy exists in order to make humanity aware that since the fourth century of the Common Era, human development has been in transition. Before the fourth century, humanity could look into the heavens and perceive the Christ as Sun Spirit in space. Now human beings must deeply experience their inner self and find the inner Sun Spirit, the Christ within the I, just as previously Christ had appeared within the physical sun. The Christ has become the bearer of the I, just as previously he had been the Sun Spirit.

In the fourth century of the Common Era, the peoples who were rooted within the Graeco-Latin civilizations began to feel drawn to the Christ in a way that could be satisfied through the written and oral traditions. Today these written and oral traditions have lost their persuasiveness among the most pioneering spirits. Human beings have to learn to find the Christ deep within the inner self, just as humanity in ancient times was able to find the Christ in the sun and its light. We need to understand the intervening centuries of transition in the right way; the soul had achieved its independence during this time, and yet it also felt as if it were empty. When the soul in ancient times had looked into the cosmos and felt endowed with the etheric body, it could not possibly have seen the universe as a mechanical-mathematical system in the way that Copernicus perceived it at a later time. Previously these things had been more deeply connected to the human being. And the world system that was being destroyed by the Copernican model was not being replaced by one that seemed better; it offered a world system that arguably was just as decadent as the Ptolemaic system seemed to be.

But when the soul no longer looked for the roots of the etheric body within the cosmic etheric, it opened the door for founding a science of the stars that did not care whether or not the human being belonged to the starry heavens. The only tribute this transformed human being paid to the ancients was to shift the center of the new model of the universe to the sun, where in earlier times the Christ had been perceived. The sun became the center point of the universe, albeit the center point of the physical and not the spiritual universe. And thus a dim recollection remained that human beings long ago had looked up at the sun, acknowledged the sun as the middle point of the universe, and felt simultaneously the Christ Being. You see, we should not concentrate our attention merely on the outer appearance of events in world history, as we customarily do today; we must never lose sight of the way in which our feeling experience is subtly interwoven with our knowledge and understanding.

If you are attentive, you will perceive a remarkable sensitivity in Copernicus. Indeed, we might describe it as a feeling element that penetrated his intelligence and understanding. He did not simply calculate mathematically; he had an inner longing to give back to the sun something it had received from the ancients. Out of this profound inner longing, active within his feeling-imbued intelligence and understanding, Copernicus articulated three laws.[†] The third law placed in question what had been laid out in the first and second laws. But over the course of time, astronomers, who preferred to see everything in a mechanistic way, ignored the third law. Copernicus proposed a law whereby the movement of the earth around the sun was not fixed as absolutely as scientists generally portray it today. Nowadays we see this hypothesis as a statement of fact, a phenomenon that can be verified in every observation. Thus if you sat on a chair that was placed far out in space (and that would have to be very far off in space), you would be able to see the sun from a great distance and the earth circling around it. Indeed we can imagine a chair placed far out into space and a schoolmaster sitting on the chair looking at the entire universe. However, this is not scientific observation. Copernicus himself did not have such an inflexible conscience in these matters as do the people in more recent times, who insist on the mechanization of the entire structure of the universe. Copernicus himself pointed out phenomena that showed that a simple notion of the way the earth moved around the sun was not absolutely and indisputably correct. But as I said, this third law was ignored or rejected by later scientists. They stayed with the first two laws: the earth rotates on its own axis, and the earth moves around the sun; and they were satisfied with a very uncomplicated system, which in this simple form is generally taught now in schools. I am not trying to raise objections to the Copernican system. But the time has come to speak about these things, as I spoke about astronomy in the natural science course in Stuttgart.[†] We must think about these things in a different way than it is currently possible to do within a strictly materialistic-mechanistic construct.

And precisely with Copernicus we have a scientist who approaches his model of the universe with a feeling-imbued understanding and perceives more than a framework of mathematics. It was not Copernicus' intent merely to construct a system of mathematical coordinates for our solar system, and to position the sun at the center point of the coordinate axes. He wanted to give back to the sun what had been taken from it when humanity could no longer perceive the Christ in the sun.

This example makes it clear that we should investigate more than merely the outwardly visible facts or external circumstances; we even should look beyond the evident changes in human thinking over the course of history. We must trace very carefully the transformation of our capacity to integrate human feeling and sensitivity into a deeper understanding of what we know. This became evident as the material-istic and mechanistic approach spread and flourished. With Copernicus and later on with Kepler,[†] too, we can still see a feeling-imbued intel-ligence at work. This kind of intelligence was particularly strong in Newton.[†] In the natural-scientific course I gave in Stuttgart, I explained that when, in later life, Newton reviewed his early contributions to mathematical-natural philosophy, it made him feel ill. After he first had observed space through a telescope, he achieved everything for a time through his mathematical-mechanical faculties; and then later when he examined the matter again, it made him feel faint. Afterward he wrote that what he had established as abstract space, with three abstract dimensions, was actually the *sensorium* or mind of God.

Only gradually over the course of time did human beings engage with the world through their capacity of thinking alone, no longer refining their intellectual creations through their feeling-intelligence and soul understanding. Newton still tested his findings through his feeling-intelligence as well as his powers of observation, abstraction, and ideation in his scientific work; Leibniz[†] did so to an even greater extent, and so did other natural-scientific researchers at this time. Anyone who examines the life of Galileo[†] finds at every turn how all of the capacities of the human being were brought into play. The scientific researcher learned how to feed the thinking apparatus with the results of observa-tions and experiments, just as one feeds a steam engine with coal; and the human being who approached knowledge in this way emerged later as the authoritative leader of scientific research, conducted without any preliminary or prescriptive hypotheses, on the grounds that any predetermined hypothesis fails to lead to real knowledge.

Thus we see that in the fourth century of the Common Era, the soul had emerged, strengthened by its autonomy from the etheric body, and yet sensing its own emptiness. In the centuries of the Intellectual Soul, the soul exercised new capacities and learned how to fill itself with many mathematical-mechanical thoughts and ideas, so that within the human I, the inner light could be found. The presence of the inner light, the thought-generating capacity of the I, meant that it was no longer possible to speak about the I in a figurative or symbolic way. The I had become the supportive essence, or core, of the strengthened soul.

Thus we learn to recognize what has happened to humanity's need for the Christ over the centuries. The longing for the Christ occurred more and more frequently. Today this need is very strong, and yet many human beings silence this impulse and push it deeply into the unconscious realms of the soul. Only through knowledge of the spiritual cosmos can the human being encounter this longing for the Christ. Above all, we must see as characteristic of our own age (the twentieth century and beyond) that the need for the Christ and the inner strength of the soul to find the Christ within the human I (and, so to speak, behind the I), is exactly parallel to what the human being in ancient times found within the Sun Spirit.

The way in which the human being stood in relation to the Sun Spirit during the Graeco-Roman era was as if it occurred by the last rays of daylight. For the Sun Spirit appeared to human beings in its full soul-spiritual radiance only during the Ancient Indian epoch. Now we are living in a time of the first light of a new day, in which the knowledge of the Christ can be generated by the powers and capacities resident within the human being. The ancient knowledge of the Sun Spirit, which Julian the Apostate wanted to solidify, can no longer satisfy the human being in any way. Indeed, the efforts of Julian were futile in the context of historical development. In the epoch beginning with the fourth century, human beings simply did not know how to experience the Christ directly. There followed centuries in which the need for the Christ could be met only through the remnants of oral or written traditions. Now in our time, we can truly understand what is written in the Gospel of John as the words of Christ to his disciples: "I have yet many things to say to you, but you cannot bear them now."[†]

The time must come in which the human being understands what the Christ meant when he said, "I am with you always, even unto the end of the world."[†] For the Christ is not dead; he lives. He speaks not merely through the Gospels; he speaks through the spirit eye, when one's spiritual eye once again is able to grasp the revelation of the secrets of human existence. To the spiritual eye, he is visible every day; he speaks and reveals himself. And we are a feeble humanity if we fail to strive in our era, so that human beings might receive and grasp what the Christ once wished to say. Two thousand years ago human beings were not constituted in a way that would have allowed them to understand what the Christ offered to them. Of course, human beings around the Christ could understand something of what he was saying. And the Gospel as oral and written tradition has continued to exist over time for all human beings, so that the words quoted above have been spread throughout the earth.

Now humanity must strive to replace the Christ of oral and written tradition with the living Christ. In our day it is unchristian if you wish only to reaffirm what has been written or passed down for centuries. For now it is so that every day the revelation of the Christ speaks out of the spiritual world and into our thinking that is striving for illumination; into our feeling hearts; and into our will-filled humanity.

2

The Task of Knowing for Today's Youth

Dornach, January 6, 1923

It would fill an entire book if I were to compile all the kind words that have been sent to us from those who feel connected with what has been lost in the recent catastrophe. [Six days earlier, on New Years Eve, the first Goetheanum was destroyed by fire.] Therefore I shall read only the names of the people who have extended their sympathy in writing. We see how deeply this has entered the hearts of those who understand what was sent out to the world from this place. It also shows the deeply felt desire and determination to rebuild and restore what we have lost. It will be a source of strength for many of you to know how widespread our work has become and how deeply our sense of loss is shared by others. For our goals should not be merely theoretical; they should find expression in work, in love toward one another, and in devoted service to humanity. And so we ought to speak here about the deeds we expect to carry out and the tasks we intend to accomplish. I shall mention only the names of persons who are not present, for what fills the hearts of those who have been here in these days of grief-filled gatherings can hardly be expressed in words, even though it is felt no less deeply or clearly. So allow me to continue without mentioning the names of dear friends who on this occasion are present, even though they, too, have expressed their condolences in writing. You know who you are. [The names were read.]

We can assume that what we have begun here is already deeply rooted in many hearts. Let us take note that a recent course† attracted a larger number of friends from outside this area who also wish to pursue anthroposophic matters here at the Goetheanum. Today allow me to turn our attention especially to the young friends who have come to this course to discover for themselves what is meant by anthroposophy, and who recently have found their way in such a fine and heartfelt manner to this movement.

We must understand what it means when young souls are earnestly striving to grasp what can be known today about science, art, and so forth, today, and also sincerely want to work within the anthroposophic movement. These young friends, who are attending this course, are among those who came here a short time ago, saw the Goetheanum, and expected to see the Goetheanum again on their return; and indeed they thought that they would see it in a different form than is now the case. And when I turn my thoughts preferentially to these younger friends, I do so knowing that those who carry the anthroposophic movement in their heart, also carry as an immediate soul concern whatever a particular group or single individual may be experiencing. For the most part the younger friends who want to find their way into anthroposophic work are searching for what is called today the life of the spirit. In particular I would like to speak to those who are pursuing the study of academic disciplines, feel an impulse to work together with others, and wish to carry out their striving within the anthroposophic movement.

Above all these young people are earnestly striving to imbue the human soul with the life of the spirit. Within anthroposophy a life of the spirit is spoken about that cannot be achieved in any easy manner, although today precisely an "easy approach" appeals to most human beings. We do not try to conceal the fact that the paths to anthroposophy are difficult ones. (Anyone who consults anthroposophic literature will also be convinced of this.) But the paths are difficult because, on the one hand, they are related to the most profound and potent human values; and on the other hand, they require people to see clearly the signs of cultural decline in our time and recognize that the anthroposophic movement is trying to move forward along a different path.

We must not lose sight of the fact that anthroposophy can be meaningful in many ways for people living in the present age. Approached with inner commitment, anthroposophy can help human beings to perceive spiritual worlds and to convince them that everything conveyed here out of the spiritual realms is based on truth. But I must emphasize, ever and again, that even as important as it is for individuals in the present to take up this earnest, difficult path, nevertheless, those who possess an unprejudiced, healthy human understanding can gain insight into the truth of anthroposophy on the basis of their own inner resources and capacities.

This has to be emphasized time and again, so that no one adopts the unfounded position that only someone who sees clairvoyantly into spiritual realms can perceive what the anthroposophic movement proclaims to be true. Intellectual life and modern civilization present so many prejudices to human beings today that only with difficulty can we trust healthy human reason. In the light of such prejudices, we are even less likely to be convinced of the truth of anthroposophy without the aid of clairvoyance.

The Anthroposophical Society should take the lead in sweeping away the prejudices so common in present-day civilization. Indeed it should work against prejudices in all of its endeavors. If the Anthroposophical Society were to set such an example, then we might be justifiably confident that a human being's inner powers of knowing can grow without clairvoyance. And those individuals who, for whatever reason, cannot strive for the exact clairvoyance that we also will speak about here, still can achieve a full confirmation of the validity of anthroposophic knowledge.

There is yet another very special path, by which academically-oriented young people can find their way to anthroposophy. You see, the study of academic subjects could and should provide the starting point from which young people can arrive at their own intuitive perception of the spiritual legacy of anthroposophy. Let me emphasize that I refer specifically to the human being's *self-generated* perception. The possibility does exist for science, knowledge, and the inner life to be integrated within our educational system.

But consider how little university students in our present civilization are inwardly connected to the field of knowledge they are striving to master. It cannot be otherwise today, for academic subjects are brought to students as something more or less external to them. They encounter a system that is not at all adapted to express or even to speak of what are often extraordinarily significant aspects of empirical knowledge.

Staggering truths, really staggering truths, are inherent today in every field of knowledge, every science or academic subject. And these are truths that, if young people were to encounter or experience them, would give them a kind of microscope or telescope of the soul. If young people were able to approach these truths through their faculties of soul, they would be able to unlock mighty secrets of existence.

The investigations that would lead to enormous discoveries if they were properly cultivated are precisely the ones that would delight the hearts and souls of young people. It would enrich students enormously if they were to find within their academic studies the acknowledgement of the depths of human nature and the individual personality. We have to point out again and again that students living within a system of indifference recognize that the subjects they study are also presented with indifference. As a result, the relationship of students to the many-faceted examples of unlocking truths or discovering new knowledge in empirical science remains at a superficial level. I would even say that some, or even the majority, of our university students go through their entire course of study without an inner experience of the academic disciplines they study. They allow the subject matter to wash over them; and then, having reviewed sufficiently beforehand, pass the required exams and find a position with which they can make a living.

It sounds almost paradoxical to say that the hearts of university students should be addressed in everything that is brought to them. It sounds like a paradox, but it actually could be so! For young people who have a subjective capacity and inclination may respond to a subject out of the depths of their own heart, even though they may encounter something in the driest book or driest lecture and cannot understand the intent of the author or lecturer. Sometimes in such a young person, the subject may penetrate the soul deeply. We notice in the best of the young friends who have come into the anthroposophic movement, that they themselves are not responsible for this; but rather through their destiny within the life of the present-day civilization, they have been offered nothing for the heart out of the current impulse toward knowledge; nor have they received anything for the head. Some of you here will not want to forgive me for saying this; but most of the students who are here will indeed understand it.

Today we have reached a time in the development of the natural sciences (I tried to describe this in the natural science course) in which the students typically have to experience in their study of the natural sciences what I would call a feeling of oppressive weight or paralysis within the soul. Indeed, science today is such that whoever studies it with diligence and discipline experiences something like the anguish that overcomes the soul when you wrestle with the philosophical problem of knowledge. Anyone who looks around at what exists in the sciences today encounters great cosmic questions embedded within the narrow descriptions of phenomena. And these detailed formulations that arise out of the truths of natural science press into the soul the impulse to articulate the riddle that has to be solved. Human beings long to solve these riddles; otherwise we feel an inner paralysis and oppressive constraint.

If only this anguish, this paralysis, could be transformed into a beneficial fruit of our study of the natural sciences! For out of the anguish that grips the entire human being, there could arise not only the longing for the spiritual world, but also the capacity to see into the spiritual world. And so when the human being has to absorb knowledge in a way that cannot satisfy one's inner being, this experience ignites a powerful impetus within the soul and heart to overcome what is inwardly so unsatisfying.

That is what one finds so terrible, so shattering in the pursuit of knowledge today: no effort whatsoever is made to understand that the current situation can work upon the entire human being in such a way that young people are prevented from reaching up to what is worthiest in humanity. Only young people acting out of their own deep longing are able to free themselves from the hindrances that have been laid in their way.

And when we turn from the natural sciences to the humanities, we discover that during this era when the natural sciences have ascended in their influence, the humanities also have been affected by the methods used in the natural sciences. If students could be guided to the humanities in a way that restores a fully human perspective to the humanities, they would experience something that I would like to call an inward soul shortness of breath. For if all of the abstract ideas, the results of documented research, and everything else that can be found typically in the study of humanities today, were brought with human sympathy to young people, it would produce a kind of soul shortness of breath in the individual. This gasping for breath would awaken the impulse, the necessity, to reach higher into fresh air, and thus enter the realm of spirit observation that supports an anthroposophic world perspective.

Whoever has followed the spirit of my lectures on the development of the natural sciences in the modern period, will not be able to say that I have given a superficial critique of modern science. To the contrary, I have tried to demonstrate that the natural sciences (and also the humanities today) are indeed significant cultural foundations; they have served and must continue to serve the bases of civilization that must be laid down and acknowledged, so that we can extend these foundations of knowledge further in the future.

But the human being cannot be anything other than a human being. In order to fulfill our humanity, each one must be fully body, soul, and spirit. Students and young people today live in a time in which they are confronted with matters devoid of a human element. Even so, the noblest and most enlivened human striving could be stirred within them, if only they would receive what is necessary; even if it were not imbued with the fullest humanity in the highest sense of the word. For if young people were offered actual knowledge at the most basic level, something would be achieved. If that were to occur, then our students would need nothing more than to hear about the accomplishments of natural science and the humanities in the places of higher learning, and they would feel not only an urgency to adopt spiritual science, they would also have the capacity to receive it. And then what would live in students and young people would grow entirely out of its own accord, so that anthroposophic knowledge would be the means by which civilization can move forward.

If our young friends carefully consider what I have said, paradoxical as it may seem, they will find that I have characterized the most important causes of suffering that they have had to endure during their studies. I believe that the cause of most of these sorrows is also the reason why they have come to us. But the suffering and pain for many of them already has a long history, and it is not possible that the situation for them as individuals can ever be fully rectified. For something that should have happened in a certain period of one's youth cannot be received in precisely the same form at a later time. What comes later, however, can serve as compensation. Indeed the compensation for what the young people among us failed to receive at an earlier time is the recognition of the importance of cultivating anthroposophic life in the present.

Take upon yourselves this task: do for the anthroposophic movement what you either already know you carry as a conviction; or what you, in the course of time, could do with conviction out of your completely individual and innermost self as something necessary for the continuance of human civilization. Then you will be able to carry and preserve in your hearts this realization, even beyond this earthly life: you will be able to sustain the consciousness that you have fulfilled your obligation, your duty, to uphold humanity and the world in an era of the greatest human difficulties. This will be a rich compensation for what may have been lost to you at an earlier point in time.

If each one of us inwardly experiences and grasps what it means to be part of the younger generation in our time, then we shall be able to understand why young people have found their way into our circles. Moreover, the capacity to build a relationship to these young people will grow and grow among those in the Anthroposophical Society who, shall we say, by virtue of their age, do not appear to belong to the younger generation.

I believe that out of our current grief-stricken situation, I can affirm to the students and young people, and say as well to the oldest members of the Anthroposophical Society, that individuals who today rightly understand themselves as human beings, can experience within the Anthroposophical Society what must occur if human civilization is to go forward and what will prevent the destructive forces from gaining the upper hand over the dawning of life's quickening forces. In the culture and civilization of the present age, it sounds almost comical to say that because human beings in their spiritual-soul nature continue to be active between the time we go to sleep and the time we wake up, we should also take care that our spiritual-soul nature conducts itself in the right way during this period of sleep. But within the Anthroposophical Society you will discover that the human spiritual-soul existence that occurs between going to sleep and waking up is regarded as the seed that we shall carry over into the eternity of the future. Our physical and etheric elements, which are visible to us as we carry out our daily tasks from morning to evening, remain in bed while we are sleeping. We also do not carry our physical and etheric elements with us through the portal of death when we enter the suprasensory, spiritual world. We do, however, bring with us into the spiritual world a delicate spiritual essence that exists outside the physical and etheric bodies during the time between going to sleep and waking up. (We shall leave aside, for the moment, the question of the significance of sleep for the human being on earth.) Through anthroposophic spiritual science, it becomes clear that this essence, this substantiality, which is imperceptible to ordinary consciousness, lives between going to sleep and waking up, and is precisely what human beings will carry with them when stepping across the portal of death, so that when we exist in worlds other than this earthly one we can continue to pursue our tasks there.

The tasks that the human being wishes to accomplish between death and rebirth will be achievable insofar as we have cultivated the spiritual-soul element during earthly life. My dear friends, just as our physical world surrounds us during earthly life, so too, in the spiritual world human soul-beings exist as a living presence, even though they do not have physical bodies. These soul-beings remain in the spiritual world perhaps decades or centuries, waiting for their next incarnation. They exist in the spiritual world just as we human beings live physically on the earth. What happens here on earth among human beings (we refer to this afterward as historical life) is influenced not only by other earthly human beings, but through the forces exerted by human souls who are living between death and a new birth. These forces exist. Just as we reach out our hands within physical reality, these beings extend their spiritual hands into the immediate present. It would be an arid historical account if the only documents we used were ones dealing with our earthly realm. The true history that takes place on earth includes the participation of the spiritual forces arising from the activity of souls in the spiritual world during the time of their existence between death and a new birth. We work together with human beings who are not currently incarnated in an earthly life.

We transgress against humanity when we do not educate young people in the right way. We transgress against humanity when we ignore the noblest efforts of human souls to accomplish deeds out of unseen worlds. We transgress against the whole course of human development if we do not nurture our own spirituality and enable it to pass the portal of death fully prepared to continue its development with ever-increasing consciousness. For when the spiritual-soul nature is not cultivated on earth, then the consciousness, which ought to be illuminated immediately after death, and ought to grow increasingly throughout the existence between death and a new birth, will remain dim. If the human being wishes consciously to reach full human potential, then the spiritual aspect must belong to the whole.

In the present age, it should be the earnest endeavor of human beings who understand the intentions of the anthroposophic movement, to know that anthroposophy is a cosmic life-legacy, a cosmic life potency and force. We transgress in the highest sense when we fail to achieve what must be developed in order for the earth and humanity to progress further. The demise of all that is connected to the earth will occur if cultivating the spiritual is neglected. In addition to our interest as individuals in the insights of spiritual science, many of us are drawn to anthroposophy by the profound earnestness of the task of forming a spiritual connection with a deeply meaningful, all-encompassing opportunity to act on behalf of humanity.

This knowledge holds true not just for a particular category of human beings. For example, it is equally valid for the young and the old. But in order for the young and the old to find their way to one another, a unified spirit must be active among all who belong to the Anthroposophical Society.

May the younger people bring their very best; may the older people understand the best offered by the younger people; may understanding be extended from one to the other. Only then shall we move forward together. Let us move beyond the solemn days we have just experienced, beyond the grief that still hovers over us. Let decisions be more than wishes or accolades. Let our decisions penetrate our hearts and reside so deeply within our souls that they become deeds. Even in small circles we shall need to perform deeds, if we are to compensate for our great loss.

The deeds of the young, when they are achieved in the right way, will be cosmically significant deeds. The greatest beauty that can be created by an older person will be manifest by working together with human beings who are still capable of accomplishing "youthful" deeds. If you grasp this, my dear friends, you shall be able to meet the younger generation with understanding. Through the beautiful examples offered by the older people to compensate for our loss, the young people will be able to see what will benefit the future and what will satisfy their own inner well-being. Let each one of us see in one another what is just and imbued with strength. Let strength generate and empower strength. Only then shall we move forward together.

3

THE EARTH'S INTERIOR AND CELESTIAL
CONSTELLATIONS IN RELATION TO
THE PHYSICAL HUMAN BEING

Dornach, January 7, 1923

Today I would like to refer to the preceding lectures, and then move forward using the results of spiritual-scientific research to show how the human being is placed within the entire cosmos. I shall speak about the human being, first of all, by looking at the physical organization, and then by considering what is called in spiritual research the etheric or life body, the astral body, and the organization of the I. But we will not understand the various aspects of the human being by merely enumerating them in sequence, for each of these elements is related to the cosmos in a different way. Only when we understand the ways in which the different elements of the human being are ordered within the cosmos will we be able to grasp the relationship of the human being as a whole to the universe.

Observing a human being standing before us, we see that the four members of the human constitution are indistinguishably joined together and united in reciprocal interaction one with another. In order to understand them fully, we first must consider each one separately in its specific relationship to the cosmos. We shall accomplish this not by using an all-encompassing approach, but by observing them one by one, from a specific point of view.

Let us consider human beings in relation to everything that exists outside the body, all the physical surroundings that extend outward to the periphery of human perception. Here we find the outwardly visible human senses. Yet we know by means of anthroposophic observation[†] that we can reach certain kinds of human sense perception only by going beneath the outer surface of the body, and entering the innermost aspect of the human being. Essentially, we have to look for these senses inside the body. These inner senses instruct us about their nature from our innermost aspect, although they do so in an unconscious way from their point of origin within the body.

With regard to all that exists outside and surrounds the human being, we can say that the outer world is connected to the senses that are found on the outer surface of the human body. We need to consider only the most visible of the senses, for example, the eye or ear, to discover that we receive impressions from the outside. It is necessary, of course, to confirm this by thorough, detailed observation and research, which, for some of the senses, we have already carried out in this very hall. But as the outer world presents itself to us in everyday life, we can already say that a sense organ, such as the eye or ear, perceives things through outer impressions.

Our upright position in relation to the earth allows us to receive impressions of our surroundings along a horizontal plane. Even a more exact observation would show that what I have just said is absolutely correct. For if it seemed as though we could perceive something from another direction, it would be an illusion, a deception. Every direction through which a sense perception is transmitted lies in the horizontal, and by horizontal I mean a line that runs parallel to the surface of the earth. If we are standing on the earth, then the main direction for receiving sense perceptions is parallel with the earth. Along the direction of the slightly curving line of the earth's surface flow all our external perceptions.

Through observation, we can say that perceptions approach us from outside ourselves; then they pass from the outer to the inner aspect of the human being. And what do we bring to these perceptions from within ourselves? We bring our thinking and our capacity for imagination to bear on these perceptions. Let this process pass before your eyes. When I perceive something through the eye, an impression comes from the outside, and the power of my thinking and imagination arise from within to meet it. From outside comes an impression when I look at a table. The fact that I can remember the table with the aid of an inner "picture" is due to my inner capacities of imagination and ideation. When we imagine a human being schematically, we see that the direction of perception moves from the outside to the inside; the direction of the idea or imagination moves from the inner toward the outer. What we envision through the eye relates to human perceptions during our everyday lives and is the way in which external earthly development reveals itself in our present era. It is what I have already identified as our ordinary consciousness today. However, if you explore anthroposophic literature, you will find that there are other possibilities for human consciousness than those that are readily available to us in everyday life.

Now try to create a picture of what can be perceived by the human being, even if it is only approximate and hazy. You see the colors present on the earth, hear sounds, feel the sensation of warmth, and so forth. You recreate the contours of what you have perceived so that you can fashion for yourself the things you have seen. Through everyday consciousness we learn to know what is in our surroundings. But there are other possibilities for consciousness that remain more or less unconscious for us today; other possibilities that are pressed into the depths of the life of the soul. And yet these deeper levels of consciousness are of even greater significance than the states of consciousness that exhaust themselves in the processes I have mentioned thus far.

For human beings living on earth, what lies beneath the surface of the earth is just as important as what encircles the earth. We can perceive what exists on the earth's periphery with our ordinary senses, and grasp what we have perceived through our senses by the power of imagination and conceptualization. This constitutes the consciousness readily available to humanity.

But now let us consider the interior of the earth. At first glance it appears that the interior of the earth conceals itself from ordinary human consciousness. Of course, we can dig into the earth to a certain depth; and within a cavity, such as a mine, we can make observations just as we do about the earth's surface. But that is no different than observing the corpse of a human being. Looking at a corpse, we see something that is no longer a fully human being. It is a residue of the human being. Indeed if you look at this in the right way, you have to say that the corpse is the opposite of a human being. The true manifestation of earthly humanity is the living, moving human being, which is manifest physically in the bones, the muscles, and so forth, carried within the human being. The reality of a living human being encompasses the bony frame, the muscle structure, the nerve system, heart, lungs, and so forth. A corpse no longer corresponds to the human being. When I have a corpse before me, there is no need to have lungs, heart, or muscle system. Therefore these elements of the body disintegrate. The various parts of the body maintain the form required of them for a short time after death. But a corpse is actually an untruth; after death it cannot be maintained. The corpse must disintegrate. It is no longer a reality. Likewise, what I find in the interior of the earth when I dig below the earth's surface is not reality. The interior of the earth affects the human being in a different way than the earthly surroundings that we perceive through the outer senses. From the perspective of the soul, you have to say that the environment of the earth is worked upon and grasped through the ordinary senses of the human being, as well as through the thinking and imaginative capacities of ordinary consciousness.

The interior of the earth works upon the human being not along a horizontal direction, but in a vertical movement from below to above. It goes right through the human being. Moreover, what works from below upward from the interior of the earth cannot be perceived in the way in which the outer senses perceive earthly surroundings. If the human being were to perceive the interior of the earth in the same way we perceive our normal earthly environment, then we would need a kind of eye or sense of touch that could penetrate the earth without digging a hole into it; that could pass through the earth as easily as we move a hand through air when we grasp something.

When you look through the air, you do not have to carve a hole in it to do so. If you had to make a hole in the air before you could look at an object, it would be the same as insisting that you must dig a mine-shaft in order to perceive the interior of the earth. But even if you do not need to dig a hole in the earth to perceive the earth's interior, you still would need to have a sense organ that could "see" without digging holes in the earth, or an organ that could perceive through feeling. Perceptions of the interior of the earth do not reach into the conscious-ness of the human being. Nevertheless, the perception of the earth's interior is conveyed through feeling. What is it that we can perceive within the core of the earth? Specifically, we can perceive the various metals of the earth.

Recall now just how many metals are contained in the earth. Every day you perceive animals, plants, minerals, and a great many human-made things in the air surrounding you. Likewise, you perceive metals within the interior of the earth. The perceptions of metals, even if they were able to enter your consciousness, would not be material perceptions; they would come in the form of imaginations. Visual impressions come to the human being along the horizontal plane. The metals do not send forth visual perceptions; rather something from the inner nature of the minerals emanates upward through the human being and calls forth imaginations or pictures. The human being does not perceive these pictures; instead the imaginations grow dim. They are suppressed to a certain extent, because our normal earthly consciousness does not perceive these imaginations. Therefore the imaginations are dimmed until they are reduced to feelings.

When, for example, you think about everything that has to do with the gold that exists in the crevices of the earth, your heart perceives a picture that corresponds to gold in the earth. However, this picture is an imagination that is not perceived by ordinary consciousness. It will be experienced only as a blunted yet living inner feeling, a feeling we are not able to articulate. The human being remains silent rather than expressing the perception of this picture corresponding to gold. This is also true for other organs in the body. The liver, for example, receives a certain picture of all that is tin† in the interior of the earth, and so forth.

All these unconscious impressions are only experienced as an inner feeling. Perceptions from our physical surroundings come to us through the horizontal plane and are met with the power of our thinking and inner imagination. Likewise, when emanations from the metals flow upward from the earth's interior and pass right through the human being, there arises within us in response, the dim consciousness of an inwardly living feeling. But at this point in the life of the earth, these human feelings remain chaotic and indistinct. We experience only an all-encompassing, life-imbued feeling.

If we were given a true gift of imagination, we would know that we have a relationship to the metals in the earth. Actually every human organ functions as a sense organ; even if we use an organ primarily for another purpose, it still functions as a sense organ. Just as our outer sense organs perceive, the inner organs also have a capacity to perceive. The human being is through and through a sense organ; and just as a complex being is differentiated in its individual sense organs, so individual inner organs also have specific functions.

The human being receives the perception of metals from below, and this perception meets a corresponding living feeling within the human being. Our feelings provide a counterforce to the influences metals have upon the human being. It is parallel to the way our thinking and power of imagination counterbalance the effect of everything in our surroundings that is conveyed to us through sense perceptions. And just as we receive the influences of the metals from below, we also receive influences from above in the movement and form of the celestial bodies in the cosmos. We experience sense perceptions from our surroundings, and we also have a consciousness that receives inspiration from every planetary circuit and every constellation of the fixed stars. As our consciousness streams out in response to the influence of celestial bodies, it has the potential of becoming an inspired consciousness. Just as we allow the power of our thinking to flow outward toward our sense perceptions, we also allow a counterforce to stream outward into the cosmos to meet the inspiration of the moving planets and the impressions of the stars. This counterforce is the power of the will. What arises in our will when we take this inspired consciousness into account we perceive as inspiration.

When we study the human being in this manner, we see that with regard to our earthly consciousness, we are in a waking state in our sense perceptions and our corresponding thoughts and imaginations. Indeed, we are fully awake only in our life of the senses, and in its counter-activity, thinking, when we stand within ordinary earthly consciousness. In contrast to this, our life of feeling is manifest only in a dreamlike state. Our feeling life is no more intense or enlightened than dreams; but dreams are made up of pictures, whereas our life of feeling, which is the soul constitution shaped by one's actual life, is made up of feeling. But the foundations of our feelings are generated by the effects of the metals of the earth upon human beings.

Even deeper, even less clearly articulated, is our consciousness of the will. We simply do not know how the human will works. I have often described this situation. The human being has a thought, extends an arm and grasps something with a hand. The thought can be grasped with one's waking consciousness. Then we see the act of grasping an object. But what lies between thought and deed? The penetration of the muscles by the will remains concealed from ordinary consciousness as if this act were experienced in a deep, dreamless sleep. In our feelings, we dream; in our will, we are asleep. But, from the point of view of ordinary consciousness, this will that sleeps is precisely our response to the impressions coming toward us from the stars, just as our thinking replies to the sense impressions in ordinary consciousness. And what we dream in our feelings is our answer to the influences of the metals within the earth.

As earthly humans, when we are awake, we perceive the objects around us. Our capacity to think and imagine gives an answer to these sense impressions. To accomplish this we use our physical and etheric bodies. Without our physicality or our etheric bodies we could not develop our capacities for sense perception and for thinking, which work back and forth in a horizontal direction. And so with regard to our waking consciousness, we can say that the physical body and the etheric body are filled with our sense impressions and our thinking activity. During sleep, the astral body and the I are outside our physical and etheric bodies. The astral body and the I are the elements of the human being that receive impressions from below and from above. The astral body and the I are asleep as they receive what streams upward from the metals in the earth and what streams downward from the movements of the planets and the constellations of the fixed stars. What becomes manifest in earthly surroundings from the horizontal direction has no influence on us during sleep; but the forces working upward from the interior of the earth and downward from the planets and fixed stars are the ones that work on us during the night.

If you attempt to move from ordinary consciousness to an imaginative consciousness during this epoch in human development, then all of the human organs will be able to grasp this imaginative consciousness to the same extent. It is not so that just the heart would be affected by this consciousness; all organs would have to be equally stirred by this consciousness. I have already said that the heart perceives the gold that exists in the earth. But the heart in and of itself can never perceive gold. As long as the I and the astral body are connected with the physical and the etheric bodies, as is the case for the human being in a normal state of wakefulness, the perception of gold can never become conscious. It is only when the I and the astral body (as in the instance of true imagination) become to a certain extent independent of the physical and etheric bodies, that the astral body and the I, in proximity to the heart, can perceive what streams forth from the metals within the earth. The center of perception that receives the emanations sent forth from the gold lies within the astral body, located in the region of the heart. The heart is able to perceive because the portion of the astral body that belongs to the heart is the part of the body that perceives the gold. The physical organ itself does not perceive gold; rather, it is the astral body that perceives it.

If we are able to attain imaginative consciousness, then the entire astral body and the whole organization of the I will be able to allow the segments of the astral body and the I to perceive their corresponding physical organs. That is to say, the human being perceives the totality of metals in the earth, albeit with differentiations. We can perceive specific details and differences, if we train ourselves and make it a particular goal of esoteric study to know the metals of the earth. This kind of knowledge is not something that should typically be sought by human beings in our era. An individual should not use this knowledge in a self-serving way. It is a universal principle that if a person wanted to use the knowledge of the metals of the earth for personal benefit, the imaginative capacity would be withdrawn.

It is possible, if a pathological condition occurs somewhere in the body, or if the connection between the astral body and the physical organs is interrupted, that the person may experience a light sleep during a waking state. Typically when we sleep, the astral body and the I draw apart from the physical and the etheric bodies. There is also a very light sleep, which individuals themselves barely notice, that may be present when a person is awake. This is very interesting to an observer because a person who is both asleep and awake at the same time may have a mysterious gaze and look somewhat "mystical." This comes about because we may experience the presence of a very light sleep even though we are wide awake. Indeed the physical and etheric bodies are always vibrating back and forth in relation to the astral body and the organization of the I. And people who experience the interaction of sleep and waking states may be able to locate metals within the earth. However, the ability to sense the presence of particular metals in the earth is accompanied by a certain level of illness.

When this capacity is placed in the service of technology and the utilization of the earth's resources, it may not seem to matter to the beneficiaries whether or not these people who can detect the presence of metals in the earth are a little ill. We may not bother to look at the human cost of procuring a desired substance. But viewed inwardly and from a cosmic perspective, when we seek knowledge not merely from the horizontal plane of what surrounds us on earth, but also want to receive perceptions directly from the earth's interior, this will always result in illness. Those who work out of direct perception of the interior of the earth cannot report findings in a conventional way. When we pick up a pen and write something down, this comes from our thinking and portrays something that is lifeless. But this ordinary capacity of imagination dampens down or confuses a perception that arises from below. In that case, it is necessary to make or draw signs that are different from ones that we ordinarily write or speak; for we perceive particular metals in the earth in an inwardly ill state. I also would like to point out that water is a metal. People in the pathological state we have been describing can be trained, not just unconsciously to perceive the existence of metals within the earth, but also to unconsciously make special signs. When you place a rod in the hand of one of these individuals, they make a sign with it. What does this indicate? It shows that there has been a slight interruption within the person between the I and the astral body, on the one hand, and the physical body and etheric body, on the other. Thus the person not only perceives what is nearby, but puts aside the usual perceptive capacities of the physical body, makes the entire body into a sense organ, and perceives the interior of the earth directly without carving out a hole in its surface. But when this occurs within the province of the feeling life, one cannot express the imagination that corresponds to the perception from the earth's interior. The individual can only indicate perceptions by making signs rather than by expressing it in words.

We also perceive what comes from above in a similar way. However, these perceptions have a different inner character. They do not correspond to the way we perceive metals in the earth through human feeling; rather, our perception comes in the form of inspiration, which is reflected from the movements of the planets or the constellations of stars. We perceive what streams down from above just as we can perceive the interior of the earth. An abnormal condition occurs in this instance, too, for the I is loosened from the astral body. We perceive from above what the flow of time and what the differentiation between segments of time give to the cosmos. We see more deeply into world events; not only in the past, but also certain occurrences that flowed out of necessity from the world order rather than from the actions of free human will. In that situation we can see prophetically into the future, into the ordering of time itself.

With these examples I wanted to indicate that a person may be able to heighten perception through certain pathological conditions. The healthy way to develop such capacities is through imagination and inspiration. We can differentiate healthy from unhealthy in this matter by looking at the following example. It is good for an ordinary person to have a normal sense of smell. A normal sense of smell allows us to perceive objects in our surroundings. But if someone has an abnormal sensitivity to a certain odor, that person can become ill in the presence of whatever emits the odor. There are people, for example, who become ill if they enter a room in which there is one single strawberry. They do not even have to eat the strawberry to feel sick. That is not an enviable situation. There could be situations in which a person with a heightened sensitivity to the smell of strawberries could identify the whereabouts of stolen strawberries or other stolen things that have a characteristic odor. They could be asked, for example, to use this unusual faculty in order to find stolen objects. If the human beings could sharpen a sense of smell as can be done with dogs, then the police would not need their police dogs. They could use instead human beings with a heightened sense of smell.

But we must not do this. You will understand this when I say that the capacity to perceive what arises from below and what descends from above should not be used in the wrong way. Developing these forms of perception and using them unwisely must be avoided, for doing so disturbs the entire organization of the human being. Training human metal detectors and human police dogs would not seem like a moral question to some entrepreneurs. Since we can receive these perceptions only in an abnormal or somewhat ill state, we should avoid the negative consequences of using these perceptions in the wrong way.

You will be able to understand all of these things that at first seemed to come to you in a confused and clouded way, or even in an overly theoretical manner; eventually you will be able to see how these things can be evaluated in the light of our relation to the entire cosmos. That is one side of the matter.

There is, however, a proper way to use these forms of knowledge. If you have attained imaginative knowledge, you must not use the feeling capacity of the astral body that is found near the heart to acquire gold for personal benefit. However, you may use this imaginative capacity in order to understand the structure, the true tasks, and the inner nature of the heart itself. You may use this capacity to enhance human self-knowledge. This also applies to the proper use of our physicality; for example, of the ability to smell or see, and so forth. And so we shall learn to know every organ of the human being as we discern each organ in relation to what we perceive from below and from above.

You will learn to understand the heart when, on the one hand, you recognize the gold within the earth as it streams upward and can be perceived through the heart. Then, on the other hand, you will learn to recognize the stream of will coming from the sun above; that is to say, to understand the counter-streaming from the sun as a form of the will. And so you can bring together the effect of the sun's streaming from above, at the point at which it reaches its zenith, together with the perception of the streams emanating from gold in the interior of the earth. By allowing the gold content of the earth to lead to imagination and the sun streams to awaken inspiration, you can achieve an understanding of the heart of the human being. You can attain a true understanding for the other organs in the same manner. If you wish to understand yourself fully as a human being, you must allow these two forms of knowledge, one from the depths of the earth and the other from the far reaches of the cosmos, to work upon you.

Today we have touched upon our relationship to the cosmos in a more concrete way than I have ever done before. If you take the lectures that I recently gave about the understanding of nature during the course of modern history, and recall my comments in yesterday's lecture, you will discover that what the human being receives from the current level of knowledge in the natural sciences is basically dead knowledge. You cannot even recognize yourself as you are in reality; rather, you can recognize only what you are in death. A true knowledge of the human being will only come to fruition through recognition of the difference between organs after death and living organs in relation to what they receive from below and from above.

To make that distinction you must acquire knowledge in a state of full consciousness. Instinctive knowledge in former times came about because the astral body and the etheric body then were more closely connected than we can experience today. Today the human being during earthly existence can become a free human being. For that to occur, however, it is necessary that we recognize what is dead in the present; that we understand the foundation of the past that arises from the interior of the earth in its metallic aspect; and that we acquaint ourselves with the life-generating effects coming from the stars and their constellations.

And in every organ a true understanding of the human being must be sought in its threefold nature: the dead or physical aspect, the foundation of life or the soul aspect, and the life-generating or the spiritual aspect. We must search everywhere, even within the smallest details of the human constitution, to discover the bodily-physical, the soul nature, and the spiritual aspect. And the reasonable starting point must be drawn out of a correct evaluation of what we have previously understood as the results of natural science. It must be recognized that the contemporary state of the natural sciences everywhere leads to the earth's tomb, and that we have to find our way back from the tomb and into the living.

Thus by taking facts into account, we can discover how modern spiritual science can bring life into the old forms of intuitions. The intuitions themselves have always been there. In the past few days, I have advised people who work in the most varied fields about any number of questions. For example, I advised literary historians who speak about Goetheanism, to remain true to the intuitions Goethe described in *Wilhelm Meister's Journeyman Years.*† There a woman appears in Book I who experiences the movement of the stars by means of an abnormal soul-spiritual state. Next to her stands an astronomer. Juxtaposed to the woman who intuitively experiences the celestial realm is another woman, who has the capacity to experience metals in the earth through her feelings. Near her, is Montanus, the miner and geologist. Montanus' intuitive knowledge of the interior of the earth was much deeper than the physical truths that have been described in the development of the natural sciences since the time of Goethe, even though the latter have been very substantial. For today natural-scientific knowledge belongs to the circumference of the earth's surface that lies easily within the grasp of the human being. Goethe, however, pointed out in *Wilhelm Meister's Journeyman Years* that the realms belonging to the human being also include the vast reaches of the stars above and the depths of the earth's interior below.

Many things may still be discovered both in the practical application of scientific knowledge and in the pure sciences. But these discoveries will be elevated to treasures of knowledge only when one takes what is offered through Goetheanism just as seriously. Spiritual science also will play its role by illuminating more fully what we find as presentiment in Goethe, or by reformulating the intuitive knowledge that Goethe brings forward in the literary form of a novel. Anticipating connections that may bear fruit over time causes a certain historical rejoicing!

I want to emphasize, however, that when we speak about the cultivation of scientific striving in the anthroposophic movement (and indeed it should be cultivated with great seriousness), anthroposophy should not succumb to the danger of being led astray by the contemporary disciplines of chemistry, physics, or physiology. Rather, the cultivation of the sciences in the stream of anthroposophic living knowledge should be brought into relationship with the specific scientific disciplines. Some would like to hear the chemist, physicist, physiologist, or physician speaking like an anthroposophist. That will not lead us forward. Nor will it be helpful if the individual specialists try to make anthroposophy speak in the languages of chemistry, physics, or physiology. That will only result in awakening opposition to anthroposophy; whereas we can move forward only when anthroposophy renders service to these specialists as anthroposophy, and not just as something that assumes anthroposophic terminology, or where scientific terminology is superimposed on what one already has in spiritual-scientific knowledge. It does not matter whether anthroposophic language or another terminology is used for hydrogen or oxygen, or if we continue to use the old terms. The question is whether one adopts anthroposophy with one's entire being. Then one will become, in the right way, an anthroposophist as well as a chemist, physiologist, or physician.

In this course I wished to present the history of natural-scientific thinking so that the knowledge of historical observations may bear fruit; for the anthroposophic movement urgently needs to be fruitfully engaged among the widest range of today's fields of knowledge.

4

Jacob Boehme, Giordano Bruno, and Francis Bacon as Representatives of the Struggle to Discover a New Knowledge of Humanity and the Cosmos

Dornach, January 12, 1923

In the course of world history, there are outwardly visible symptoms that reveal forces of inner development; and these symptom sometimes show how the outward expression is connected to the inner developments. The interrelatedness that permeates the universe, the interwoven worlds of the spirit, the soul, and physical matter, are of such a profound nature that often what merely seems to be outwardly apparent, upon closer examination actually corresponds to inner reality. And in that sense Giordano Bruno's death in 1600 (he was condemned to death and burned at the stake) was an outward manifestation of a most significant inner development for humanity. Indeed the flames of this pyre illuminate for the historical observer a clearly legible flame-script recording an inner transformation that became important for the entire development of human history.

We must not forget three personalities who were significant for every subsequent period: a Dominican, Giordano Bruno;† a shoemaker, Jacob Boehme;† and a Lord Chancellor, Francis Bacon.† These men were significant for every subsequent period because they embodied characteristics of humanity's transition from the sixteenth to the seventeenth centuries. These three men had very dissimilar personalities, but precisely in their distinctiveness, one from another, each one reflected a different aspect of what was emerging in the new worldview and what was waning in the older worldview during this time of human development.

Jacob Boehme came from the humblest origins in his society; and yet even as a boy his finely attuned, soul-sensitive ear could hear much of the folk wisdom that during his lifetime still lived within the peoples of middle Europe. This folk wisdom was more closely linked to what a person could feel inwardly than it was to learning the secrets that lay behind natural processes. The folk wisdom at that time, which was still audible to Jacob Boehme's soul-sensitive ear, had already reached a state in which its profound wisdom could no longer be clothed in language or expressed adequately in words. Aside from all of Boehme's greatness, we observe how Boehme "chewed" his words, tried to press and wrest out of them what he experienced through his feelings and had drawn into himself out of the wisdom still present in folk traditions.

Next we consider Giordano Bruno, who was steeped in the teachings of the Dominican Order. These teachings were based on an ancient wisdom that also brought forward insights, in finely chiseled ideas, about the relationship of the human being to the universe. These insights contained a certain strength and intensity of knowledge, but these qualities had faded under the influence of church tradition. We see in Giordano Bruno the longing and passion for knowledge that was characteristic of the transition from the sixteenth to the seventeenth centuries, and was forged within the soul with Faustian force. Giordano Bruno was entirely a child of his age, for in addition to his Dominican heritage, he was also a contemporary citizen of the world in the most refined sense possible; one who brought forth vivid, clear-cut, and yet carefully cultivated ideas. In all likelihood no one embodied the character of his age more fully than did Giordano Bruno. We can see that he wrapped the subtle ideas he encountered during his student years in the cloak of poetry. For Bruno, who wished to speak out of the fullness of universal consciousness, had to work within the narrow confines of the human souls of his day. He became a knowledge-imbued poet, a poetic scientist. Such a rich soul content lived within him that whenever he tried to say something this rich, soul-filled substance burst through the constraints of lifeless ideas. Bruno had to give himself over to the poetic in order to express the fullness of light.

Now we can look at our third representative, Francis Bacon, Lord Verulam, a man who lost entirely the ground beneath his feet and was completely engulfed by the outer material life of his age. He was a statesman who served James I as the Lord Chancellor of England. A man of great intelligence, he was not rooted in any specific spiritual or intellectual tradition, and thus could personify what the philosopher Fichte[†] later derided as the banality of reason, the banality of rationalism.

Francis Bacon indeed did introduce banality into philosophy. He had completely lost the ground of the spiritual under his feet. Since he was not rooted in any particular tradition, he regarded as real only what his outward senses showed him. He was not willing to assume anything spiritual on the basis of his sense experience. Bacon was the opposite of Jacob Boehme. Boehme wanted to extract out of an old spirituality what could, in fact, no longer be understood: the spark of the soul as well as the spark of the material. He wanted to find the secrets of the soul and matter in the old traditions, which he then struggled to clothe in words hardly adequate to the task. Francis Bacon found no such desire within himself. His soul existed as a *tabula rasa*, an empty slate, in contrast to the outwardly perceived sense world. Bacon used the banality of ordinary human reason, not the healthy form of reason, to meet the outer world of the senses. Out of this approach arose a knowledge based entirely on sense perception, a knowledge devoid of every aspect of the spiritual.

These three personalities were contemporaries. Boehme was born in 1575. Bruno, born in 1548, was the oldest of the three. Lord Bacon was born in 1561. Each in his own way represented a different aspect of the initial stage of modern civilization.

Today, when forces pressing downward are at their strongest, it is difficult to understand what was inwardly weaving and living within such souls as these. A great deal of what lived in these souls as real and genuine spiritual perspectives has now died out. At some point in the future, looking back to our time period, it will be possible to see our era as a culmination of materialism, which carries within it a corresponding moral counterimage of materialism. And this moral counterimage shows an increasing level of immorality as well as indifference toward everything spiritual. I draw attention to this indifference because during the three lectures this weekend I wish to build toward a culmination on Sunday[†] in which I shall speak about the opposition to the anthroposophical worldview. Therefore I am laying the foundation for this today and tomorrow through historical examples and observations.

The indifference toward everything spiritual raises the question of why people in our era still find something remarkable in Goethe's *Faust*. It would be easier to understand if human beings in our time said that *Faust* belongs to an epoch that has already been superseded. Indeed, they could say that Goethe's *Faust* reveals little more than superstition; it often deals with magic, and even features a pact with the devil.

It is easy enough to say in our day that all of this is simply poetic embellishment. And yet many willingly acknowledge that Goethe, in the character of Faust, wanted to portray a representative of humanity. We have to admit that it may be easier to adopt the position taken by the prominent scholar DuBois-Reymond,[†] who regarded *Faust* as nothing more than nonsense. DuBois-Reymond advised Faust to do the "honorable thing"—marry Gretchen—and focus his attention on inventing the electric machine and the air pump. That is an honest expression of what most people today think about *Faust*, but few say. Many praise *Faust* only because it is popular to say that Goethe's *Faust* is a great work that should not be dismissed. But this only reflects indifference; they do not bother to take a stand about something that does not matter to them.

One should be clear about the attitudes that might be expressed today if they were not influenced by judgments from the past. If Shakespeare had not written his *Hamlet*, and the play had appeared as one written only recently by an obscure poet, then we would see what people would honestly say about this play now.

We really have to think seriously about these things in order to understand our own day and time. Indifference lets you make an observation about Mephistopheles in Goethe's *Faust* because you may feel too timid to do otherwise, or because it allows you to say all manner of insignificant things about magic in the play. But to penetrate what was really present as a soul-spiritual atmosphere in a time when a matter decisive for the spiritual life of modern civilization was at stake is almost impossible in the present time. And yet that was precisely the case in the era in which Giordano Bruno, Jacob Boehme, and Francis Bacon lived.

Above all, if we want to look into this matter objectively, we must acknowledge the tremendous ideas that arose in earlier epochs; and they are remarkable especially in comparison with ideas today. Ideas that once were held in enormous regard are treated with indifference today. At best they only shed light on a literary or historical context.

We look back to the medieval era and see a figure such as Merlin.[†] Karl Leberecht Immermann[†] tried to bring this figure back to life for his own era. Yet what had once been larger than life images lost all of their grandeur in Immermann's prosaic verse.

Let us take the straightforward story of the Merlin legend. What was Merlin supposed to become? He was supposed to be the antithesis of the Christ. According to the medieval legend, Merlin was to be the exact opposite of the Christ. The scriptural tradition tells us that the Christ came into the world without physical procreation. Merlin was also supposed to incarnate in the same manner. But Christ entered the world through the overshadowing of Mary by the Holy Spirit. Merlin was supposed to enter the world because the devil overshadowed a virtuous nun as she slept. The devil wished to create an antipode to the Christ in Merlin; he overshadowed a pious nun as she was sleeping. But Merlin did not become the Antichrist because the nun was too virtuous. The devil's intent was frustrated by the purity of the nun's morality.

What do the lines of thinking in a medieval saga imply? They project an inner dauntlessness in the medieval worldview, an inner energy within human thought processes. If we compare this with what is said in our time about the origin of evil in the world (with the exception of what may be said in anthroposophic circles), about the origin of corruption in the human being, we must admit that what has taken hold in recent times is trivial and narrow-minded. Finally, apart from inner philosophical rigor, with which the origin of evil is sometimes spoken about today, some of the things said about evil are trivial in comparison with the impact of the creation of Merlin, who is a misbegotten son of the devil and therefore can never become evil enough.

Remember that Merlin is one of the leaders of the Arthurian circle. The legend used the figure of Merlin to illuminate a characteristic of an era. But the bards could not find anything on earth from this period of time that would capture adequately what they wished to portray.

Therefore the legend went beyond the earthly realm, soared above it into the suprasensory and the evil; and used a misbegotten son of the devil to explain something of an earthly nature.

I am not saying that we have a need for a similar mythic element for our own era. I am not saying that in order to capture something of this magnitude, we would have to speak in a similar way. Nor do we need to attribute the origin and source of philistinism in the modern period to something earthly. For philistinism has the peculiar characteristic that it fails to grasp its perniciousness, even as it lacks an understanding of its usefulness.

We find, for example, that controversy over the Lord's Supper or Communion was already widespread during the High Middle Ages [ninth through the thirteenth centuries c.e.]. I have already pointed out[†] that people began to debate questions about the Lord's Supper only when they no longer knew what was contained within the sacrament. One begins to debate a matter only when one knows nothing about it. As long as we know something about a matter, we do not need to discuss it. For those who can look with even a little insight into a world secret, discussion is always a sign of knowing nothing. Thus when people sit down and begin to discuss and argue about something, it is an indication (to a person who has insight) that no one knows anything. As long as reality exists—and it is possible to know something only about what is real—no one needs to have a discussion about it. I have never heard that when a rabbit is placed on the table at mealtime, there is a discussion as to whether or not it is a real rabbit; or where the rabbit may have originated; or whether the rabbit exists in time or eternity. Instead people sitting around the table eat the rabbit. There may be debates over its ownership, but not over existential questions. But behind the historical controversies over the Lord's Supper or Communion there lies something very different that allows us to experience the enormity of ideas for human beings in an earlier era. These ideas provide a great contrast to the philistine ideas of today, which are sometimes no less devilish, but in any case still are philistine ideas.

Individuals such as Trithemius von Sponheim,[†] Agrippa von Nettesheim,[†] Georgius Sabellicus,[†] and Paracelsus[†] were not slandered in an ordinary manner. They were accused of forming covenants with the devil and of practicing the art of magic, which people so feared. We also recognize a fear of the magical behind the controversy over the Lord's Supper, or Communion. The fear of magic accompanied the emergence of a new period in history, whose signature may also be found in individuals such as Francis Bacon, Giordano Bruno, and Jacob Boehme.

What did it mean if someone was called a magician? A magician was someone who could draw a kind of knowledge out of his inner being that supported the capacity to control nature and even other human beings. But the spirit of modern civilization moved toward the suppression of the inner knowledge that had formerly existed and had carried a remnant of ancient esoteric knowledge into the early modern period. Instead, the spirit of modern civilization allowed only the knowledge drawn from external nature to flourish, and put aside knowledge arising from the human being's innermost being. In an earlier time human beings stood in abject fear of anyone who handled things in a way they could not understand; that is, putting together machines, and so forth. In the modern era we know that if you can watch someone do something, you have an idea of how the knowledge entered another person's mind, and can grasp it yourself. Today that process is a given, and no one is afraid of magic anymore. The fear no longer exists because the inner sources of knowledge have been pushed deeply into the human being. Today it seems immaterial whether one listens to someone who imparts knowledge that is truly a part of the speaker or watches a person who operates machines in the laboratory. In either case, one thinks one can see how knowledge comes into another individual's mind, and does not admit that the other person's mind can contain anything else. We always have to be able to see exactly what a person has in his or her head. Today this seems to be self-explanatory. It just "stands to reason."

In the time of Francis Bacon there were still human beings who possessed a wealth of inner activity. So it was worthwhile for Francis Bacon to launch a campaign opposing the abundance and worth of an inner life of the soul, and to point out the wealth of what could be gained from one's external surroundings. Here again, we look back to the previous era, in which people presumed that the human mind could be filled with content; and they wanted to know what that content was because they were convinced that what the mind contained could not be found in nature that surrounds the human being. And then Bacon came and explained that the presumption that the mind generated content from within was ridiculous. The human head is completely empty; everything the mind contains has to be drawn into it from without, from nature itself.

That was Francis Bacon's theory. But in the early Middle Ages the great fear prevailed that in human beings something of an independent knowledge could grow within the soul, and even that the spirit could grow within the human being. No wonder the understanding of the mystery of the Eucharist died out completely, for it presumed that a real transformation occurred within the human being, a transformation in which physical matter could become something entirely different.

Thus we see that during the controversy over the Eucharist something remarkable occurred. In the early periods of Christianity, the transformation of the bread and wine (transubstantiation) enabled certain ideas to be accepted as both possible and real. By the sixteenth century the power of these ideas no longer existed. Therefore human beings began to ask what can the mystery of the Eucharist be? And henceforth the ceremony and its components were seen in a purely external manner. The external and material conveyed the essence of what was being expressed through the ritual, so that the adherents of the Reformation argued about the manner in which the bread and the wine should be served as well as about the nature and significance of the ritual itself. The spirit was driven out of the ceremonies.

That was the first phase of the era of materialism. Materialism in modern civilization surfaced initially in the debate over Christian sacraments. Materialism first burst forth in this religious context. And during this time, the period in which Bruno, Boehme, and Bacon lived, the seed for a *new* spirituality should have been planted. But this modern era showed humanity only spiritless matter in the laws of nature. As a result, human beings had to search for the spirit by means of their own capacities. In this first phase of materialism, the spirit was extinguished in the life of the mind; and above all, it was extinguished in all aspects of religious ritual. And then the dissolution of the spirit continued even further into all of the secular areas of life.

Goethe was aware of this and created in his *Faust* an echo of what still lived in the vigorous ideas that arose in the transition between the sixteenth and seventeenth centuries. What did Goethe want to represent in the character of Faust? The form is poetic, but above all he wanted to bring to light the universally human. It is not difficult to say what Goethe wanted to achieve in *Faust*. He wanted to place the complete, full human being before humanity. When the impulse to write *Faust* arose in Goethe, he could find only limited and incomplete traditions regarding the historical Doctor Faustus. But he chose this Faust-figure from the sixteenth century because Goethe's perceptive feeling sensed the mighty struggle in the sixteenth century to rediscover something that had been lost; namely, the human being.

The discovery of the true nature of the human being was what each of the three men I mentioned earlier in this lecture also tried to achieve: Giordano Bruno, Jacob Boehme, and Francis Bacon. The Dominican Giordano Bruno outgrew Scholasticism, in which ideas had faded into externalized abstraction. Bruno expressed his ideas in poetics, elevated them into an art, and filled them with feeling and meaning. He tried to bring the ideas with which he struggled back to life. How is the universe found within the human being? How is the human being found within the cosmos? This is how it was with Giordano Bruno.

This was also the goal of the shoemaker Jacob Boehme. He, too, sought for the human being; but he did so among the humble people with whom he had grown up, whose qualities seemed more human than people among society's elite. He did not find the essential human being he sought, so he immersed himself as deeply as possible in folk wisdom; what he also sought was the universe revealed in the human being, and the human being revealed in the universe.

Among the three, Francis Bacon was the only one who did not consciously search for the essential human being, although he looked for the human being in a certain way. He wished to understand the human being in the way leading investigators of nature have always looked for this knowledge. Bacon wanted to characterize the human being as a kind of mechanism. Condillac[†] and La Mettrie,[†] natural philosophers of the nineteenth and twentieth centuries, constructed the human being out of atoms, and various natural processes, just like a mechanism. These thinkers produced nothing more than a ghost of the human being, a ghost that was not alive; rather, it was just a sack filled with abstractions. Bacon, too, spoke about the human being as if he were carrying around a sack stuffed full of abstractions. Even so, it still represented something. Bacon did search for the human being, even though he was unconscious of it. He did not realize it, but he also sought to understand the universe in the human being and the human being in the universe.

Now what do we mean when we say that each one of these individuals, Jacob Boehme, Giordano Bruno, and Francis Bacon, in his own way, was searching for the human being within the universe and the universe within the human being? If we look at Jacob Boehme, we see that he tried to speak about a human being that simply does not exist. Through his faltering concepts we find a profile of a human being that is nowhere to be found on earth. Nevertheless, this apparently non-existent human being had an inner capacity, an inner power of existence. When we try to take Jacob Boehme's human being into account, we have to say to ourselves that Jacob Boehme speaks about the three elements of life within the human being: salt, sulfur, and mercury. And yet this is not the human being we see before us in the modern era. But what Jacob Boehme forms and shapes is a *being*. You cannot say he puts it together piece by piece, but rather that he forms and shapes this being. And in a spiritually-scientific manner you ask what relationship the human being has with respect to the being portrayed by Jacob Boehme? And then we realize that this being is the human being in its pre-earthly existence. When we consider it from a spiritual-scientific point of view, we discover remarkable correspondences between the pre-earthly existence of the human being and the being Jacob Boehme tried so haltingly to describe. On the earth, a human being in its pre-earthly form as it was described by Jacob Boehme cannot exist. But in its pre-earthly state of being, this being did have a plausible existence. Nevertheless, Boehme's description does not entirely agree with the actual pre-earthly human being.

When we enter fully into Boehme's description of the human being, then on the basis of anthroposophic knowledge we sense that Jacob Boehme is portraying the pre-earthly existence of the human being.

That is indeed so, but Boehme described the pre-earthly existence in such a way that it remains a theory; not externally, but inwardly a theory. It is the pre-earthly human being that cannot become fully human and perishes spiritually, before the pre-earthly human being can be born on earth. This form of the human being cannot come into earth existence.

What Jacob Boehme portrayed of the pre-earthly human being shows that he wanted to reach a memory of what a person once could have experienced; but no matter how hard he tried, he failed to draw the memory into conscious awareness. For Jacob Boehme, the capacity to conjure up again the pre-earthly human being had been lost. In earlier ages, the human being could know pre-earthly existence. Boehme had found this kind of wisdom in folk traditions. But he was unable to produce anything more than a stillborn soul image of the pre-earthly human being. He no longer had the capacity to portray the human being as a living reality in pre-earthly existence.

Let us now turn our attention to Giordano Bruno, who was not only a child of his time, but a person for whom only the present mattered. You have the feeling with Giordano Bruno that the present was everything; the grand present, the present that encompasses the Cosmic All in space. With Bruno, there was nothing of the past and nothing of the future. He experienced the cosmos entirely in the present. He represented the Cosmic All as something present, and wanted to portray the human being, as well, within the context of the present through his halting poetic words. Bruno could not accomplish this any more than Jacob Boehme could attain his goal of characterizing the pre-earthly human being. But the seeds are present in Bruno to place the human being of the present (that is, the human being between birth and death) in an accurate way, so that the human being can be correctly understood.

Thus we see the limitations of human capacities and persistence in mastering a true knowledge of the whole human being. And the knowledge and understanding of the human being must be won, because only *from* this knowledge may our understanding of the pre-existent and post-existent human being spring forth. We know very little of the post-existent human being. This form of the human being was entirely closed and invisible to Francis Bacon.

During sleep, the I and the astral body are outside of the physical and etheric bodies, which continue to live in the same world that we see with our eyes and perceive with the entire apparatus of the senses. During sleep, our soul-spiritual kernel takes into itself what is needed for the future, and what will unfold after we go through the gate of death. What is taken from this life and is carried over from the present into the future; is veiled to ordinary consciousness. Similarly, to the first beginnings of modern scientific knowledge, which are evident in Francis Bacon, the future was closed from view; and yet, even though its existence was denied, an awareness of the future lived in the knowledge of the senses at an unconscious level. Indeed, by means of a knowledge gained through sense perception, we must recreate knowledge of post-existence; that is, an understanding of our existence after death. Bacon could not accomplish that, for he had no spiritual capacity to do so. He portrayed the human being as if it were a sack of ideas stuffed full of abstractions. It is the most imperfect and lamentable result that emerged in the transition to the modern era—that the human being had to strive to reach the spiritual out of the knowledge of nature; indeed, the knowledge of the spirit had to be wrenched from the knowledge of nature. That is what occurred in the life of Francis Bacon.

We see that Jacob Boehme was trying, however imperfectly, to reach a picture of the pre-earthly human being. In Giordano Bruno we find a grand and yet equally incomplete picture of the earthly human being in the present, in the time between birth and death, drawn out of the World-All. With Bacon we have an unconscious attempt to see what should someday come to life, but instead produces only a completely dead product. The human being, as portrayed by Bacon, cannot live on earth; his form of the human being is a ghost on the earth. However, when the role of the soul-spiritual in sleep and in human existence between death and rebirth is rightly understood and comes to fruition, then humanity will become aware its own post-earthly existence.

When we look at these three spirits, a truly remarkable trefoil presents itself at the turn of the sixteenth and seventeenth centuries. They came from diverse origins: Jacob Boehme was a man of the common people; Giordano Bruno was steeped in the spiritual schooling of the

Dominican order; and Francis Bacon outwardly attained the highest social station, but inwardly had completely lost the foundation under his feet. When we take into account the social circumstances of each one, and how each in a different way came to his own perspectives, then we discover what remarkable destinies were fulfilled in their lives.

We see the man of the common people, Jacob Boehme, fighting his entire life for what still lived within the folk traditions; but these remnants lived in an inarticulate form and even provoked persecution. The struggle also existed within the common people, but in a latent form. Jacob Boehme himself never left the spheres of folk tradition.

Francis Bacon was a remarkable intellect and an advocate of the modern worldview. Morally he lost his way. Bacon was representative of the risks of modernity, at least insofar as this kind of science may open the way to moral waywardness.

And between the two is Giordano Bruno, who pointed not to something from the past, nor to something out of the future, but wanted to seize within the immediate present the kernel that would grow into the spiritual perspective of the future. In Bruno this still appeared in embryonic form. But those who were tied to the old traditions were determined to suppress this seed in its moment of birth. And so we see how the flaming pyre in Rome was a remarkable historical monument. Bruno himself declared that his execution would be significant in the future: "You may kill me, but my ideas over centuries cannot be extinguished—ideas will live on." So here the outer symptoms of historical development actually reveal the inner development of humanity in a profound way. And if we really understand the context of the old, then we also understand that the flames consuming Giordano Bruno bore witness to the new impulse, which of necessity had to arise out of the old. I wanted to describe for you what actually, inwardly, took place in this event, what those flames were meant to destroy.

Now in our day a physical memorial in honor of Giordano Bruno has been erected where the pyre was lit. We want to be sure that we understand what was extinguished in that event; and what should and must continue to live and continue to develop in a living way, albeit not in precisely the same form in which it once transpired.

5

Salt, Sulfur, and Mercury Processes in the Inner Human Being

The Dissolution of Ancient Clairvoyance through Spiritual Observation of Nature

Dornach, January 13, 1923

I would like you to recall the three individuals I characterized yesterday (Giordano Bruno, Francis Bacon, and Jacob Boehme), because their significance for the transition from the sixteenth to the seventeenth centuries carries over into our own time. Each one struggled to understand the human being anew, to articulate the essential nature of the self. And yet at the same time they were unable to arrive at the clear insights they were seeking. This is a common characteristic of the age in which they lived, and one that now may be seen very clearly. I pointed out that although the old knowledge and wisdom about the nature of the human being had been lost, even the most earnest struggles of these prominent intellectuals of the sixteenth and seventeenth centuries could not achieve a new understanding of our essential being.

In a strange, almost incomprehensible language, Jacob Boehme conveyed a yearning to understand the universe in the human being and the human being within the universe. Above all, what Boehme brought together in his understanding of the inter-relatedness of the human being and the universe now illuminates today's anthroposophic knowledge of the human being during pre-earthly existence. Nevertheless, a complete and clear representation of the human being before we enter earthly life is not to be found in Boehme. He haltingly portrayed the rudiments of a pre-earthly human being, but the human being Boehme described as a soul-spiritual being would have had to die in the spiritual world before descending to earthly existence. Thus Boehme was unable to fully grasp the existence of the universe in the human being and the human being in the universe.

When we look at the poetic phrases of Giordano Bruno, we find a person whose knowledge of the universe is painted in grand pictures. He places the human being within a majestic worldview, and also tries to discover the universe in the human being and the human being in the universe. But Bruno likewise fails to reach a full understanding. Giordano Bruno's mighty pictures are indeed grand and beautiful. On the one hand, his pictures sweep into the vastness of infinity; and, on the other hand, they plunge into the deepest reaches of the human soul. But they remain indefinite and nebulous. Ultimately, everything that Giordano Bruno says reveals his striving to place human beings of the present within the spatial universe, and to describe the nature of the cosmos as well.

Even as Jacob Boehme gave an inadequate description of the pre-earthly existence of the human being, so too, Giordano Bruno offered an incomplete picture of the human being living in the present on earth in relationship to space, and even to the cosmos. A truly thoroughgoing view of the relationship of the human being to the cosmos in the present era would give us a picture of both the pre-earthly and the post-earthly existence of the human being, just as I presented here a short time ago in the course on philosophy, cosmology, and religion.[†]

Looking once again at Francis Bacon, we see that he no longer has anything like a traditional idea of the human being. Bacon gives no evidence of older notions about human nature from ancient esoteric traditions or the old mystery wisdom. Bacon turned his glance out into the world where the senses can directly perceive; and he gave human reason the task of combining observations of phenomena and sense-perceptible objects to discover the laws of nature. He placed the human soul in the soul-state that exists between the moment of falling asleep and its subsequent awakening, but he assigned to this state only pictures of a non-human nature. These pictures, when you take them in the logical and abstract way used by Bacon, reflect only what is external to the human being. If, however, these pictures are experienced in a living way, then they could be transformed into something that reveals the nature of human existence after death. For out of a modern knowledge of nature, it is also possible to achieve exactly what esoteric perception can establish about the nature of the human being after death. Thus

Bacon is among those who struggled to reach a new knowledge of the human being in the universe and the universe in the human being at the turn of the sixteenth and seventeenth centuries. But his efforts were insufficient for the task he wished to accomplish. For Bacon, only the images or pictures remained of what had, in former times, been a living reality experienced deeply in the life of the soul. Bacon, lacking the vitality of soul experience that existed in ancient and medieval times, could no longer intensify the pictures and suffuse them with living experience. Bacon stood at the threshold of recognizing the nature of life after death, but he was unable to reach beyond the threshold and grasp this knowledge.

Thus we can say that drawing upon traces of old traditions Jacob Boehme still had some knowledge about the pre-earthly existence of the human being, but it was incomplete. Giordano Bruno stood at the brink of describing the universe in a way recognizable to human beings today; he saw humanity with its life of soul on one side, and humanity standing before the expanse of the entire cosmos on the other side. But Giordano Bruno defended an inadequate view of the cosmos and an equally insufficient description of the life of the soul, which for him had shrunk into a living monad.

Lord Bacon shows us how the natural sciences would have to develop. Indeed, natural science based entirely on the material aspect could draw out the spark of the spiritual in matter through an unfettered approach to human knowledge. He pointed humanity in the direction of this freely won human knowledge, but assigned to it no specific content. If Bacon had sought for relevant meaning, he would have illuminated the post-earthly nature of the human being. That he was unable to do. His capacity to reach true knowledge also remained incomplete.

Everything that in earlier epochs had enabled human beings to draw living knowledge from within was extinguished by the early modern period. The human being became inclined to remain empty when looking within and wanting to draw knowledge about the world out of the inner life of knowing. Human beings, one could say, had lost their connection with a living inner experience of knowledge. What remained was a point of view focused upon the outer world, upon an external nature not directly connected with the human being.

Jacob Boehme drew out of folk wisdom three principles associated with the fundamental nature of the human being, which he referred to as salt, mercury, and sulfur. His words meant something very different from the meaning these words have today in the language of modern chemistry. If we tried to connect Boehme's understanding of *salt*, *mercury*, and *sulfur* with the terminology of the modern science of chemistry, we would entirely miss Boehme's insights. These words are used in quite another way. Why did Boehme use this terminology? What did these words mean in the context of the traditional folk wisdom that was the source of the terms used by Boehme? This is important because when Boehme spoke about salt, mercury, and sulfur with respect to the human being, he meant something concrete and real.

When we speak about the life of the soul today, we often speak in abstract terms, for what once was a real, living experience has disappeared from our conscious awareness and concepts. Even Jacob Boehme was able to collect only the last crumbs of what once was a reality. External nature, perceivable through the senses and accessible to human powers of reasoning, was spread out before the human being in the seventeenth century. We have learned about processes in nature, and built upon this expanding knowledge, until today we know a great deal about nature. We can also learn about the nature of the human being through outer observation. When we try to understand human nature by external observation alone, however, without realizing it, we build up concepts about human physicality without examining whether the concepts correspond to the actual physical nature of the human being.

When we take processes in nature perceived through our senses and apply these processes to the living human body, we create only a phantom human physicality. This approach cannot reveal what occurs beneath the skin of the human being. Similarly, when we speak about the human being in terms of Thinking, Feeling, and Willing, these expressions, too, are abstractions, shadow thought-images, which are supposed to be filled out by our inner experiences. When our inner experiences are merely mirror images of external nature, we no longer have any notion of how the soul-spiritual aspect penetrates human physicality. Nor do we have any understanding of what once was passed on as remnants of ancient esoteric knowledge.

What does anthroposophic spiritual science say about this? Let us consider our physicality with respect to internal processes that occur simultaneously with sense perceptions. Take, for example, the process of metabolism that sustains our living physical organism. We see that metabolism coincides with sense perceptions. When we eat, we physically assimilate our food. At the same time we also taste its flavors. Thus our perception of flavor is mixed together with a process in which a substance from nature is assimilated into our physicality.

In the metabolic process, perceiving the flavors of the food we eat accompanies the nourishment of our organism. Tasting food is the first step in the digestive process. Then the physical elements in the food are dissolved into the fluids that are present in the human organism. Plants take matter out of lifeless nature and transform it into another form. The basic form for matter in lifeless nature is crystalline. Matter that does not appear to be in crystalline form and seems to lack any form, such as dust and other such matter, is actually made up of shattered crystals. Plants take matter out of crystallized, lifeless nature and reconstitute it in a form that they can assimilate. Likewise, the animal takes plants into its metabolic processes and changes them into a form it can use. Thus we can say that in nature everything has its specific form. When the human being takes in matter for nutrition, the substance is dissolved and reconstituted. This is the basic nature of human metabolism: the human corporality dissolves the forms that exist in nature. We transform nature's elements into liquid or fluid forms.

But even as we dissolve what we eat into a fluid state, we also inwardly reconstitute these original forms that were broken down in the metabolic process. We recreate these original forms. When we eat salt, we dissolve it in the fluids of our organism, but then we form within us what the salt once was. When we eat a plant, we dissolve the substance of the plant into fluids, but inwardly we reconstitute it again. However, we do not recreate it in a fluid form; we reconstitute it within the etheric body of the human being.

If you were to imagine yourself living in ancient times, you would see yourself as a human being taking salt into your body. You would dissolve it and reconfigure it again in your etheric body. During those ancient epochs, you would have perceived the entire process; that is, you would experience the form of the salt in your thoughts. You would eat the salt, dissolve it in your physicality; the salt crystal would exist in your etheric body and you would know that the salt had the form of a crystal. This you would have perceived inwardly; and just as you experienced the process of metabolism within yourself, you also could experience nature inwardly. Cosmic thoughts became your thoughts. What you experienced as an imagination, as a dreamlike imagination, would be represented inwardly as etherically reconstructed forms, which were also cosmic forms.

Then the time came when human beings lost the ability to inwardly experience the processes of physical dissolution and etheric reconstitution. Increasingly, we looked for explanations within nature itself. No longer could we inwardly experience that salt has the form of a hexahedron. We tried to discover the form of a salt crystal by investigating outwardly visible nature. We became severed from inner perception and more firmly connected to outer physicality. This radical shift away from inwardly perceiving cosmic thoughts through perceptions generated in one's etheric body was completed by the beginning of the fifteenth century, and it increased in its intensity until it reached its height in the time in which Giordano Bruno, Jacob Boehme, and Francis Bacon lived.

Jacob Boehme still could grasp the crumbs of folk wisdom, which spoke to him in the following way: the human being dissolves everything that is consumed of outer matter. It is a process similar to dissolving salt in water. We carry this "water" within our life fluids. Everything material that nourishes the human being is "salt." It dissolves itself. Thus the cosmic thoughts of salt find expression in reality on the earth. And the human being reconstitutes these cosmic thoughts within the etheric body. That is the nature of the salt process. Jacob Boehme articulated what in ancient times was perceived and recognized through inner experience. If it were not for anthroposophic insight today, it would not be possible to unlock the meaning of Jacob Boehme's halting expressions. Without anthroposophic insight, all manner of nebulous or mystical interpretations can be attributed to Boehme. It is clear that Jacob Boehme brought together the process of thinking (through which the human being imagined the cosmos in pictures) and the process by which salt is first dissolved in the physical body, and then is subsequently reconstituted in the etheric body. That represented the salt process as Boehme understood it.

Sometimes it is almost moving to see that some people today read Jacob Boehme's explanation of the salt process and think they understand what he said. In fact, they do not grasp his words at all, and only reveal their own arrogance by saying so. They hold their noses high in the air and say that they have read Jacob Boehme and know that he brings us an unbelievably deep wisdom. But these interpretations do not contain any element of living wisdom. If it were not for the arrogance of these people, we might be moved by the regard they claim to have for Jacob Boehme. But they act as if they understand something that Boehme himself did not fully understand, for he struggled to express mere traces of insight that had passed into folk wisdom. Boehme himself did not fully understand the true significance of the processes he tried to describe.

Boehme pointed us in the direction of an entirely different science and wisdom that existed in ancient times; wisdom that was experienced by the human being as self-perception of processes in one's own etheric body, which inwardly reconstituted cosmic thoughts. Ancient people recognized that the cosmos embodied the process of crystallization on earth and understood that this process echoed cosmic thoughts. They recreated the process of crystallization within the etheric body and accompanied the process knowingly. This was inherent in ancient knowledge, but in the course of human history it eventually disappeared.

Imagine that you yourself were present during an ancient initiation ceremony and listened to the description being given to a new initiate out of the Cosmic All. With soul-spiritual sensitivity you would listen to the words being spoken:

Everywhere in the Cosmic All, cosmic thoughts are at work: The Logos is at work! Observe crystallization on the earth! Crystallizations are the manifestations of individual Words within the Cosmic Word. The sense of taste is just one of many senses. What the human being hears and sees may be treated in the same way that salt in its etheric form may be physically perceived. The human being takes in through human physicality what is embodied in the salts, reconstitutes its cosmic form in the etheric body, and experiences the entire process consciously within. The cosmic thoughts repeat themselves within human thoughts; thus the human being recognizes the cosmos in the human being, and the human being in the cosmos.

With extraordinary intuitive perception, the ancient initiate could experience with concrete intensity this dreamlike and visionary understanding of both the cosmos and the human being.

During the High Middle Ages, this ancient knowledge disappeared behind a logical wisdom that was very significant but had nevertheless withered within the framework of Scholasticism. The ancient knowledge trickled down and became folk wisdom. What formerly had been an elevated cosmic and humanistic wisdom was reduced to folk sayings, repeated by the common people, who understood very little of its substance but still felt that at one time it must have contained something of enormous value. Jacob Boehme lived among the common people, absorbed this folk wisdom, and through his own strenuous effort brought it alive within himself. He was able to say more about the remnants of the ancient wisdom than the common people; and yet he, too, could express it only in a faltering way.

In Giordano Bruno there lived nothing more than a general feeling that humanity had to recognize both the cosmos and the human being. But he lacked the capacity to say:

Cosmic thoughts exist, and the Cosmic Word incorporates itself in crystals. Human beings assimilate cosmic thoughts in that they perceive the salt that dissolves in the human physicality, and then reconstitute the form of the salt within the etheric body. Thus the human being experiences the concrete aspects of the many-faceted cosmos and creates concrete thoughts within the human being, from which sprouts an etheric inner world as rich as the one the cosmos emits in the Cosmic All.

Cosmic thought and human thought melted together for Giordano Bruno and became a general description of the cosmos, sweeping outward into infinity, but in a way that was entirely abstract. And what lived within the human being as the recreation of the cosmos melted together with a description of a living indivisible entity, a monad, which amounted to nothing more than an elaborated point.

What I have described to you was knowledge for the sages of the ancient mysteries. It was their science. But in addition to the fact that these sages of old could extract such a science out of their dreamlike methods, they also had the capacity to form real connections with the spiritual beings of the cosmos. Just as we today enter consciously into a relationship with another person, so it was that formerly these sages established connections with the spiritual beings of the cosmos. From these spiritual beings they learned about another, singular capacity of the human being. They learned from these spiritual beings that only the human being is capable of creating something in the etheric body whereby the human being inwardly is a replica of the cosmos: a smaller cosmos, a microcosm, indeed, an etheric rebirth of the macrocosm. And just as these sages had inwardly replicated the cosmos in the etheric body, it was also possible for them to gradually extinguish the microcosm as the element of air was drawn into the physical body and expelled again during breathing.

Thus the human being could learn how the universe was reborn inwardly in various forms, and could also experience inwardly these different forms of the universe. In ancient times, out of one's inner living fluidity, the etheric of the entire cosmos was evident. That was an aspect of the ancient occult vision. But it remains an actual process as well. This same process is present in humanity today, although we cannot inwardly experience it.

The spiritual beings who entrusted ancient sages with this knowledge pointed out to them that in addition to perceiving their inner Life Fluidity (water), out of which the microcosm was born, they also perceived the Life Air, which we take in as breath and then spread throughout our entire organism. What thus has been spread throughout the human organism is poured over the entire microcosm, causing the originally clear etheric forms to become indistinct. The wonderfully formed etheric microcosm begins to become less distinct because the flow of the breath begins to interfere with or obscure the etheric forms. What had been many forms became a single one. The human astral aspect lives within the air, just as the human etheric aspect lives in the watery element. The astral human being lives in the airy element, and by breaking up the etheric thoughts and transforming the etheric thoughts into human capacity and strength, the human will is born out of the astral aspect inherent in the Life Air. The powers of growth accompany the birth of the will, for they are closely related to the will.

What I have just described is not equivalent to our modern use of the word "will" as an abstraction; here we have a concrete process. The astral seizes the air-forming process and spreads it out over the etheric fluidity. This process presents itself outwardly in nature when something is burned. In earlier epochs burning was associated with the sulfur process. What was experienced in the soul as the human will was regarded as a manifestation of the sulfur process.

In previous eras human beings did not use the abstract word "thinking" for something that arose in the mind in pictorial form. Rather, when people who were truly knowledgeable spoke of thinking, they referred to the salt process. Nor did they speak in an abstract way about the will; rather, they referred to the astral forces penetrating the airy element in the human being and to the sulfur process in which the observable will has its origin. They pointed out that the balance between the two processes (for the two are opposite processes) was achieved through the mercury process, which is both fluid and formed. The mercury process moves back and forth between the etheric and the astral, between the formative capacities of water and air.

Abstract ideas, which the Scholastics taught and modern science has assimilated, did not exist for the ancient thinkers. If thinkers in ancient times had been confronted with our concepts of thinking, feeling, and willing, they would have felt like a frog that found itself in a jar pumped empty of air. That is how it would have seemed if an ancient thinker had come across our abstract ideas. They would have thought: *this manner of thinking does not allow for a soul-filled life; in such an atmosphere one cannot breathe soul-permeated air.* For them it would have seemed like an empty void. They did not speak of an abstract thinking process or an abstract will process. Instead they spoke of a salt process and a sulfur process, and meant by this something that was soul-spiritual on the one hand, and something material-etheric on the other. For them this was a unity, and they perceived the cosmic order as one in which the soul worked everywhere in physicality, and the physical was everywhere permeated by soul.

Writings from the Middle Ages, and even those from the thirteenth, fourteenth, and fifteenth centuries, were still influenced by remnants of an ancient perspective that was filled with substance and knowledge based upon inwardly living experience. This knowledge had died out by the time Giordano Bruno, Jacob Boehme, and Francis Bacon lived. Ideas had become abstract ideas rather than living ones. Human beings no longer looked within themselves for knowledge; rather, they looked outward into nature. I must say to you that the ancient thinkers would have looked at our ideas no differently than a frog gasping for air in a vacuum. But we ourselves are capable of understanding these ideas. When people today speak about thinking, feeling, and willing, they do not think that these processes are mirror images drawn from external nature, which also happen to occur in human beings. Nonetheless, in our modern era we can achieve something that the ancients could not fully understand. One is able now, out of one's own autonomous capacities, to draw knowledge out of one's own self. But in the time between the fifteenth century and our present day, human beings could no longer arrive at knowledge simply by looking within their inner being. Rather one looked outward into nature, from which one would draw abstract ideas. But now these abstract ideas can be intensified, can once again receive substance, because they can again be experienced in a living way. It is true that this human capacity is still in its beginning stages, but this beginning can also lead to anthroposophic spirit knowledge.

All of these processes that I have referred to, the salt process and the sulfur process, for example, are processes that do not take place outwardly in nature. They are processes that we can recognize only in our inner being. In outer nature they do not take place. However, there does occur something in external nature that is related to the contrast between processes in a corpse and processes that occur in a living person.

If the chemistry we are familiar with today were to speak of the sulfur and salt processes that Jacob Boehme could still acquire out of folk wisdom, it would characterize what occurs in a corpse rather than what occurs within a living human being. Today's chemistry is completely dead, whereas the perceptions of the ancients were inwardly alive. The human being formerly saw into a world that was different from the one surrounding earthly humanity. With the help of self-generated understanding, the human being had the capacity to see something that was not in the environment surrounding the human being on earth, but something that belonged to another world. When a human being living in an earlier era achieved an understanding of these salt and sulfur processes, that individual could see into the pre-earthly life of humanity. For earthly life is differentiated from pre-earthly life in that the living sulfur and salt processes that are visible now in our outer world of the senses appear as if they were dead. What we perceive between birth and death through our senses are, in fact, the living sulfur and salt processes that we experienced in pre-earthly existence. That is, the processes that Jacob Boehme dimly understood but expressed with difficulty actually correspond to what one can perceive in pre-earthly existence.

Jacob Boehme did not speak about pre-earthly existence because he did not have a clear understanding of its reality and could express what he grasped only in faltering words. The capacity of the human being to look into pre-earthly existence had been lost. Moreover, the connection humanity had with the spiritual beings of the cosmos, which could help us to see in the sulfur process the reality of post-earthly existence, had been severed. The entire constitution of the human soul is different now from what it was in ancient times. And Giordano Bruno, Jacob Boehme, and Francis Bacon all lived during the time of this transformation of the soul.

Yesterday I mentioned the fact that today people no longer have any idea how differently human beings in ancient times saw themselves in relation to the world. In our day people can barely appreciate accounts that date back further than the relatively recent past. I have pointed out that the grandiose notion of the origin of Merlin is an example of this. We can also look at other examples. In Dornach we have performed the Oberufer Plays[†] several times. But the story of the visit of the Three Kings to the Jesus child can also be found in the much earlier Germanic lay of the *Heliand.*[†] This narrative poem originated in central Europe and dates back to the early medieval era; that is, the ninth century C.E. There we notice something very remarkable. Something quite unusual is attached to the visit of the Three Kings from the East. The Three Kings in the *Heliand* account came from a place and a people that were entirely different from the people living at the time that the story was being told; that is, the kings had come from the era at the very beginning of our time reckoning. And they were the descendants of people who were immensely wiser than the people to whom they appeared in the story. The Three Kings said that they had descended from an ancestor who had lived in the distant past, when a few people still had the power to speak with the gods. When their forefather approached death, he assembled all of the members of his vast family and told them what his god had revealed to him: there would come a time when a World King would appear, and this event would be accompanied by the appearance of a star.

If we look for other sources for this tradition, we find mention of Balaam,† the son of Beor, in the Book of Numbers in the Old Testament. The Three Kings from the East may have been referring to Balaam, for the scriptures relate that he conversed with his god and ordered his entire life according to these exchanges. Furthermore, in the time in which the *Heliand* originated in central Europe, there still lived a dim recollection of human beings who once spoke with their gods. A real concept of this occurrence lived within human beings during the ninth century. Thus we once again have seen how people in earlier epochs still experienced a living world, whereas at the present time we have moved away from this reality.

You can see what a dramatic change has occurred in the souls of human beings. At one time the human being knew that individuals had occult knowledge, even if it was in a dreamlike form. At an earlier point, humanity looked within and beheld processes such as the sulfur and the salt process. Through their occult capacity they were able to perceive pre-earthly existence.

Certain people who wanted humanity to move backward rather than forward, and were themselves initiated to a certain degree, foresaw that this capacity to see into pre-earthly existence would be lost, and that one day human beings would no longer be able to draw out of themselves any knowledge of pre-earthly life. Thus it was introduced into the canon of church doctrine that there is no pre-earthly existence whatsoever, that the human soul is created at the time of physical conception. The fact of pre-earthly existence was dogmatically veiled in darkness.[†] That was the first step, the first stage, by which humanity on earth was led into ignorance of a fundamental aspect of the human being. A piece of one's essential humanity was taken away—the knowledge of the human being's pre-earthly existence.

Jacob Boehme, Giordano Bruno, and Francis Bacon lived during the time in which the knowledge of pre-earthly life was still concealed. They lived when it was not yet possible to grasp what they should have been able to discover through the spiritual observation of the outer world. The human being soon would be able to find in the outer world what could no longer be found in one's inner being.

Again there were initiates who wanted to lead humanity backward rather than forward; initiates who did not want to allow this new form of insight, which is the opposite of the ancient esoteric knowledge, to flourish. They tried through a dogmatic approach to substitute a belief in the afterlife for the new knowledge. And thus in the time in which Giordano Bruno was active, an intervention came to suppress the knowledge of pre-earthly human existence,[†] and to suffocate as well the knowledge of human existence beyond earthly existence. Giordano Bruno struggled with great determination to gain knowledge, and he surpassed the efforts of both Jacob Boehme and Francis Bacon. Bruno stood as if he were a man of the present, but he just could not reformulate what was given him out of the Dominican wisdom he had received to create instead a real cosmic perspective. He could only express poetically what had come to him in an uncertain way of a true worldview.

And yet, the knowledge Giordano Bruno portrayed in a nebulous form did give birth to a new understanding of the cosmos revealed in the human being, and the human being revealed in the cosmos. This did not come out of a renewal of an older esotericism; rather, it arose out of the freely generated spiritual activity that can be acquired by all human beings.

Thus I have characterized for you what had to come about in the course of human development. And today the human being stands before the fact that the will to allow this new knowledge to arise is despised and deeply hated by a great many human beings who are enemies of this possibility. This can also be grasped from a historical perspective. It helps us to understand how the fierce opposition to an anthroposophic worldview has come out of the very depths of its active opponents.

6

The Sleep of Civilization in the Present Era

Dornach, January 14, 1923

Today I would like to continue with the themes of the last two days: *Giordano Bruno, Jacob Boehme, and Francis Bacon* on January 12; and *Salt, Mercury, and Sulfur* on January 13. Let us look at the developments leading to the spiritual life of the present time, so that we can recognize that the anthroposophic worldview is a necessity in our time; and yet we must expect that anthroposophic insights will have vigorous opponents. I do not wish to mention the specific objections of this or that opponent right now. I prefer to approach the theme in a general way. It is more important to point out that if the Anthroposophical Society wishes to continue to exist, if it wishes to take its place consciously in today's life of the spirit, and to contribute something to it, the society has to consolidate itself. This is not the first time I have said this. Several weeks ago I explicitly pointed out that the consolidation of the Anthroposophical Society is an absolute necessity.[†]

We have to be clear about the relationship Anthroposophy has to our present-day civilization. The roots for contemporary civilization in Europe and America go back as far as the fourth century of the Common Era. We must keep in mind that the spread of Christianity and the entire way in which Christianity was grasped and understood in the third to the fourth centuries was fundamentally different from what it became later.

We often think that in our present era we can trace historical events backward, and move through successive historical periods as if there were a fundamental continuity running through them. For example, we could move backward through the modern period, and that would lead us back to the medieval period. From there we would revisit the

67

great migrations of peoples, then the Roman Empire, and afterward the culture of ancient Greece. We think and feel about the ancient Greek civilization in the same way we do about the Roman Empire, the Middle Ages, and the modern developments in European and American history. In fact, that assumption is not valid. There is a deep chasm between the continuity extending from modern civilization to the Roman era and the fundamentally different ancient Greek civilization. Let us bring this matter before our souls. When we recall the Greece of Pericles or Plato or Phidias, or the Greece of Sophocles and Aeschylus, we are looking at a soul-consciousness that is rooted in the ancient mystery culture and ancient spirituality. Above all, in ancient times classical Greece culture still had within it what I characterized yesterday as a living experience of the real inner processes of the human being, including what I referred to as the salt, mercury, and sulfur processes. The ancient Greek way of thinking and the Greek way of experiencing the human being was closer to the reality of the human constitution than any of the characterizations put forward since the fourth century C.E. And we would include the three individuals we spoke about in the last two days among examples of those who had represented a transition to the complete loss of a true understanding of the human constitution in modern consciousness.

Personalities such as Giordano Bruno, Jacob Boehme, and up to a certain point, Francis Bacon, struggled to achieve a true understanding of the human being. They were unable to reach the full understanding they sought. When we go back further than the Roman era and enter ancient Greece culture, any talk about the limits of knowledge of the human being had no meaning, for the ancient Greeks could grasp the nature of the human being and understood humanity's place within the cosmos. On the other hand, the Greeks did not have the mechanistic view of nature that now holds sway in scientific circles today. We could say of the ancient Greeks that they saw clouds and rain streaming down; they watched the mist ascending upward. These processes were expressions of the earth's fluidity. When they turned with acute awareness to the movement of the human blood circulation, they saw it imbued with an essentially living quality. The ancient Greeks did not perceive a difference between the rise and fall of water in nature and the movement of blood within the human body; that is, however, a distinction made in modern science. The ancient Greeks still experienced what lay behind the words, "The cosmos is revealed in the human being; the human being is revealed in the cosmos."

These are things we must take very seriously, because they lead us to a soul consciousness that now appears only in a fragmented form, at least in terms of the outwardly visible sources of historical documentation. We have to remember that in the fourth century C.E., efforts were set in motion to utterly destroy all remnants of esoteric culture. Certainly we know something of this occurrence on the basis of archeological excavations. But we have to realize that what later gave impulse to western civilization arose out of the ruins of Hellenism; a Hellenism that spread not just across southern Europe but all the way to Asia as well. We must not forget that from the middle of the fourth to the middle of the fifth centuries C.E., innumerable temples were burned to the ground; temples that were filled with the most important, the most priceless treasures of everything that Hellenism had nurtured and conveyed. Humanity today, which typically is interested only in written documents, can no longer see any of these treasures of Hellenism. We must remember what was recorded in a letter† written by a contemporary in the fourth century: "The ancient times are coming to an end. Not one sanctuary remains in the fields that were cultivated for the sake of the temples. They have all been destroyed. How can the peasants working in the fields find joy in their work?"

Today it is unimaginable how much was completely destroyed between the mid-fourth century and the mid-fifth century. The destruction of temples and monuments went hand in hand with the efforts to extinguish Greek spiritual life, a process that received its bitterest blow when the Athenian school of philosophy was closed in 529 C.E.† We have many resources (artistic and architectural, as well as literary and documentary) that help us to look into Roman society, but it is not possible to recreate ancient Greek civilization in its outward manifestations. It is true that a great deal of ancient civilization was consciously preserved right up through the medieval period. The Benedictine Order, for example, participated in this. But even Saint Benedict† built the first Benedictine cloister on a site that at one time was held sacred by pre-Christian peoples. Whatever had a connection with the past had to disappear, and indeed these traces *did* disappear.

If you think of so-called normal human feelings, it is difficult to understand the impulse for destruction that swept across southern Europe, western Asia, and North Africa. We can understand it only if we recognize that the entire consciousness of humanity during that period was completely different. I have often pointed out that it is simply incorrect to say that "nature or world history[†] can never make a developmental leap." In human history such a leap can take place. The soul constitution of civilized humanity in the second and third centuries C.E. was, without a doubt, very different from what came later.

Now I would like to show you how this kind of change functions. When we speak about the transition between waking and sleeping we say that the physical body and the etheric body remain in bed during sleep, and the I and astral body leave the physical body. To put it another way, the soul-spiritual aspects of the human being leave the physical and etheric body. Such a description would not have been used in ancient India; human beings then would have said exactly the opposite. In sleep, they would have said, the spiritual-soul aspects of the human being enter the physical body more deeply. That is, the process was exactly the opposite of what I described as the present-day constitution of the human being in waking and sleeping states.

This difference is seldom noticed today. For example, when the Theosophical Society was founded,[†] some of the founding members heard about spiritual truths from the Indians they met, and the early theosophists adopted what they heard as their own. They heard something about the astral body and the I leaving the physical body. Certainly, an Indian in the nineteenth century would have said such a thing, for in India one can often observe what is real. But afterward, when people from the Theosophical Society repeated this, they claimed that the departure of the astral and the I during sleep was part of ancient Indian wisdom. This is not so, for the ancient Indian actually said just the opposite: the soul-spiritual goes more deeply into the physical body during sleep. That was an accurate description of the human being during ancient times. To a certain degree this knowledge was present in the consciousness of the ancient Greeks, who experienced that during sleep the soul-spiritual entered the physical body more deeply than it did when the human being was awake. In this the Greeks manifested a certain stage in the development of humanity.

Today, when we describe the consciousness of human beings of another time, we must characterize it from our own immediate spiritual perception. And so we rightly say that the sages of ancient times, and also the ancient Greeks, possessed an instinctive dreamlike clairvoyance. That is what we would say from our perspective. But those who lived in ancient times would not have regarded their experience as dreamlike. They felt as if they were awake during their form of clairvoyance. When they perceived the world in mighty pictures, as I described it yesterday, it felt as if this was an intensification of their consciousness. They also knew that when they sank into their inner being and saw what occurred within the human being, they experienced themselves in relation to the universe; they knew that the processes within the human being were equivalent to the processes in the universe. During sleep the ancient Greeks perceived that the human being dipped more deeply into the physical body. In deep sleep, their heightened consciousness once again would be silenced, dimmed, and even become unconscious. They attributed this to the influence of the physical body that surrounded the soul and led it into sinfulness, into iniquity. Precisely this intuitive perception gave rise to the ancient consciousness of sin or iniquity. The Greek consciousness of sin led back to an even more ancient perception that the soul's descent into the physical body prevented the soul from having sufficient freedom to live in the spiritual world.

If you think through all that I have said about this, you would have to say that the human being in ancient times was conscious of being a spiritual being living within a physical body. It would not have occurred then to anyone that the physical body was the defining characteristic of a human being. The essentially human quality in that era was expressed as "the thinker."† The human being was not just a being with ruddy or pale countenance, two arms and two legs; the human being was a soul-spirit being living within a physical body.

The consciousness of the soul-spiritual nature of the human being in Greek civilization is still evident in the remnants of its artistic portrayals of the human archetype, seen in every wonderful sculptural form left by classical Greek culture. When gazing at the ruins of a Greek temple, we have to say (though the cults practiced may have fallen into decadence), that even in the ravaged images of the Greek gods and the temples, evidence of the ancient constitution of the soul still exists. Indeed, the old soul-spiritual consciousness of the human being was writ large in the forms that were destroyed.

If an initiate from the Greek Mysteries of the early Greek era came to us and spoke to us with the consciousness of a Greek incarnation and not from a subsequent one (that inevitably would be different from that of the ancient Greek era), the initiate would say to us:

> *You modern human beings are the ones who are asleep. We were the human beings who were awake. We were awake within our physical bodies. Yes, we were awake as spiritual human beings living in physical bodies. We knew that we were human beings, because we could distinguish our humanity existing within the physical from the physical body itself. What you call being awake, was for us being asleep. When you are awake and order your senses within the outer world, and explain something from the point of view of the world of senses, you are asleep in relation to what is the essence of your humanity. You have fallen asleep; we are the ones who were awake.*

That is what an initiate of the ancient Greek Mysteries would say to us, and from a certain point of view, would be correct. For today we presume we are awake from the time we wake up until the time we go to sleep; that is to say, when we are in our physical bodies as soul-spiritual human beings. But we are not consciously aware of ourselves in that sense, and thus we are asleep with regard to our own essential nature. When we are within the cosmos that exists outside us, we are sleeping; for that happens between the time we go to sleep and the time that we wake up. We need to learn how to be awake when aspects of our being are out in the cosmos. With the same intensity with which the human beings in ancient times were awake within their bodies, the modern human being has to learn how to be awake when the astral and the I are outside the physical body; when we are actually within the outer cosmos.

We are in a state of transition. Compared with the human being in ancient times, we have been asleep with regard to the essential aspects of our humanity. Now we are at the point when we should awaken in a new way, to a new kind of conscious wakefulness. And what role does anthroposophy play in this? Anthroposophy simply wishes that the human being would learn how to remain awake outside of physicality. And so anthoposophy comes along and tries to awaken the modern human being—the person the ancient initiate regarded as asleep. Anthroposophy wants to awaken the modern human being, but this sleepyhead refuses to wake up!

Anthroposophy wants to sound the alarm! In the Oberufer Nativity play, the shepherd named Huckle† tries to awaken his fellow shepherd Buckle. He calls out, "The birds are already singing." Buckle rolls over, "Let 'em sing. They've got little heads and they don't need much sleep." Huckle tries again, "The sky is falling! The sky is falling!" Buckle ignores him, "So what! Let the sky fall in! It's already been up there long enough." That of course is not exactly what anthroposophy is saying. Rather the call is: "The spiritual world wants to come in! Wake up! Let the Light of the Spirit shine!" Anthroposophy wants the sleeper to wake up. Modern civilization needs an awakening. But humanity wants to go right on sleeping!

I want to remind you that Jacob Boehme, who was filled with folk wisdom, and Giordano Bruno, who stood within a spiritual community, preserved a great deal from ancient times and lived within a memory of the ancient state of wakefulness. Francis Bacon, however, had the impulse to justify the sleepiness of modernity. That is, he grasped more deeply than we have been able to do in these past two days what is characteristic of our era. The modern human being cannot reach as deeply into the physical as humanity could in ancient times. For modern human beings during sleep do not enter more deeply into their physical body; instead, we go out of our physical body during sleep. But modern human beings must also learn to come out of their body during the waking state, for only thereby can we be in a position to know ourselves once again as human beings. Nevertheless, the temptation to prolong our sleep is very great. "Buckle, the riders are already galloping along the roads." "Let 'em gallop, they still have a long way to go."

Du Bois-Reymond[†] said (and I am not speaking now of the shepherd Huckle in the Christmas play), "Human knowledge has its limits. You cannot force your way into the phenomena of nature, nor into the secret workings of nature. You have to accept the limits to human knowledge." But anthroposophy says, "We must strive to go further and further: The impulse of the Spirit already is sounding." Du Bois-Reymond would reply, "Let the impulse of the Spirit resound; it still has a long way to go. It will take natural science until the end of time on earth before all of the secrets of nature will be revealed."

Human beings already have a justification to stay asleep. The argument to admit to the limits of our knowledge of nature is reason enough for remaining asleep and not bothering to pursue knowledge of the nature of the human being either. There are plenty of sleeping pills in our present age, and you may hear them spoken about right here. Whenever possible, people prefer to listen to what is easily understood, just as if they were watching a film. People do not like it when they have to pay attention and work on something inwardly. Most people prefer to dream about cosmic mysteries rather than to engage them with their inwardly active thinking. The path to waking up, however, begins with thinking, for a thought wishes to become more developed through its own activity. That is the reason why I dealt with thinking so vigorously in my book *The Philosophy of Freedom*,[†] several decades ago.

My dear friends, I want to bring something to your attention. Think back over the dreams you have had and see if you ever have had a dream in which you did something that you would have been ashamed to do during the day. I mean that seriously. Admittedly, there may be a number of people sitting here who have never had such a dream; but even they will know someone who can tell them of such an experience. There will be those here who can admit that sometimes they have had dreams about doing something that they would not have done in a waking state, which would have made them feel ashamed if they had done so. Let us look at the pervasive, overpowering sleep of our entire civilization, in which people just want to dream through all manner of cosmic secrets. Here comes Anthroposophy saying exactly the same words as the shepherd Huckle cries out to his fellow shepherd, "Buckle! Wake up!" And the people who are dreaming today are supposed to wake up! I can assure you that some things people do during this great sleep of civilization, they would not do if they were really awake. That is a fact. But instead the dreamer says, "How am I supposed to believe that?" The dreamer does not give a second thought to what the impossible things that occur in dreams would look like if they were carried out during a waking state. But, unconsciously, many fear that there are things they must not do when they are awake. Naturally, I don't mean this in a trivial or a narrow-minded way. Nevertheless, there are many actions that we consider perfectly acceptable and normal, which we would see in a completely different light if we were really awake.

There is a deep-seated fear of awakening and being shocked by what is deemed acceptable in the sleep of civilization. If we had awakened from this profound sleep, we would no longer feel comfortable dissecting a liver, side by side with the brain. We would feel desperately ashamed to follow some of our current research methods, if we truly had awakened in an anthroposophic sense. But we can hardly expect that individuals who stand right in the midst of today's research methods would awaken from one day to the next and suddenly adopt an anthroposophic sensitivity toward research methods without any explanation.

We certainly notice the willingness of people to justify the sleep of civilization. Think about the immense joy a dreamer has when something that was dreamed actually occurs a few days afterward. It is immediately evident that these superstitious dreamers are overjoyed when an event in a dream becomes a reality; and that actually occurs occasionally. Dreamers among scientists and mathematicians, whose ideas affect entire civilizations, calculated a specific orbit for the planet Uranus according to the Newtonian law of gravitation, and the elaboration of the Newtonian formula by later mathematicians. But the actual orbit of Uranus does not correspond to the orbit based upon this calculation. Such mathematicians then dream that the real orbit has been diverted by the existence of another planet, which might possibly exist. The entire process has been dreamed, for it has really been calculated without the impulse or necessity of inner assurance and authenticity. When in fact Dr. Galle[†] discovered the planet of Neptune, it seemed as if the dream had become a reality. Afterward, the sequence of a projected existence of a planet and its subsequent discovery is called a scientific method applied in the world of nature. In fact, the existence of Neptune was projected in a dream and then, thereafter, it appeared. That is really how it is with the dreamers, when something presents itself after it first has been dreamed. Or recall how Mendeleev[†] calculated the existence of a new element in the periodic table of elements. That kind of dream is actually not so difficult to propose, because when there is an empty place in the periodic table, it is quite easy to fill in the space with a new element and attribute a few characteristics to this invention. Nevertheless it is a dream! If the new element does exist, then the method of its discovery is no different than the example of the dreamer who dreams of something that happens to the dreamer a few days later in a waking state; the event in waking life is claimed to be a verification of the dream. The ordinary dreamer does not describe the event in real life as a verification of the dream, but scientists do say that they have been able to verify what previously had been imagined.

We must, first of all, fundamentally understand how our modern civilization has become a civilization asleep, and how an awakening is absolutely necessary for humanity. Above all, everyone who feels drawn to spiritual science must see right through the tendency toward sleep that permeates our present time. At any moment you, as a dreamer, may realize that you are asleep. It may suddenly come to you: I am dreaming. Humanity must be able to experience deeply what the philosopher Johann Gottlieb Fichte[†] expressed so energetically: "The world that is spread out in front of the human being is a dream; and everything the human being thinks about the world is a dream of a dream."

But we must not fall into the error that we find in the philosophy of Schopenhauer.[†] There is little to be gained if we simply turn to a theory of knowledge and declare that everything is a dream. It is not our task to point out that the human being dreams, and that the human being can never do more than dream; for if we came to the boundary of these dreams, then on the other side is the thing-in-itself, which by definition can never be reached through the senses. It is interesting to consider what Eduard von Hartmann,[†] who otherwise was an outstanding thinker, had to say about dreams in contrast to reality. He said that the human being dreams everything that is present in consciousness, and that behind the dream lies a "thing-in-itself" about which the human being knows nothing. Hartmann pushes the thing-in-itself to the limit.† The table-in-itself is contrasted to the table we see before us. The table that we see in front of us is a dream; and behind it is the table-in-itself. Hartmann actually differentiated between the table as appearance and the table-in-itself, between the chair as appearance and the chair-in-itself. But he is unconscious of the fact that the chair on which he himself is sitting has anything to do with the chair-in-itself; for it is difficult to actually sit on a chair that is only an appearance of a chair, one that is no more than a dream. Likewise the dreamer has to lie down on a real bed. However, this whole play of words that proposes that the world is no more than a dream can be very useful as a preparation for something else. What would that be? It prepares us for an awakening, my dear friends. The point we are making is not to persuade you that the world is a dream; the discussion of the idea becomes the spur to awaken within ourselves. And awakening begins with an energetic grasp of our thinking, an active seizing hold of our thinking. An awakened thinking is precisely what leads you into everything else.

The impulse to self-awakening is imperative today. Certainly, anthroposophy can be placed before the world. But if the Anthroposophical Society wants to be a community, then this community must be real. If you, as an individual, wish to live in the Anthroposophical Society, you also must experience the Anthroposophical Society as a reality. You must be permeated by the will to awaken, and not take it as an insult when someone says to you: "Wake up!" Your wakefulness is imperative. Allow me to say this again in just a few words.

The misfortune that has just befallen us, the burning of the Goetheanum, must be a summons to each individual to wake up; a summons to the Anthroposophical Society to take action, a summons to make our society a reality. The real Being of the society is precisely the Being we have experienced, which I characterized at the end of the Christmas course of lectures.† The living streaming from person to person within the Anthroposophical Society must be real. A lack of love between one another, rather than mutual trust, has become widespread in the newest phase in the life of the Anthroposophical Society, and if this lack of love gains the upper hand, the Anthroposophical Society will collapse.

Building the Goetheanum has brought many beautiful qualities living within anthroposophists to the surface; but parallel to this, the society itself should have been strengthened. It is true that many fine qualities were reaffirmed at the end of the recent course of lectures, similar to the qualities that were evident during the construction of the Goetheanum. And these qualities surfaced again during the night of the fire. But these qualities must be cultivated. Above all, if you have a task to do within the Anthroposophical Society, a task that goes above and beyond being a member, you really must carry this task out with real personal interest and real commitment. A deep sense of personal interest and real commitment toward the work of the society are unfortunately exactly what is missing; we need people who are ready to carry out a specific task or take on a particular responsibility for the society.

No service for the society may be viewed as a small matter, including what one person can do for another. The smallest deed becomes worthy because it is also service to the greater whole. That fact is something that is too often forgotten. The society should be deeply grateful when a great misfortune inspires us to act out of our finest qualities of character. But we must not forget how quickly many lose their interest and commitment to a task in the face of the need to continue their efforts on a daily basis. Some take on a task one day and then quickly forget about it. Therefore I want to remind you of the enormous magnitude of the opposition that exists in the world today toward anthroposophy. Indeed, the level of antagonism is often overlooked and underestimated.

We must realize that antagonism exists, that opposition exists. We can see this within the course of world events. Sometimes I am amazed how little inner awareness and sympathy there is on our part, especially when the opposition is rife with untruths. We have to remain matter-of-fact and objective in the positive defense of anthroposophy, when we are dealing with concrete matters. But we also have to understand that anthroposophy can only survive in an atmosphere of truthfulness. We need to develop a feeling for what it means when so much untruthfulness, so much condemnation, is directed against anthroposophic positions. To be prepared to meet these situations, we really need to depend on our inner life. Be assured that we will have plenty of opportunities to stay awake. The impulse to awaken may expand in other ways as well.

When we see someone sleeping, even though the flames of untruthfulness are everywhere in evidence, then we won't be surprised when an ordinary human being sleeps on.

Now I would like to take what I have shown you in miniature today and place it before you in its fullest magnitude. Think! Feel! Meditate on being wide awake! Many long for what they believe is esoteric, even as slander is being nailed on the windows. Dear friends, the esoteric is within grasp. Take hold of it! But the most esoteric task that exists within the Anthroposophical Society today is the will to awaken. This will to be awake must take precedence in the Anthroposophical Society. An awakened Anthroposophical Society will be the ray of light that will ignite the will to awaken our entire present-day civilization.

7

TRUTH, BEAUTY, AND GOODNESS

Dornach, January 19, 1923

Truth, Beauty, and Goodness, the three universal ideals of humanity, have existed throughout all eras of conscious human development. Arising at first from an instinctive consciousness, the true, the beautiful, and the good have been the highest goals as well as the definitive characteristics of human striving. In ancient times you would have understood more about the true nature of human beings and their relationship to the universe. The ancients spoke more concretely about truth, beauty, and goodness than we today are able to express, given our deep affinity for abstractions. Anthroposophic spiritual science, however, once again speaks concretely of these ideals. This approach is not widely welcomed in our time, for people now much prefer what is inexact, undefined, or nebulous, especially when they are asked to go beyond everyday experience. Today let us clarify how the deeper reality of the words truth, beauty, and goodness are related to the essential nature of being human.

When we place before the eye of the soul the essential nature of the human being, first of all we have to look into the physical human body. In our day, the physical body of the human being is considered only in its outward form. No one is conscious of the fact that the various aspects of the physical body have been built up during pre-earthly existence. Of course the human being lived within a purely spiritual world during pre-earthly existence. In the spiritual world the human being worked out the spiritual prototype, the spiritual form of the physical body, in union with higher spiritual beings.[†] What we carry with us on earth as a physical body is a reflection, a physical expression of a kind of spirit kernel that we ourselves crafted during our pre-earthly existence.

Here during earth existence we experience our own physical body. Even with all that accompanies our sensations and the direct experience of our physicality, we are not fully conscious of our physical body. We speak about truth, but we do not understand how our sensitivity for the truth, our feeling for the truth is directly related to the experience we have of our physical body. When you are confronted with a simple fact, you either form an idea of the fact that exactly corresponds to it, and is therefore true, or you adopt a false idea that has nothing to do with the fact and reveals nothing about it. The false idea may come about because of ineptitude, inner laziness, or even as a result of direct and intentional opposition to the truth. When you contemplate the truth about a specific matter, you find yourself in harmony with the feeling that your physical body experiences in relation to its pre-earthly existence. We only need to formulate an idea out of laziness or willful lying, or put forward an idea that does not correspond to a fact, and it is as if we had carved out a hole in what connects us to our pre-earthly existence. When we surrender to an untruth, we sever threads in the fabric connecting us with our pre-earthly existence.

This connection is a delicate spiritual fabric, if I may say it in that way; a fabric that we have woven during our pre-earthly existence, a fabric that shapes the form and contours of our physical body. I would like to put it this way: it is as if our physical body was connected by many threads to its pre-earthly existence, and when we surrender to untruthfulness, it severs these threads. The purely intellectual consciousness that has become prevalent since the beginning of the era of the Consciousness Soul is so appealing to human beings that we are not even aware of being torn away from our pre-earthly existence. This is one of the reasons why human beings today have so much difficulty understanding how the human being stands in relation to cosmic existence.

We are most likely to be aware of our physicality when something disrupts the health of our bodies. But in fact when we surrender to untruth, we sever threads that connect us to our pre-earthly existence. This affects the physical body, especially the constitution of the nervous system. It is through the feeling we receive from the physical body that we also receive our feeling for our spiritual being within the cosmos.

In order to experience ourselves as spiritual beings in the cosmos, it is necessary that the threads connecting the physical body to its pre-earthly existence have not been severed. If the connection has been broken, then for our very sense of being and existence we have to create a substitute for a healthy feeling of our spiritual being. This we do unconsciously. But humanity has reached an inner uncertainty with regard to this feeling for one's own being, which has penetrated right into the physical body. This pure sense for our spiritual being, which is an essential characteristic of being human, formerly was more and more evident the further back we go in human history. And we ask ourselves today if it is still strongly present in us.

Think, for example, about the many things people take into account when planning for the future, except for their original spiritual inner life. Too often a person chooses a profession in order to be known as a secretary or a notary, and thinks that if other people identify him or her as having a particular profession, they are able to describe who the person really is. Actually the only thing that matters is whether we understand our true being through an inner feeling life quite apart from outer appearances.

What assurance do human beings have of the reality of the self, the feeling for our own existence? During earthly existence we live in a world that is only a reflection of true reality. We shall understand this physical world only if we recognize that it is a reflection of true reality. However, we must experience true reality within ourselves; we must *inwardly* experience our relationship to the spiritual world. That is possible only when we sustain our relationship to our pre-earthly existence.

We can keep our connection to pre-earthly existence intact through our love for pure truth and unwavering truthfulness. Nothing strengthens the genuine feeling of our humanity more fully than the cultivation of the truth and truthfulness. To feel responsible to test everything you say; to feel responsible to know the extent to which you can stand behind something you say, these are measures that support the inner consolidation of the worthiness of your inner being, of your very existence. And the integrity of your inner being is connected with your capacity to experience the spiritual within your physical body. Thus we shall see that a close relationship to the physical body also helps us to recognize, to experience, the ideal of truth.

In recent lectures I have described how we acquire the etheric or life body,[†] that is, the formative forces of our body, a short time before we descend from our pre-earthly into our earthly existence. We gather together forces shaped in the cosmic etheric substance in order to form our own etheric body. In earlier epochs of human development, humanity had a better understanding of the etheric body than people have today. Today we have a poor understanding of this etheric body. In fact, many people ridicule any mention of the reality of the etheric body. Nevertheless, it is through our capacity to perceive and feel this etheric body that we shall strengthen our experience of beauty.

When we strive for a real experience of truth and truthfulness, we discover this within the physical body. When we wish to develop our feeling for beauty, our experience of beauty in the right way, we discover this in our body of formative forces; that is, the etheric body. Beauty is connected with the etheric body just as truth is connected with the physical body.

You can understand the relationship of beauty to the etheric body of the human being by thinking of the significance of beauty revealed in the artistic creations of humanity. And what I wish to draw to your attention here holds true for all the arts. When we see a living human being, we know that this person is just one individual among countless other human beings. One person has no meaning without the many others who surround the person. The one belongs to the many; and the many belong to the one. Just imagine how weakly rooted in existence we would be without our fellow human beings. When we apply this example to an artistic portrayal of a human being (it does not matter if the work of art is a sculpture, painting, or drama) we see that the artist tries to create something that is sufficient within itself; something that encompasses in and of itself an entire world. This is exactly parallel to the human being who gathers together etheric forces out of the entire cosmos, in order to present something real in earthly existence by means of his or her individual etheric body.

In ancient times humanity had a strong sense for beauty as they understood it. Certainly they had a better sense for beauty than we do today. However, even now we cannot consider ourselves to be fully human without an experience of the beautiful. To have a sense for beauty, we must acknowledge the presence of the etheric body. When we are insensitive to beauty, it means that we ignore and fail to recognize the etheric body.

Today people feel none of this in their consciousness. Ancient Greeks who approached the temple and stood before a statue of a god or goddess became inwardly warm, and felt as if they were experiencing an inner sunlight. Indeed, the ancient Greeks inwardly felt forces streaming into each internal organ. Standing before a statue of one of the gods in a temple, the ancient Greeks uttered from the depths of their heart, "Whenever I stand before this statue, I feel my fingertips in the outermost periphery of my body more clearly, more distinctly than I have ever experienced them before. I have never been so inwardly aware of the arch of my forehead before I entered the temple and stood in front of a statue of one of the gods." In the presence of beauty the ancient Greek felt permeated with warmth, inwardly illuminated, and divinely endowed. This was nothing other than experiencing the love of beauty.

The ancient Greek also had a completely different feeling for ugliness than a modern human being experiences. The feeling for ugliness in modern times occurs in a very abstract form, as if it was concentrated and localized in a countenance or face. Ugliness was experienced as coldness by an ancient Greek, and in the presence of extreme ugliness, the ancient Greek had goose bumps. This experience was actually felt within the etheric body; it was something that in ancient times the human being felt in a pronounced way. In the course of human development we have lost a part of our capacity to experience ugliness so powerfully. These physical sensations have become unconscious for modern human beings, who are drawn toward rational understanding and abstraction, and thus are inclined to focus attention on their heads where the powers of reason and abstraction reside. What was previously experienced in a living way in the etheric body now remains unconscious to modern human beings.

Enthusiasm for truth and truthfulness produces a feeling for our pre-earthly existence in the depths of our unconscious. An era in which human beings have no feeling for their pre-earthly existence will also lack the right sense for truth and truthfulness. An energetically cultivated feeling for the truth, which connects us strongly with our pre-earthly past, inevitably causes sadness in our increasingly intimate experience of the present. As you develop an enthusiasm for the truth and then experience a certain sadness living in the present age, your soul will be comforted and illuminated by the warmth of experiencing beauty. Through beauty we once again receive joy to balance the sadness that sweeps through us as we try to develop our enthusiasm for truth and truthfulness. Whenever we cultivate our feeling for truth there arises in us the following realization: In this earthly life we experience merely the echo of truth, for truth exists only in pre-earthly existence. Because we have left our pre-earthly existence, we have lost our complete immersion in the substance of truth. Only through our enthusiasm for truth and truthfulness can we expect to maintain our connection to pre-earthly existence.

By cultivating a genuine feeling for beauty we can reestablish our connection to pre-earthly existence during earthly life. We should never underestimate the importance of beauty in education and all aspects of culture. Surroundings filled with ugly machines, smokestacks, and billowing smoke create a world devoid of beauty and prevent humanity from making a connection with pre-earthly existence. Indeed, such an environment tears human beings away from their pre-earthly existence. A highly industrialized city provides a convenient way-station for all of the demonic beings who want to make human beings forget that they once had pre-earthly existence in the spiritual realm.

But if you give yourself over to beauty, you have to acknowledge that something we consider beautiful is not as rooted in reality as is beauty itself. If an artistic portrayal of the human being is formed in an ever more beautiful, sculptural, or painterly manner, it only becomes clearer that this does not correspond to external material reality in earthly existence. We receive comfort from a beautiful semblance; however, the comfort that arises from a beautiful semblance can last only until the moment we pass through the portal of death.

The spiritual world in which we were fully immersed in our pre-earthly existence still exists and is always present. We only need to stretch out an arm and extend it into the world around us; what exists around us is also the spiritual world in which we spent our pre-earthly existence. Even though this spiritual world is always there, the human being has a connection to it only in the deepest levels of unconsciousness, when one glows with enthusiasm for truth and truthfulness. And a connection is also made between earthly existence and the spiritual world whenever a human being is warmed by something beautiful, and by beauty itself.

As we aspire to reach our full, our true, humanity from a higher spiritual perspective, we should never forget that we have lived a pre-earthly existence in the spiritual world. When we glow inwardly in the presence of beauty, we can experience within our souls the image of renewing our connection with the spiritual world of our pre-earthy existence. How can we strengthen the capacity to enter directly into the spiritual world, a world we left when we descended from pre-earthly existence into earthly life?

We build up the strength to enter spiritual worlds when we fill ourselves with goodness and extend good deeds to other human beings. It is not enough to merely know about, or to be interested in, or to have a feeling for, an impulse to do a good deed. It matters only that you manifest the good in your actions; that you convey your own soul to the individuality of the other, to the inner being of the other, into a living experience of the other. Goodness encompasses all of the capacities and will forces within the soul. And these capacities and will forces come out of the art of permeating the human being on earth with the full expression of a person's humanity, acquired during pre-earthly existence. You connect yourself through the image of beauty in earthly life to the spiritual, which you left behind when you entered your earthly existence. So, too, you will be able to connect your earthly life with post-earthly existence, by being a good person. A good human being is one who is able to give something of his or her own soul to the soul of another human being. The capacity to take something of your own soul and give it to the soul of another is the foundation of all true morality. Moreover, no social configuration on earth can be sustained without the element of true morality.

When this morality leads you to the most significant will impulses in your life, and your highest moral actions become a reality, then these moral capacities begin to permeate and direct the impulses of your soul. Thus you will be inwardly moved and able to read the concerns written on the face of another person; and the concerns visible on another's face will be impressed upon your astral body. Just as the feeling for the true is manifest in your physical body, just as the glowing experience of the beautiful is impressed upon your etheric body, so the good enlivens your astral body. Your astral body cannot be healthy, cannot stand upright in the world, when you are not able to be permeated by goodness.

Truth is related to the physical body; beauty, to the etheric body; and goodness, to the astral body. Here are concrete relationships between the living human being and the three abstractions: Truth, Beauty, and Goodness. Now we can form a connection between the real being of the human being and what we instinctively perceive as the three ideals.

These three ideals will be manifest only to the extent that we are able to develop our full humanity. We reach our full humanity when we perceive that truth is planted within our physical bodies, and is not simply derived in a conventional way. We can bring our full humanity into existence only when we are increasingly able to use our feeling for beauty to enliven our etheric bodies. We will not have the right sense of beauty until we feel quickened inwardly when we gaze at beauty, just as the ancient Greeks naturally experienced beauty. My dear friends, you can stare at beauty, or you can live it, experience it. In our day most people just stare at beauty. Then they do not have to awaken their etheric bodies. Staring at beauty is not the same thing as experiencing beauty. As soon as beauty inwardly quickens you, so too, is the etheric body affected.

It is possible for us to do something good out of habit. Similarly, someone might avoid doing something very evil for fear of punishment; or someone might do something bad to another person because the person did not show respect. However, we may also do something good out of real love for the good, in the sense that I described several decades ago in my book *The Philosophy of Freedom.*† To do good deeds out of an inner experience of what it means to embrace the good leads us to an appreciation of the importance of the astral body. We will experience this only when we act out of an inwardly generated and deeply-experienced sense of the good. Otherwise the good remains knowledge in the abstract, or simply talk about the good; and neither leads to an experience of the astral body.

The living experience of the good is not the same as the experience of beauty, which creates a connection with pre-earthly existence through images that will no longer exist after the human being passes through the portal of death. Truly experiencing the good provides a real link between the human being and the spiritual world that is always present, and into which we can stretch out an arm. We are separate from it during material existence. However, the experience of the good is a real link directly to the spiritual world we enter when we cross the threshold of death. What an individual during earthly life practices while trying to live in the good makes it possible for a person to create forces that remain on earth, even after crossing the portal of death.

Basically, the sense for truth and truthfulness, when it becomes truly rooted in us, is a legacy of our pre-earthly existence. Our sense for beauty, when it is imbedded in our innermost being, gives us an image of the pre-earthly connection with the spiritual world, which we wish to renew and sustain. Truth implants in us the necessity not to sever ourselves from the spiritual, but rather to embrace a real connection to the spirit; to express it through doing what is good and to develop a will force that is truly human.

To be united with the true means that we must remain connected to our spiritual past. For beauty to have meaning, we must not deny that the spiritual and the physical worlds are interwoven. To be guided by the good means that we shall plant a seed on behalf of the spiritual world for the future.

The three concepts, past, present, and future, when placed in the context of human life expressed in its fullest humanity and grasped as concrete reality, receive even greater significance through their connections to the ideals of Truth, Beauty, and Goodness.

Untruthful human beings deny having had a spiritual past and sever the thread between the self and their own spiritual past. The person who disregards beauty wishes to live where the sun of the spirit never shines, and wants to wander about in shadows forever void of the spirit. The human being who denies the good abandons and renounces the spiritual future, and expects to receive the benefits of the spiritual future by way of an externally generated means of healing.

Long ago, Truth, Beauty, and Goodness arose out of the deepest human instinct and became the three greatest ideals that inspired human striving. In modern times these ideals have almost become empty words, but we have the possibility of taking these ideals and giving them, once more, real meaning and substance.

And now, my friends, having laid the foundation for exploring Truth, Beauty, and Goodness today, I would like to speak about these ideals again tomorrow.

8

THE HUMAN BEING AND THE SPIRITS OF NATURE: IMPLICATIONS OF AN ANTHROPOSOPHIC WORLDVIEW

Dornach, January 20, 1923

Recently we have been speaking about the relationship of the human being to nature and the entire cosmos in earlier epochs; and about the connection humanity has today to the natural world and the cosmos. I have pointed out that in former times human beings experienced nature in a real, concrete, and living way, because they were able to feel and experience their inner being in a fully enlivened way. For example, I indicated that human beings at one time could experience thinking as if it were a process of extracting salt from their own organism. When a person was thinking, it felt as if a hardening process were taking place within the physical body. It seemed as if one's thoughts were streaming through the body and generating a kind of etheric-astral bone structure. A person could also *feel* the difference between a crystal that was shaped like a cube and one that came to a point. Thus, a human being felt inwardly as if thinking were a hardening process. Exercising the will, on the other hand, felt like a fiery process that generated a sensation of warmth streaming through the physical body.

Because in earlier epochs human beings experienced so fully their inner being, they also felt inwardly and deeply what occurred in nature and what lived concretely within the natural world. In the present time, we know little more about the inner human being than we receive in mirror images of our perceptions from the outer world. We experience these mirror images as if they were memories. We know of these images what we experience or have experienced with our feelings, although our feelings themselves are very abstract. But we no longer experience or receive knowledge in a living manner; a manner that flashes up, rays outward, warms through, or illuminates the physical organism from within. Human beings today readily accept what a physician or a scientist tells them about their physicality. A real inner experience of one's own body no longer seems to be available. Since human beings today do not know very much about themselves, except what the scientist or physician has to say, they confine themselves to abstractions about nature and the world. Nevertheless, everything you know about the outer world corresponds exactly to what you can recognize and know through the experience of the inner world of the human being. As long as people today are content to know only what a physician or scientist tells them, they can have only an abstract perspective of the world.

People today inform themselves about the laws of nature based only upon abstract thoughts. But a living experience of nature is still present at an instinctive level and cannot be denied. Human beings have gradually lost sight of the elemental forces that are at work in nature. A rich realm of nature has been lost to humanity.

What used to be understood as the life of nature is now referred to as myths and fairy tales. These myths and fairy tales contain pictures that point to a spirituality that permeates nature. This is an elemental spirituality within uncertain boundaries, but spirituality nonetheless; and one that reveals a still higher spirituality. Humanity in earlier times was not dealing just with plants, stones, and animals; human beings formerly were also in contact with elemental spirits, which lived within the earth, water, air, and fire. As we have lost our awareness of the inner human being, so, too, we have lost a living experience of nature spirits.

In our time it would not be a good idea to revive a dreamlike consciousness of these nature spirits, for that would lead to superstitions. We have to find a different way to relate to nature, one that can be grasped by modern human consciousness. We have to be able to say to ourselves that there was a time when human beings could look deeply within themselves, and they had a lively capacity to experience what occurred within the depths of their own being. Through this capacity they also became acquainted with elemental spirits. This older way of gaining knowledge out of inner experience spoke to these human beings in pictures, which today still affect us with their elemental poetic power. For when these people looked within themselves, spirit beings began to whisper and to speak to these human souls.

These elemental beings made their homes, so to speak, within human organs. One of them would dwell in the human brain, another in the lungs, and yet another in the human heart. In earlier times you would not have perceived your inner physicality in the way that an anatomist describes it today. Then, you would have experienced your physical being as a living, elemental spirit being, and the elemental beings who lived in the various human organs could speak thus to the human being. Today if you were to search a path to these elemental beings by means of initiation science, you would have a certain feeling for these beings, a very particular understanding of them. At an earlier time, these elemental beings could speak through various internal organs to the human being. In fact, they could not move beyond the confines of the human skin. They lived on earth only in that they lived within human beings. They existed within the human being, spoke to their human hosts, and conveyed to them their knowledge. Human beings learned about earth existence in so far as they could learn from the elemental beings who lived within the human skin.

When humanity moved toward freedom and independence, these elemental beings lost their dwelling place within human beings on earth. They could no longer embody themselves in human flesh and blood. These elementals still exist in the earthly realm, and they still have to reach a certain goal together with humanity. That will be possible only when we express our indebtedness and gratitude to them for what they have given us in the past. At one time these elemental beings bestowed knowledge on humans, and then nurtured it; we have them to thank for much that we have become. In our previous lives on earth they were present in us and permeated our earthly existence. Through them we have become what we are now. They no longer have physical eyes or physical ears; in times past they lived within us. That is no longer the case, and yet they are still present in the earthly realm.

We need to say to them, "You were once our teachers, but you have grown old. Now we must give back to you what you once gave to us. We will only be able to do that when we, in our current stage of development, impress nature today with the spirit." We must not just look at nature through the prism of abstract understanding. Instead we must look more deeply for the pictorial inherent in nature, which is not accessible through dead judgments of knowledge. We must look for what we can reach in the fullness of life and through a feeling-imbued knowledge.

If we search for the living experience of what elemental beings may bring to us (and this we can activate through the spirit of an anthroposophic perspective), then these beings will come to us again. Elemental beings observe and listen when we deepen our connection to nature through anthroposophic insight and understanding. Then they receive something from us, whereas they receive nothing from conventional physiological and anatomical science. Indeed, they suffer in the face of modern sciences. They get nothing at all from anatomy lecture halls or anatomical dissections; nothing from chemistry and physics laboratories. In these settings, elemental beings have the feeling, "Is the earth completely empty now? Has it turned into a desert? Isn't there a single human being still alive to whom we now can give what we used to give to human beings? Wouldn't human beings like to bring to us again what they alone can give to the realms of nature?"

There are elemental beings that are waiting for us to unite ourselves with them, just as we unite ourselves with other human beings and share with them a genuine feeling for the experience of knowledge. Similarly, these elemental beings could participate in our learning about how to deal wisely with nature. When we study physics or chemistry in a conventional way, we cannot receive from the elemental beings what they once generously gave us out of their knowledge of nature, and thus helped to make us who we are. To them, we appear ungrateful. Faced with what is currently unfolding in human consciousness, these elemental beings are freezing in the earthly environment. We will be able to express gratitude toward these caring beings when we again search for the spirit in everything that we see with our eyes, hear with our ears, grasp with our hands. For these elemental beings are able to share in the perception and experience of the spiritual element that permeates the world of human senses. Whenever we grasp something in a solely materialistic way, elemental beings cannot experience it. They are excluded from this kind of knowledge. We can give to the elemental beings the gratitude that we owe them only when we work together in all earnestness with human beings who share the spirit of an anthroposophic worldview.

Let us take two examples of observing nature from an anthroposophic perspective. Imagine that you have before you, a fish and a bird. At first you look at the fish and likewise the bird with your physical senses. Those who are egotistical in their perception might not bother to go beyond these first sense impressions. But you shall want to overcome and go beyond an egotistical awareness of nature. You may begin by going beyond simply watching the fish in water and the bird in the air. You can consider carefully the form of the fish and the form of the bird; and then try to understand how the form of the fish reflects its life and movement in water, and how the form of the bird corresponds to its life and movement in the air. We can consider flowing water not just with the understanding of a chemist who looks at the water and says this is a chemical union, two atoms of hydrogen and one of oxygen; rather, we gaze at water as it actually is in reality. Then we can look carefully at a fish in the water and observe that it has a soft body with remarkable breathing forms toward the front portion of the body. Within the body there is a soft bone structure and a delicate jaw that is produced by the fish's life and movement in water. The bodily substance takes its form as a result of the movement of the fish through water, which is also penetrated by the rays of the sun. If you perceive the rays of the sun entering the water, emanating light and warmth, you can then visualize the fish swimming against streams of light-filled and sun-warmed water. This will give you a feeling of what the fish experiences swimming against the current of the water that has been softened by the sun's warmth and illuminated by the sun's light.

If I imagine that the fish is swimming toward me, I can see that its teeth carry the light and warmth-filled streams of water into its bodily substance and connect it to its breathing organs. In a unique way the form of the head provides an ideal covering for the jaw as the fish swims into the sunlit and light-warmed water.

Next I feel that something else is active in the tail of the fish. I experience that the flow of water along the tail of the fish contains a much weaker level of light than the water flowing up against the head of the fish. The light-filled flow of water around the head of the fish encourages the fish's bodily substance to remain soft. The water around the tail, which flows under subdued light, produces a tendency toward hardness. Observing both these phenomena, I learn that the head of the fish encounters what is sun-like, and that the more rigid tail of the fish has been affected by the moon as it reflects light. Thus I am able to place the fish in the fullness of its connection to water.

Next I gaze at the bird, which has not had the opportunity of forming its head by moving and swimming through sunlit and sun-warmed water, but instead is dependent upon the air. I discover the exertion that is required for the bird to breathe. Unlike the fish, the bird's breathing process is not supported by being surrounded by water. The warming and illuminating powers of the sun work in a different way in the air than they do in water. I notice that the jaw of the bird is forced back into its bodily substance. I become aware that it is as if all of the flesh that would have surrounded and supported the teeth was forced backward, and the jaw pressed forward and became hardened in its form. I discover why the bird thrusts its beak forward, whereas the fish in a softer way supports its jaw within the bodily substance. The head of the bird is a creation of the air; and yet the air, too, is affected by the inwardly glowing, illuminating presence of the sun. I recognize what a great difference there is between the sunlit and sun-warmed water that creates the form of the fish, and the sunlit and sun-warmed air that shapes the form of the bird. I begin to understand that because of the specific configuration of the elements in which the bird lives, it receives its unique form. Just as the fins of the fish receive their ray-like form through the element of water, so, too, the bird's feathers look a certain way, depending on how they are ruffled by the air and are affected by the light and warmth of the sun.

In this way I can go beyond a simple, naïve act of looking at something; and instead I can strive for a living comprehension of a creature within nature. I can exert myself rather than being lazy. If I see a fish lying on a table, I can, at the same time, picture it moving within water; if I see a bird in its cage, I can immediately visualize the air surrounding it in flight. I do not have to watch a bird flying in the air in order to feel and perceive the powerful, formative force of the air upon the very form of the bird itself. In this way what lives in the form of the bird is enlivened and spiritualized within me. That is, I can experience and perceive the forms of the fish and the bird inwardly; they become enlivened and spiritualized within me. Likewise, I can perceive in a living way the difference between a thick-skinned animal like the hippopotamus and a thinner-skinned animal such as a pig. I can see that the thick-skinned hippopotamus is attracted to direct contact with sunlight, whereas the thin-skinned pig prefers to withdraw from sunlight. To put it briefly, I learn to behold the many ways in which nature rules and manifests in each individual created being.

I would like to move now from examples in the animal kingdom and speak about what we call the elements in our physical world. I shall not take the path of the chemist who says that water consists of two atoms of oxygen and one of hydrogen. I shall put aside the scientist's observation that the air contains oxygen and nitrogen. I prefer to go directly to concrete observation. I see a body of water filled with fish and the relationship between water and fish. It is merely an abstraction to say that water is made up of hydrogen and oxygen, for that ignores a great deal. The reality is that water together with the sun and the moon create a fish; and furthermore, the fish speaks to my soul about the elemental nature of water. It is just an abstraction when I describe air as a mixture of oxygen and nitrogen, for the sunlit and sun-warmed air presses the flesh back over the bird's beak, and shapes the breathing organisms of both fish and bird into very different forms. The elements speak to me through the fish and the bird as they each reveal to me their unique characteristics. Think about how natural phenomena become inwardly richer with this approach, and how everything is inwardly impoverished when we speak about nature from only a materialistic point of view.

I would like you to take note that what arises out of anthroposophic spiritual science will provide many opportunities to change attitudes toward conventional modes of thinking as the examples I have just described indicate. For what we will bring forward through anthroposophic spiritual science will not be the same as the products of our present civilization; rather, what we have to offer will be a stimulus to develop a fuller understanding of the world.

If people began to inwardly experience the changes in the conventional attitudes that I have tried to characterize, then a new consensus would enable them to form a community, such as our Anthroposophical Society, which is truly based upon reality. Then everyone who belonged to the Anthroposophical Society, for example, would be able to say:

I am a person who feels grateful to the elemental beings who once worked actively in my being, and have made me who I am today. In former times they dwelt within my physical body and spoke to me through my very organs. The elemental beings have lost this capacity to speak to me through my organs. However, if I am able to observe everything in the world in the manner just described, and to recognize that phenomena are formed out of nature in its totality; if I take seriously the characterizations given to me through anthroposophy, then I will be able to speak out of my soul in a language that elemental beings once again can understand. I wish to become a human being who expresses gratitude to these spiritual beings.

I want to emphasize that in the Anthroposophical Society it is not enough to say that here we speak about the spirit—the pantheist also says that. In the Anthroposophical Society we must consciously *live with the spirit*. If we are able to do this, then quite naturally we shall be able to *live in the spirit* with other human beings as well. Furthermore, it would be recognized that the Anthroposophical Society is carrying the responsibility to repay the nurturing elemental beings for what they have done for us in former times. We also would be aware of the reality of the reigning Spirit that is present in the Anthroposophical Society. Much of the old feeling that still lives as traditions among us would disappear; and a real feeling would develop for the unique task of the Anthroposophical Society in our present day. Everything else would gradually be understood in its true meaning and value.

We may say with a certain inner satisfaction that the Goetheanum, which now has been brought to a tragic end, was built through the cooperative labor of seventeen nationalities, even though it was constructed at the same time that the peoples of Europe were waging war against one another. But the Anthroposophical Society will become a reality only when people strip away what they cling to in the narrow confines of nationality. Then anthroposophic cohesiveness can become a reality, and it will become something more than an abstract striving expressed in the founding of the Anthroposophical Society. In order to accomplish this, however, very specific preparations are necessary.

To a certain degree the reproach coming from the outside world regarding anthroposophists is justified. The anthroposophic movement talks a great deal about making spiritual progress, but in fact we see very little evidence of spiritual progress in the lives of individual anthroposophists. Progress certainly is possible. A careful reading of specific books opens the possibility of true progress in relationship to the spiritual. But in order for this to take place, the matters we spoke about yesterday must be taken seriously, must become real. We need to recognize that the physical body will become properly constituted through truthfulness; the etheric body will be realized through beauty; and the astral body will be refined through the sense for the good.

Speaking of truthfulness, I wish to point out that all who wish to unite themselves with the Anthroposophical Society must prepare themselves by cultivating truthfulness. Truthfulness must be acquired in life experience, and that will be something different for those who wish to express gratitude to the elemental spirits in nature, who have nurtured humanity since ancient times, than it would be for those human beings who know nothing about elemental beings, and do not wish to know anything about our indebtedness to them.

Those who do not wish to know anything about a deeper perception of reality prefer to present phenomena and events according to their personal prejudices. They would like to say this or that has occurred— if and when it seems right to them. They like to say that this or that person has particular qualities, but only when it corresponds to their own preference. But if you wish to discipline your inner truthfulness, you must not go beyond what speaks to you out of the reality and actuality of the outer world. You must be strict with yourself; remain watchful of your thought processes; be precise in the formulation of your words, so that with regard to the outer world you articulate nothing other than a verifiable fact or state of being.

Just think how common or fashionable it is in today's world for people to assert that what appeals to them, or whatever has been suggested to them, is precisely true. Anthroposophists must not become accustomed to this approach; rather, they must strictly exclude their own prejudices from the actual facts of a matter and describe only the pure phenomenon or event. Then anthroposophists, through their own efforts, would become a kind of corrective in society, which would challenge the prevailing confusion between what is opinion and what is fact.

Think of what is typically reported in newspapers today. Newscasters and journalists feel obligated to report everything whether or not it has been verified, and then say that it actually is thus and so. We often suspect that when we are told something, the person speaking has not taken the trouble to find out if the facts of the matter have been verified. Often an account is justified by saying, "Well, that certainly could have happened." Regarding the world around us, we often hear that this or that is presumed to be so: "Why shouldn't this actually have occurred in this way?" But with this approach we can never achieve a sense of inner truthfulness. When we, as anthroposophists, educate ourselves in the observation of the outer world of the senses, we must stand strictly behind what is verifiable and what corresponds exactly to what appears before our eyes in the world of the senses. If such a goal were embraced in our world today, it would cause a remarkable change in our society. If a miracle like that occurred and people actually had to make certain that their words corresponded to the facts, this would produce utter silence. Unfortunately, much of what is talked about today has not been verified; rather, it is filled with all kinds of opinion and is infused with apathy and indifference for what is real.

We also must be aware of what happens to us when we do not strive for complete and utter truthfulness in our lives. If we add anything to what we actually perceive through our outer senses; if we convey anything that does not correspond to the pure and accurate course of events or phenomena we observe; and if we allow these to enter our ideas and convey them in our representations to other people, our capacity to acquire higher knowledge will be extinguished.

There was once an occasion in a college of law[†] in which a carefully planned scene was enacted in front of about twenty law students. The students who had observed the interaction were asked to write down what they had witnessed. The scene had been carefully planned ahead of time to the smallest detail, and so it was possible to know how the event unfolded. Among the twenty students who wrote down what they had seen, three of them wrote accounts that were about half correct, and seventeen wrote descriptions that were inaccurate. And so in a classroom of law students, only three out of twenty students were able to observe accurately a brief scene. If we were to pick randomly any twenty people who observed an event, and afterward listened to one after the other of the witnesses, none of them would come close to an accurate description. I shall put aside situations when a person is in extraordinary circumstances. It does occur under the intense pressure of battle that an evening star glimmering through the clouds has been taken for an enemy plane. That kind of thing can happen in a moment of agitation. And in a situation like that, the consequences of an error may become greatly magnified. In the small details of everyday life, however, such errors are constantly occurring.

We speak about cultivating an anthroposophic way of life and making it a reality. This realization will depend upon the extent to which we develop an understanding of facts based on the utmost accuracy. You have to educate yourself in order to recognize and master what is factual. If you are able to do this, then you will be able to see the reality behind the outer facts; and you will not paint a phantom over the reality when you later wish to describe an event. You only have to read the newspapers today. Supposedly we have swept aside all of the ghosts that might haunt us, but what is reported as certainty in newspapers is actually full of phantoms and ghosts of the worst sort. The accounts people tell each other are likewise filled with illusions. That is the reason why the basis for ascending into higher worlds today is to first acquire an accurate sense for what happens in the world of sense perception. That is the only way you can arrive at truthfulness in the way I described it yesterday.

Yesterday I tried to demonstrate how you can develop in a living way a true feeling for beauty. This you can do by observing nature and perceiving how a certain creature was shaped by its physical surroundings. For example, through observation you can see and understand why the bird has a beak; and why, looking carefully at a fish, its head is drawn forward in order to protect its delicate, soft jaw. Really learning to live into these phenomena helps to develop our sense for beauty.

Spiritual truth cannot be reached without the element of goodness, without a true sense for the good. The human being must develop the capacity to have a genuine interest in another human being; to feel empathy for someone else, and to be willing make a sacrifice on behalf of another person. Morality begins when your own astral body receives the impress of the lines of worry and concern on another human face. That is the moment when morality begins; otherwise morality is merely the imitation of polite behavior or custom. What I have described as a moral deed in my book *The Philosophy of Freedom* is directly connected with experiencing in your own astral body the deep lines of worry and concern on someone else's face; or the lines on the face of a person who is smiling. Unless we immerse own soul in the soul of another person (and that is inherent to the art of living together as human beings), we cannot develop a life imbued with true spirituality.

A strong foundation for developing spirituality would be established if within the Anthroposophical Society it were really true that whenever you met someone, you could experience in a living way what the two of you share through anthroposophy; and neither of you would bring into the Anthroposophical Society today's all too commonly-held misguided feelings and prejudices. If the Anthroposophical Society really were to become a new creation, then, above all else, each one would affirm every other person as one's equal and as a fellow anthroposophist. Then, indeed, our society would exist as a reality. We would not find cliques being formed within the society. Attempts to encourage antipathy toward someone in particular, or toward a group of people, would cease, even though situations like this have become all too common outside of our society. The relations between individuals would be based upon experience of the spiritual that flows among us. But in order to begin our self-education to recognize what is true when we stand before facts and events, we must observe with exactitude, and then take full responsibility for giving an accurate account every time we report a fact or describe an event or relate what another person has said.

Cultivating truth is our first task. Entering into the reality or experience of every living creature you encounter in nature is the second responsibility. Here we learn to cultivate, for example, our feeling for the importance of water for a fish, and the significance of the air for a bird. To these examples we can add the empathy and understanding we extend to our fellow human beings. Third, cultivating and heightening our sensitivity to the good by experiencing everything that interests another human being and all that is living in the soul of another person. If we were to develop all these capacities as individuals, then the Anthroposophical Society would become a place where people strive to educate the physical body, etheric body, and astral body according to the appropriate goals and nature of each one of these human elements. Then it would be possible to initiate what I have ever and again characterized as necessary when I say that the Anthroposophical Society should not be a society that merely issues a membership card showing a person's name, affirming membership in a society, and indicating the person's number on the membership list. Rather the Anthroposophical Society should be permeated by a common spirituality that can grow stronger and stronger, and ultimately will demonstrate that it is more important for a person to feel the anthroposophic spirituality of another human being than it is to know if another person has a Russian, English, or German spirituality. Only then will a sense of community and common purpose truly be present in our Anthroposophical Society.

We do not always grasp the significance of the present moment in history. But in this modern era we understand that we live within the course and the context of history. We know that now we must take seriously the Christian principle of universal humanity, the principle of a shared community across humanity; for without this the earth will not fulfill its purpose and meaning. We can assume that at one time elemental spiritual beings existed who cherished and fostered humanity, and whose existence we should recall with gratitude. In recent centuries in the so-called civilized world of Europe and the Americas, human beings have lost their connection to these elemental beings. Humanity once again must learn to regard the spiritual world with gratitude. It will be possible for human beings to bring about healthy social relationships on the earth only when we develop a deep gratitude and a strong love for the elemental beings of the spiritual world. These conditions can come about only when we, too, acknowledge these elemental spiritual beings as something concretely real. Then the feeling of one human being toward another will become completely different; and it will resemble again the way that relationships in previous eras were cultivated, but which in the last centuries has languished. In recent times, one typically experiences another human being as someone alien to oneself, and regards one's own self as more important than anything else. And yet we barely know who we are today. We have no answer for the question, "What is it within you that you love above all else?" We reply that the natural scientist or the physician can explain why we love ourselves most of all. But in terms of our feelings, we are quite unconscious, and live only within ourselves.

But if we continue to live merely within ourselves, we shall manifest exactly the opposite of what a living anthroposophic community is capable of generating on behalf of humanity. We absolutely have to recognize that the human being must come out of the self. We must become as interested in the characteristics and capacities of every other person to the same degree that we are interested in ourselves. If we are unable to do that, an Anthroposophical Society shall never come into being. The society as an organization can accept members and exist for a while because the rules for membership have been laid out; but that is not equivalent to a reality. The society will not become a reality because it accepts members, and the members are given membership cards that say that they are anthroposophists. Realities do not exist because something has been written down or published; realities come into being only when they are alive. What we write down or publish has to be an expression of life. When our words arise out of living experience, then a reality is present. If what has been recorded or published remains no more than what appears on paper and is simply conventional in its meaning, then it soon will be apparent that what has been written down is only a corpse. As soon as I write something down, it is as if I "molt" my thoughts. When a bird molts, that is, sheds its feathers, the cast-off feathers are dead. The bird has to grow new feathers. Today human beings often do no more than shed dead thoughts when they write something down; they are eager to commit every thought into writing. But it would be very difficult for a bird, once it has cast off its old feathers, to turn right around and molt its feathers again. If somebody were to try to restore a canary that has shed its feathers, then they would have to find a way to attach artificial feathers. We have the same situation today with human thoughts in relation to the written word and genuine reality. When people are easily satisfied with writing down molted thoughts and sending dead thinking to the publishers, we are inundated with artificial realities that have nothing to do with true realities. Unfortunately, for the most part, we are producing artificial realities.

It is disappointing when we cannot see what true reality is; when we do not notice that we rarely hear the voice of a true human being. We rarely have anything to say out of our true universal humanity. Instead of speaking out of the core of our common humanity, we speak as individuals, and only out of one or another role we assume in our outer lives, such as a government representative, or as a lawyer. But these roles are merely abstract categories. Today it is no longer important to know that it is a woman or a Dutchman or a Russian who is speaking. We must begin to look beyond the fact that a cabinet member or government official, or Russian, German, Frenchman, or Englishman is speaking; we must be aware only that a true human being is speaking.

In order to do that, we ourselves as human beings must be fully self-aware and completely present. We shall never fulfill our true humanity, however, if we are concerned only with self-knowledge. For in our era the individual self must be linked to a common universal humanity; this is the only relevant reality for human beings. Look at the truth of our reality. We know that we cannot live by breathing in air that we have already taken into our own bodies. Likewise we cannot live as human beings solely by what exists within our own selves, by feeling just what arises in our own souls. Try to breathe in the air that you breathe out. You cannot do it! Similarly you cannot live as a real human being by living entirely out of your own inner self. We can live as human beings only by living in our social life, by living in association with others. We must experience who other human beings really are; and what they, too, experience with their fellow human beings. We can live within the experience of another human being only when we ourselves can sense what fills the other human being; when we ourselves can feel what another person is feeling within. That is true human community; that is being truly human in your own life and within the life of humanity. Wanting to live only within what one creates in one's own self would mean that one would prefer not to breathe in the air around, but would rather breathe into a container of one's own breath. Then you would soon die, because the physical reality is less merciful than the spiritual. But if you continuously were to breathe only the air around yourself; if you wished to live only within your own experience, then you would die. It is just that we do not realize that we have died within our souls, or at least spiritually.

Above all, we must realize that the real founding of the Anthroposophical Society and the anthroposophic movement will be accomplished only when we take to heart the words we hear when the shepherd Huckle in the Christmas play admonishes his sleepy companion, "Buckle, wake up!" I have pointed out that adopting the anthroposophic life should awaken you; this life should be an awakening. At the same time it also must be an ongoing avoidance of the death of one's soul and a continuing call to liveliness in the life of the soul. In this way, the Anthroposophical Society will, in and of itself, generate the inner strength necessary to make it a reality.

9

THE INTELLECTUAL FALL OF HUMANITY

ENLIVENED THINKING AS A PATH TO

THE SPIRITUAL WORLD

Dornach, January 21, 1923

In recent lectures I have spoken about human consciousness in our time; it poses one of the tasks for the Anthroposophical Society that must be accomplished. Modern consciousness can be achieved only when the tasks of culture, and indeed of civilization as a whole, are grasped from a spiritual-scientific point of view. On several occasions I have tried to characterize what religions mean by the Fall of Humanity.† Religions often say that the fall (a fall from divine grace, or a fall from innocence through the knowledge of evil) marks the beginning point of the historical development of humanity. Over the years I have pointed out that the fall encompasses a significant change that has occurred during the course of human development: the growing independence of the human being from the immediate guidance of divine-spiritual powers.

We know that consciousness of this independence, this autonomy, appeared when the Consciousness Soul emerged during the first half of the fifteenth century of the post-Christian or Common Era (C.E.). We have spoken about this turning point on many occasions. Actually, the entire course of human development preserved in history and myths was a preparation for this moment in which the individual became conscious of human freedom and independence; a preparation for humanity's struggle on earth to develop its self-generated capacity to discern and to make decisions, rather than to depend upon the direct guidance of divine-spiritual powers. Religious statements of belief point to a cosmic-earthly event when the spiritual and soul instincts, which guided human morality in ancient times, disappeared as the human capacity for decision-making arose. With regard to the moral impulses of humanity, the way in which religions understood it, human beings placed themselves in opposition to the guiding spiritual powers portrayed in the Old Testament as the *Jahve* or Jehovah Powers. It is as if human beings, from a certain point, no longer felt that the divine-spiritual powers were active within individuals, and instead that individuals had to become active themselves.

Thus with regard to the overall morality of humanity, human beings felt as if they had become sinful, whereas if they had remained under the instinctive guidance of divine-spiritual powers, it would have been impossible to fall into sin. During the time in which the human being was incapable of sin, he remained as sinless as a creature of nature. However, the human being became capable of sinning by virtue of the gifts of freedom and independence in relation to the divine-spiritual powers. At this point the consciousness of sinfulness appeared in humanity. As a human being I can be without sin only if I find my way back again to the divine-spiritual powers. Whatever I decide entirely on my own bears a sinful element; I can reach a sinless condition once again only by finding my way back to the divine-spiritual powers.

The consciousness of human sinfulness was at its strongest during the Middle Ages. And that is precisely the time during which an awareness of the intellectuality of the human being began to develop as well. Previously the intellect had not been regarded as a separate human faculty. And so as the human being became aware of the faculty of the intellect and began to develop the substance and content of intellectual activity, the intellect—with some legitimacy—became infected by the parallel awareness of the consciousness of sin. Initially human beings did not say that the intellect, as it developed during and after the third and fourth centuries c.e., was infected with a consciousness of sin. Only much later, under the influence of scholastic wisdom during the High Middle Ages, was the consciousness of sin linked to the intellect.

The scholastic wisdom of the Middle Ages said that no matter how ingeniously the human intellect can be put to use, we can apply it only to the external physical realm of nature. Through the intellect we can *prove* the existence of divine-spiritual powers, but the intellect cannot lead us to a direct knowledge of divine-spiritual reality. We can, however, *believe* in divine-spiritual powers, and we can also believe what has been revealed to us through the Old and New Testaments.

Thus the human being, who in earlier times had felt morally sinful (that is, removed or alienated from divine-spiritual powers), felt an intellectual sinfulness as well as a moral sinfulness during the period of medieval Scholasticism. Scholastic wisdom acknowledged that the human intellect could know the physical, sense-perceptible world. But during the High and Late Middle Ages [1100–1450 C.E.] human beings thought that as human beings, they were too base, too limited in their own powers to reach up into the region of knowledge in which they could grasp the spiritual. Even now, we do not notice how independent the intellectual fall is from the more general moral fall. But Scholasticism transferred the sense of moral sinfulness and human baseness to the intellect. To limit the use of the intellect to the sense-perceptible world was an extension of moral sinfulness, one that by implication disqualified the intellect from investigating spiritual reality.

When scholastic wisdom passed into the modern natural-scientific perspective, the connection between Scholastic wisdom and the old moral sinfulness was completely forgotten. Indeed, the direct connection between Scholasticism and modern natural-scientific knowledge is often denied. Now the newer natural sciences also say that there are limits to human knowledge, and that the human being has to be satisfied with using the intellect to investigate only the phenomena of the sense-bound physical world. Emil DuBois-Reymond, for example, claimed that there were limits to scientific research and even to human thinking.[†]

That claim is, however, a direct continuation and extension of Scholasticism. The only difference is that Scholasticism assumed if the human intellect is limited, then the human being must turn to something other than the intellect, namely revelation, when humanity wishes to know something about the spiritual world. In contrast to Scholasticism, the modern natural-scientific perspective takes one half rather than the whole. It is willing to take revelation as a given, at least if a person presumes the validity of revelation. But then modern science goes further and asserts that the human capacity to know is simply too base, too limited, to be extended to the divine-spiritual world.

When Scholasticism was in full bloom during the High and Late Middle Ages, the constitution of the soul was not as it is today. At that time, it was assumed that with your intellect you could obtain knowledge from the world of the senses; but you also felt that you could still experience the flowing together of the human being and the sense world by using the intellect. Scholasticism also thought that the human being could rise to revelation when seeking to know something about the spiritual realm that, by definition, could not be grasped intellectually. But it was not taken into account consciously by the Scholastics that into the ideas they put forward about the sense world there also flowed living spirituality; and that is what we must recognize fully today. The concepts of the Scholastics were not without spirit, whereas today concepts about the sense world exclude the spiritual. The concepts that the Scholastics brought forward about the world of nature did not exclude the participation of the human being, for the Scholastics were of the opinion (at least those who were among the scholastic realists), that thoughts came to human beings from without and were not fabricated from within. Today it is often presumed that thoughts do not originate outside the human being; rather, they are fabricated entirely within the human being and arise out of one's innermost being. Through this fact we increasingly have come to ignore everything that is not related to the external world of the senses.

Charles Darwin's theory of evolution showed the extent to which scientists in the nineteenth century had dropped everything that was not related to the sense-perceptible world. Previously, Goethe had moved toward a real theory of evolution, at least with regard to plants, and up to a certain point with regard to animals, too. However, he did not extend his ideas to the human being. When you examine his writings to see if he might have pursued this direction,[†] you will see that he stumbled whenever he tried to find implications for metamorphosis within the human being. He formulated an outstanding theory of plant metamorphosis, and also wrote with insight about animals; but he came to a standstill when he tried to speak about human development or metamorphosis over time. Human intellect, when it is permitted to deal only with the world of the senses, will not be able to discover the full, the true, the essential human being. It is indeed astonishing that Goethe could never say anything about the development of the human being. Goethe himself never applied his theory of metamorphosis to humanity. Guided by anthroposophic insight today, we expect to apply Goethe's theory of metamorphosis[†] far beyond his applications, and still remain true to the originator's own methods and principles.

How far forward has modern intellectualism brought natural science? It has reached the evolution of animals only up to the apes, and then added on the human being without being able inwardly to make any headway regarding humanity. The closer investigators come to the higher animals, the greater the difficulty they have forming adequate concepts. It is simply not true that human beings today really under-stand the higher animals. People merely *believe* that they understand them.

Thus our understanding of the human being has been separated from our understanding of the world, because real understanding has been torn out of the concepts we use. Our concepts have become less and less spiritual, and the prevailing spiritless concepts, which view the human being merely as the end point of the sequential development of the animal realm, now permeate the substance of all thinking. These ideas already flow into children in the early years of their schooling; and if this becomes part of general education, we shall no longer be able to observe the essential nature of the human being.

You know that once I tried to approach the entire question of knowledge with a different goal in view. I am referring to my book *The Philosophy of Freedom*[†] and its precursor *Truth and Knowledge;*[†] although a resonance is already apparent in *Goethe's Theory of Knowledge*[†] published in the 1880s. I have tried to turn the discussion in a completely different direction. I wanted to demonstrate that in the modern era we can put aside a traditional approach to thinking, and out of our own inner activity we can arrive at pure thinking. We can discover that a purely will-based capacity for thinking is something positive and real when we allow it to work within us. And furthermore, in *The Philosophy of Freedom*, I tried to reach humanity's moral impulse out of this purified thinking.

Over time, human development has proceeded so that we have increasingly accepted the assumption that the human being is too base, too flawed, too weak, to act morally; and from that we assumed that the base and limited nature of the human being applies to the intellect as well. We have developed in such a way that what individuals knew about their true humanity became "thinner and thinner." But, beneath the surface, there continued to develop a capacity to go beyond abstract thinking, a capacity in human thinking that is alive and real.

There came a point at the end of the nineteenth century, however, when this capacity to go beyond abstract thinking was not being noticed by human beings; and at the same time human beings typically believed they no longer had a connection with the divine-spiritual. Consciousness of human sinfulness had torn the human being away from the divine-spiritual; and the historical forces that came afterward were not yet able to draw humanity back into relation with the divine-spiritual.

However, in *The Philosophy of Freedom* I wanted to say, look into the depths of your soul. There you will find the remnant of a genuine and energetic thinking arising out of the inner self; a pure thinking that is more than ordinary thinking, a thinking that can generate a feeling-imbued knowledge, a thinking that lives in the human will. And this enlivened, pure thinking, working together with the will, can become the impulse for moral actions. In this context I have spoken about a moral intuition that can be inspired by and permeated with moral imagination. But this can become a living reality only if the path you choose (even in the face of the increasing separation of the human being and the human intellect from the divine-spiritual) is the path that leads you once more to the divine-spiritual. If you can discover spirituality in nature, then you also will find the spirit in the human being.

I said some years ago during a lecture in Mannheim† (and it was a lecture, I might add, that has not received much attention) that humanity in its present stage of development is capable of reversing the fall of humanity into sinfulness. The fall of the human being was understood first of all as a moral fall, which was extended later to the human intellect in a way that limited the human capacity of knowing to the realm of nature. But let me emphasize that the human being can achieve knowledge of the spiritual when it has been filtered through pure thinking. In this way the human being can reverse the moral fall and ascend to the divine-spiritual through the spiritualization of the intellect.

We have considered what in older epochs was known as the moral fall of the human being. Then we have traced the influence of this moral fall upon the course of human development over time. As a result of our explorations, we now can think about an emerging ideal for humanity; we can think about creating a compensation for the fall along a path that leads to the spiritualization of knowledge and to the renewal of our recognition of the spiritual nature of the cosmos. Through the moral fall of humanity, we have separated ourselves from the gods. Now by means of a new path of knowledge, we can find our way to the gods again. We must transform descent into ascent. By drawing pure spirit out of your own being with your own inner energy and strength, you shall be able to grasp firmly the goal and ideal to take seriously the fall of the human being. Indeed you must take the fall seriously. Understanding the fall will lead you right into the discussion of the knowledge of nature in our present day. You will need courage in order to use your powers of thinking and understanding to add to the older understanding of the fall; to find the possibility of overcoming the fall through self-generated renewal. You will need courage to manifest what can become of the human being who pursues a genuinely spiritual-scientific knowledge born out of our own day and time.

As we look back upon the development of humanity, we see that human consciousness places the fall of humanity on earth at the beginning of its historical development. Nevertheless, the fall requires compensation; a balance has to be found by lifting humanity out of sinfulness. And this renewal, this redemption, can occur only during the age of the consciousness soul. Only in our modern era has the historical moment arrived in which the highest ideal of humanity can be achieved through spiritual renewal. Without this development, humanity cannot proceed further.

This is what I explained in the lecture I mentioned earlier.† In the modern period the concept of the moral fall of the human being was carried over from the medieval era, and as the natural-scientific perspective arose, the intellectual fall of the human being was added to the moral fall. The intellectual fall was the great historical sign, the historical evidence that the spiritual rising beyond the fall would have to begin.

What does this spiritual rising beyond the fall, this spiritual ascendance imply? It means that we must come to a true understanding of the Christ. Those who still grasp something of this understanding (who have not lost the Christ under the influence of newer theology) have said that the Christ is a Higher Being who came to earth and was incarnated into an earthly body. They have drawn upon the written traditions that proclaimed the Christ. They have even spoken about the Mystery of Golgotha.

But now the time has come in which the Christ must be genuinely understood. People resist a genuine understanding of Christ, and the way this occurs is characteristic of our time. You see, even if only a spark of Christ is living within them, what must follow from it? They would have to be clear that Christ as a heavenly Being came down to earth; he spoke to human beings not through an earthly language; rather, he spoke out of a cosmic perspective. We, too, would have to exert ourselves to understand him; we would have to learn how to speak a cosmic language, one that would carry us beyond our earthly experience. We could not limit knowledge to the earthly sphere, for our planet was a new land for Christ. Our knowledge would have to encompass the entire cosmos. We would have to learn to understand the elements, the movement of the planets, and the constellations of the stars and their influence in relationship to what occurs on earth. Then we could draw nearer to the language spoken by Christ.

Expanding our knowledge so that it encompasses the cosmos as well as the earth belongs to our spiritual rising beyond the fall. For why did it come about that the human being felt compelled to understand only what exists on earth? This occurred because of our consciousness of the fall. We presumed that the human being was unworthy to grasp, to know, to understand the cosmos in the spirituality of its existence beyond our planet. That is the reason why it is said so often that the human being only has the capacity to know what is directly related to the earth. I gave you several examples of this yesterday. It is presumed that the human being can understand the fish only as it lies on the table, or the bird in its cage. The consciousness that the human being can rise above a purely earthbound knowledge does not exist in our so-called civilized natural science. Science typically makes fun of anything that is not earthbound. If you begin to talk about the stars, even that draws ridicule from people with the natural-scientific point of view.

If we want to hear what is really important about the relationship of human beings to animals, we have to look beyond the earthly sphere. The earthly plane can help us to understand plants, but it is not sufficient to understand the animals on earth. I have already said that we do not fully understand apes; neither are animals in general comprehensible to us. If you really wish to understand animals,† you already have to look beyond the narrow confines of the material earth, for animals live under the influence of cosmic forces. I showed you the example of the fish yesterday. I pointed out that the forces of the sun and the moon on water affect the fish; indeed, the water creates or determines the form of the fish. The same is true for the bird in relation to the air. As soon as you enter the elements, you come into contact with forces that are active within the cosmos. The whole world of animals may be understood by taking into account what lies within the earthly sphere as well as what exists far beyond it. With regard to the human being this is even more so. But as soon as you begin to speak about what lies beyond the earthly realm, you are met with ridicule. In order to have the courage to speak about what lies beyond the earth, you will have to develop a truly spiritual-scientific perspective. As a spiritual-scientific researcher today, the strength of your courage will be more important than your intellectuality. Spiritual-scientific research is fundamentally a moral task because it is a moral fall that has to be overcome and set aside.

First of all we must learn the language of Christ, the *ton uranón*; that is, the "speech of heaven" in the sense of classical Greek culture. We have to learn this language again in order to understand what the Christ wanted to do on earth. What until now has been referred to as Christendom and what has been described historically as Christianity have played roles different from the task we have today. We must learn to understand the Christ as a Being whose origins lie beyond the earthly realm. This task is identical with the ideal of raising the human being beyond the grasp of the moral fall of humanity.

However, there is a problematic element about formulating this new ideal; you recall that the consciousness of the capacity to sin once made the human being feel humble. In contrast, during our modern period human beings very seldom show humility. Often those who think of themselves as the most humble are in fact the most proud and arrogant. The greatest arrogance is found in those who strive for utter simplicity in their lives. They set themselves above everyone else, even above the humble soul searching inwardly for spiritual truths; they say that everything must be sought after in its purest simplicity. Such naïve natures (who also view themselves as naïve natures) are often the most proud and arrogant of all. Nevertheless, during the time of genuine consciousness of the fall of the human being, there used to be truly humble people; and humility was regarded as something valuable in the human being. Since then people have become more and more arrogant without there being any justification for this. Why? That can be expressed in words I recently brought to your attention. Why has pride become more and more prevalent? Because many, just like the sleepy shepherd in the nativity play,[†] have ignored the admonition, "Buckle, wake up!" Instead, they fall asleep. There was a time in which human beings felt their sinfulness with wakeful intensity; but now people fall into a drowsy sleep and only dream about a consciousness of the fall. Previously, one awakened to the consciousness of the fall and realized that human beings will remain sinful if they do not take measures to bring themselves back to the path that leads to divine-spiritual powers. In the past that realization has awakened human beings. Today, everywhere you look, you will find that individuals have been awakened to a knowledge of sinfulness. But people doze off again. The dreams come and whisper, "Causality reigns in the world. What happened in the past gives birth to its consequences in the present." And so we look up to the stars in the heavens as if they themselves cause affinities and antipathies among the heavenly bodies, a pattern of thought that we follow even down to forces between atoms and molecules, which are regarded as a miniature cosmic system.

And the dreaming went further. The dream ended at the point when it was said that we cannot know anything that lies beyond our experience of the senses. Whenever human beings go beyond the realm of sense experience, modern culture calls this "supernaturalism." But where supernaturalism begins, there science is said to end. Then the strident tirades of these dreams are brought into the congresses of natural-scientific researchers. We hear DuBois-Reymond's discourse "On the Limits of the Knowledge of Nature." And when the last sounds of the dream fade (sometimes the traces of a dream are not pleasant, and it really turns out to be a nightmare); when the speaker in the dream declares that where supernaturalism begins, there science comes to an end, not only the speaker but also the whole body of natural-science researchers slip into a blissful sleep. Listeners no longer need to activate an inner process of knowing; everybody can comfort themselves with the certainty that human knowledge is limited to the natural world; and furthermore, there is no possibility whatsoever that the human being can ever reach beyond the limit. The time has come when one can really hear the cry, "Buckle, wake up, the sky is falling!" But modern civilization just yawns, "Let it fall; it is old enough to let go." That is the state of society today; we have allowed our grasp of knowledge to fall fast asleep.

Today's spiritual-scientific anthroposophic understanding of knowledge can penetrate this sleepiness and resound in a new way. It is possible for the human being to rise beyond the moral fall through self-generated effort; this has to be drawn out of genuine knowledge. And the awakening of human beings today may very well be linked with the growth of pride and arrogance that was formerly only present in a dreamlike manner. Although some anthroposophic circles are not yet ripe enough to rise beyond the moral fall, there is still a lamentably high level of arrogance and false pride. It is part of human nature that the shadow of pride is more likely to prosper than the light-filled potential of human beings. And so, alongside the realization of the need to raise ourselves beyond the moral fall, we also must undertake our own education in the spirit of humility, and we must take in everything in a state of full consciousness. And it is possible to do so. But if pride seems to arise out of knowing, that is a sign that something has gone awry. For when understanding and knowledge are truly present, humility follows quite naturally. It is arrogance to prescribe a program for reform, as if you are implying that you know a social movement, or the women's movement, from the inside out; and therefore know exactly what would be possible, or correct, or necessary, or the best way to proceed. In such an instance it is as if you know everything, the issues and the ways to solve them. But in such a case you do not recognize your own arrogance because you explain matters as if you know everything. However, if you have achieved a real understanding of a matter, you remain humble, for genuine knowledge can be achieved (I will express it now in a simple way) only over the course of time.

If you are alive with real knowledge and understanding, you know that even the simplest truth can be mastered only with difficulty; and through effort that sometimes lasts for decades. Thus the process of inwardly working through a matter prevents you from becoming arrogant. But we must pay attention within the Anthroposophical Society of being fully conscious of the greatest ideal for humanity today—rising above the moral fall—and at the same time be awake and watchful to avoid the corrosive influence of pride and arrogance.

Today the human being needs a strong commitment to truly grasp the Being of Knowledge, so that we are not satisfied with just knowing a few anthroposophic catchwords about the physical body, the etheric body, reincarnation, and so forth, in order to appear to be a model of anthroposophic wisdom. Wakefulness helps us to guard against pride, and it must be cultivated as a new moral quality. It has to be taken into our meditation. Then the rising beyond the moral fall can really come into being; for the experiences that we have in the physical world are the ones that also lead us over into the spiritual world. These experiences must guide us toward devotion to the innermost capacities and strengths of the soul rather than to promulgating the "truths" of a particular program. Above all, we must have a sense of responsibility toward every single word that we express about the spiritual world. We have to strive to carry the truth that we have first encountered in the sense-perceptible world into the realm of spiritual knowledge. If we are not accustomed to working strictly with the facts that can be learned in the physical sense world, and to supporting what we say with observable facts, then we will not be ready to speak with truthfulness when we talk about the spirit. We cannot expect to grow accustomed to truthfulness only after we enter the spiritual world. Truthfulness is something that we have to bring with us.

On the one hand, within the consciousness of civilization today, facts are seldom taken into account; and on the other hand, science rejects the facts that could lead research in the right direction. I want to point out just a few instances from among many examples of this phenomenon. There are insects that are vegetarian when they are fully grown.† They never eat flesh, not even other insects. But when the female of this certain kind of insect looks for a place to lay her fertilized eggs, she places them inside another insect. The host insect is filled with the eggs of the insect mother. After a time of incubation, the eggs release the larvae within the body of the host insect. The larvae, which will gradually change into adult insects, are not vegetarian. They cannot be vegetarian, for they must feed upon the flesh of the host insect. Only after they have completed their metamorphosis into mature insects are they able to go without eating the flesh of the host insect.

The insect mother is herself a vegetarian and knows nothing of eating flesh; but she lays her eggs for the next generation within the body of another insect. Moreover, if these larvae would eat, for example, the stomach of the host insect in which they were embedded, then the larvae would soon have nothing more to eat. If they ate any organ of the host that was essential for the life of the host insect, the host would die and so would the larvae. And so, what do the insect larvae do when they emerge from their eggs? They reject eating any organ that is essential for the life of the host and eat only what is not needed to keep the host insect alive. When the larvae become insects and are mature enough to leave the host insect they become vegetarian and continue their lives in the manner of their adult mother.

You can see in this example that a remarkable intelligence holds sway in nature. When you really study nature closely, you will discover this commanding intelligence everywhere. Then with regard to your own intellect, you can think with greater humility; first of all, your own intelligence is not nearly as great as the intelligence that guides nature; and second, human intelligence is like a little bit of water that you take from a lake in a pitcher. The human being is actually like the pitcher that is filled with intelligence taken out of the much greater intelligence of nature itself. Intelligence is everywhere in nature; and everywhere this intelligence consists of wisdom. Whoever attributes the origin of intelligence to the human being is just about as clever as someone who says, "You are telling me there is water in that lake or in that stream? That is nonsense. There is no water there. There is only water in my pitcher; the pitcher has produced the water." Similarly, the human being who thinks that intelligence can come only from within the human being is incorrect, for in reality we merely draw intelligence out of the general sea of intelligence.

It is necessary that we really take into account the facts of nature. But the facts of nature are put aside when Darwinian theory is insisted upon, or when the facts are forced into the molds of modern materialistic perceptions. The real facts challenge every corner and crevice of modern materialistic presumptions. Today we suppress the facts. It is true that facts are reported, but only anecdotally, as an aside to mainstream science. Therefore the real facts of nature that are presented only as anecdotal "asides" in the study of science do not carry sufficient weight in the scientific education of the general public. The facts and observations of the natural world need to be available to the common person. The real facts that are known are not presented in their true significance, and untruthfulness is used to justify leaving out or suppressing the most striking and convincing phenomena.

When it comes to rising beyond the moral fall of humanity, however, we must first educate ourselves about truthfulness in the world of sense perception; and then we shall be able to carry over this education, this accustomed way of approaching the world of the senses, into the spiritual world. This prepares us to be truthful in the spiritual world as well. Otherwise we are in danger of telling other people the most unbelievable stories about the spiritual world. The person who is accustomed to approaching the physical world inaccurately, untruthfully, and inexactly, shall be able to relate only untruths about the spiritual world.

If we really grasp this ideal, it can consciously become a reality in the Anthroposophical Society; and if we can authenticate what arises out of such a consciousness, then the derogatory assertion that the Anthroposophical Society is a religious sect will evaporate. Of course the critics of anthroposophy will say all kinds of things that are untrue. But as long as we give them some cause for their criticisms, we cannot be indifferent to the truth or falsity of what opponents are saying.

The Anthroposophical Society has worked its way out of sectarianism, although it may be said that it had such roots during the years it was connected to the Theosophical Society. That prejudice can be laid to rest since the founding of the Anthroposophical Society in

1913. However, many members of the Anthroposophical Society have not taken this into account and still love sectarianism. It has come about that some long-term members of the Anthroposophical Society who almost wanted to break away from the society when it wished to transform its sectarian origins into a society conscious of its worldwide tasks have more recently made a different leap. Equally distant from sectarianism, if you look closely at its essential being, is the movement for religious renewal.[†] But the movement for religious renewal has given a number of long-term anthroposophists the opportunity to say that although Anthroposophical Society has continued to weed out its sectarian aspect, in the movement for religious renewal we shall be able to practice and nurture the religious aspect of anthroposophy. And so it may come about through anthroposophists themselves that the movement for renewal could become a desert of sectarianism, something that does not need to occur.

We can see that if the Anthroposophical Society wishes to become a reality, the courage to lift ourselves once again into the spiritual world must be actively cultivated. Then both art and religion can blossom in the Anthroposophical Society. If we take into account the nature of our artistic forms, we shall recognize that they live in the Being of the anthroposophic movement itself, and time and again must be discovered anew.

Likewise, the true deepening of religion lives within those who find their way back to the spiritual world, and who take seriously the rising beyond the fall through their own efforts. But we must also eliminate in ourselves any dependence on sectarianism, for the inclination to sectarianism is always egotistical. That will help us to avoid the problem of pressing forward into spiritual reality just to satisfy a mystical appetite, which basically amounts to egotistical excess. All the talk about the Anthroposophical Society becoming too intellectual is put forward by those who want to avoid an experience of spiritual substance and would much rather enjoy the pleasure of nurturing their soul appetite within a mystical haze of nebulousness. Selflessness is a requisite for true anthroposophy. It amounts to a kind of soul egoism when anthroposophic members themselves resist true anthroposophy and enter only into a sectarian existence, which satisfies a feeling of delight in the soul that is completely egotistical.

These are the things that we must take into account if we are to accomplish our tasks. We shall not lose our warmth toward anthroposophic striving, our sense for the artistic, or our religious sensitivity. We shall avoid what must be avoided: an inclination toward sectarianism. This attraction to sectarianism has introduced a quality of disintegration within the society, for it often draws us into forming cliques. Cliques within the anthroposophic movement seem to be an expression of relationship; but they actually lead to a negative kind of relationship—that of sectarianism.

We must come back to the cultivation of a world consciousness, so that our opponents, who with full intent want to say what is untrue, are the only ones to say that the Anthroposophical Society is a sect. We must strongly resist the characterization of the anthroposophic movement as a sect. We should also object to describing the movement for religious renewal as sectarian, for the movement itself is not conceived of in this way.

These are the matters that we must clarify in our thinking. We have to understand the innermost being of anthroposophy and recognize that anthroposophy can give human beings a cosmic consciousness. Most certainly this is not a sectarian perspective. For these reasons it has been necessary for me to speak about avoiding a narrow definition of the tasks of the Anthroposophical Society.

10

Rising Beyond the Intellectual Fall of Humanity through Inner Discipline

Materialistic Science Aligned with Medieval Thinking

Dornach, January 26, 1923

In recent lectures I have spoken about the fall of the human being and the emerging human capacity to rise spiritually beyond the grasp of the fall. Within the general consciousness of humanity in the present era, this spiritual rising beyond the fall needs to be recognized as an ideal for human striving and willing. I have pointed out the aspect of the fall that has played into intellectual life during our time. When one speaks about the limits of the knowledge of nature today, it is based on the view that human beings no longer have the capacity to reach the spiritual, and neither should we strive to rise beyond the fall through the intuitive perception of the earthly. And I pointed out that when the limits to the knowledge of nature are spoken about today, it is merely a modern intellectual way of referring to the sinfulness of the human being, which was carried over from older periods of history, especially from the medieval era in Europe. Today I want to indicate that humanity in our epoch cannot fulfill the true goal of earth evolution if we continue to hold these older views about knowledge and our intellectual development, which are still accepted in the modern era. Popular consciousness today is deeply permeated by the historical legacy of the fall. Intellectualism has already degenerated so significantly that if our acceptance of it remains as it is now, we shall not be able to speak about goals for the future of humanity. Today it must be our highest priority to acknowledge that deep within the human soul there exist capacities with a potential that far exceeds what can even be imagined in popular consciousness.

In order to understand the significance of the forces nascent in the human soul, we have to understand the nature of contemporary consciousness. Modern consciousness originated, on the one hand, out of a particular view of human thinking and, on the other hand, out of a specific notion about the human will. Human feeling lies in between these two, and we observe our feeling whenever we perceive either human thinking or human willing. Human beings today use thinking to understand the full scope of the world of nature, and the world of humanity, too, at least as far as one uses the art of thinking in the way it is applied to the natural realm. Human beings are taught to think in the way that thinking is applied to the natural sciences. We also examine social life with the kind of thinking we use today in the natural sciences.

Many people believe that the thinking used in the study of nature is impartial and unprejudiced. We often hear about the absence of preconceptions in scientific investigations; but I have often emphasized that the presumed objectivity of science is not very advanced. The kind of thinking currently used by the scientist during scientific investigations, which is also the kind of thinking used by ordinary human beings to conduct their lives, is an outgrowth of a much earlier kind of thinking. Specifically, modern thinking has developed out of medieval European thinking. Moreover, what is said today by the critics of medieval thinking is itself a product of the method of thinking that emerged during the medieval era. An essential characteristic of medieval thinking that has carried over into contemporary thinking is the presumption that thinking can be observed only as it is applied to the phenomena of the natural world; that the thinking process itself cannot be observed, and there is no basis for contemplating the scope or potential of human thinking. No notice is taken of the thinking process itself, or of the inwardly living quality of thinking.

Our lack of awareness of the living nature of thinking is a natural consequence of the observations that I have just presented. The thoughts that modern human beings have about nature are actually corpses of thoughts.† When we reflect about the realm of nature, we are thinking dead thoughts, because the living aspect of these corpses of thoughts was present in the pre-earthly existence of the human being. The thoughts that we now develop about the natural world, and also about human life, are dead thoughts. However, these thoughts were once living thoughts in our pre-earthly existence.

In our pre-earthly existence, before we descended into our physical, earthly incarnation, the abstract, dead thoughts, which we develop on earth according to the custom of our time, were living, elemental beings. In pre-earthly existence we experienced these thoughts as living beings, just as we here on earth experience life within our own blood. Here during earth existence these thoughts die and become abstract. As long as we continue as we are today and use our thinking only to observe external nature, our thinking will focus on dead thoughts. As soon as we look within ourselves and allow what is living to reveal itself to us, then it also works further within us, albeit unconsciously in comparison to our ordinary consciousness. But the living aspect of thinking that was part of our pre-earthly existence reaches into us and continues to work within us. The forces of these living thoughts are those that we possess by virtue of the forming of our physical organism for our earthly incarnation. The forces of the living thoughts residing in our pre-earthly existence cause us to grow and form our internal organs. When, for example, theoreticians speak about thinking, they are speaking about dead thoughts. If they wished to speak about the true nature of thinking and not about dead thinking, they would have to acknowledge that they must look within themselves, and in their innermost being take note that thinking is not something that begins at the birth or the conception of the human being. They would have to recognize that the inner activity of thinking is a continuation of a living pre-earthly thinking.

When we observe the very young child living in a dreamlike, sleepy state (for the time being I do not wish to speak about the child's life within the mother's womb), and if we are able to understand what is really happening within the child, then we recognize that the living powers of pre-earthly existence are still active within. Then we can see that the very young child remains in a dreamy, sleepy existence for a time, and only later begins to have specific thoughts. That is actually so; for in the first period of life, in which the young child dozes dreamily, the entire organism is seized by thoughts. As the organism becomes more fully grounded in itself, thoughts no longer are held within the solid and watery aspects of the organism. Rather, thoughts find expression in the formative qualities of air and warmth. So we can say that in the very young child all four elements (earth, water, air, and fire) are imbued with thoughts. During later development, thoughts are grasped by the formative elements of air and fire. As we mature, the power of thinking is brought into the fully developed breath and warmth-generating processes that permeate our body.

Thus the power of thinking moves from the more solid aspects of the physical organism into the fleeting, lighter, airier parts of the body. That is how thinking obtained its independent element, which accompanies us during our life between birth and death. When we are asleep, that is, when the power of thinking that is achieved on earth weakens, and is less likely to be directed into the warmth and air of the physical organism, the pre-earthly power of thinking reasserts itself. Only after you go further, and achieve a true contemplation of the inner self, will it become clear to you what the true nature of thinking is. Theories of knowledge are nothing more than abstractions. When you really look closely at this process, you will have to acknowledge that if you examine closely the conceptual and thinking processes, pre-earthly existence will reveal itself everywhere you look.

In contrast to what I have just described, medieval thinking (which still wields influence today) was forbidden to admit the possibility of pre-earthly existence. The pre-existence of the human being was declared to be heresy.[†] After centuries of being required to deny human pre-existence, humanity developed a habit of avoiding it. Think back to 1413 C.E.,[†] when the modern human being was beginning to emerge. Humanity in western societies had become accustomed to avoiding the possibility of pre-earthly existence. Indeed, they were basically disinclined to orient themselves to pre-earthly existence. If humanity had not been forbidden to think about a pre-earthly existence up until 1413, a very different development would have taken place. For example, then it would not have been just a possibility but almost a certainty that the Darwinism that appeared in 1858[†] (which outwardly was based on the observation of development in the natural world) would have had a very different form if nature had been investigated through the prism of pre-earthly existence. If that had been the case, Darwin could have founded a natural science in the light of the pre-existence of the human being. Instead, humanity was disinclined to think about the possibility of pre-earthly existence, and there emerged a natural science in which the human being was regarded as the culmination of the animal kingdom. And so the view of the human being in a pre-earthly, individual life could not come forth, because the animal does not have a pre-earthly existence.

Thus out of the old perspective of the fall was born the prohibition against speaking of the pre-existence of the human being, and that was reinforced just as modern intellectualism was beginning to emerge. This is how it came about that natural science was the child of a misunderstood notion of the fall. We have a natural-scientific tradition that is connected to the fall of humanity; that is, a natural science that emerged directly out of a misunderstanding of the fall. If this perception of natural science were to continue, then the earth itself would not be able to fulfill its true purpose. Humanity would develop a consciousness that is not connected to its divine-spiritual origin; instead, human consciousness would be separated from its divine-spiritual origin.

We have spoken concretely rather than theoretically today about the limits of knowledge of nature. We have indicated why, under the influence of modern intellectualism, humanity has sunk below the level that is within its capacity to reach. If we were to speak in the language used during the medieval period, we would have to say that natural science has "gone to the devil."

History speaks to us very clearly. Just as natural science came forward with its brilliant results (which even today should not be disputed by me), people today who still have some understanding of the true nature of the human being see that natural science is also capable of leading human beings astray. What once caused fear and trembling (it glimmered faintly in Faust as he bid farewell to the Bible and turned to nature) is now the fear that human beings still approach the knowledge of nature under the sign of the fall, rather than from the prospect that they can rise beyond the fall through their own enlivened capacity for thinking. This matter goes much deeper than is usually presumed. When the medieval period was just beginning, traditional approaches to knowledge were already haunted by the fear that Faust's "devilish poodle" was nipping at the heels of the investigator of nature. And yet now in the modern period humanity simply dozes off and does not even bother to think about these things any more.

Contemporary indifference is not a trivial matter. It is not theoretical small talk to recognize the influence of the fall upon today's discussion of the limits of the knowledge of natural science. The unperceived residue in human thinking that denies the presence of the fall in modern ideas about intellectual and empirical areas of knowledge really exists. If this corrosive influence were not present, then we would not be taught the theory of animal and human development that is currently prevalent; that is, a horizontal sequence of development from fish to lower mammals, to higher mammals, and then to the human being. This is what is typically proposed as the line of development in animal and human evolution. And yet, this does not accord with the facts of the matter. If you look closely at the developmental sequence, you will discover that it is not supported by actual observation.

The research carried out in the natural sciences today is remarkable, but what the scientists say about the research is not correct. If scientists would grasp the meaning of what they observe, they would *reverse* the direction of the line of animal and human development:[†]

Human being—Higher mammals—Lower mammals—Fish

(With this, I am obviously leaving out some details.) In this sequence you go from a time in which developmental stages *begin* with the human being, proceeding through higher mammals, lower mammals, and fish to a point of origin, in which every animal is still spiritual. Here you see that the human being is a direct descendant of higher spiritual beings and will continue to take on greater and greater similarities to higher spiritual beings. Likewise, the lower animal beings also have their origins from higher spirituality, but as lower beings they have not assumed higher spiritual natures.

We would have received accurate interpretations of these facts if the recognition of human pre-existence (that is, the acknowledgement of pre-earthly life) had not been suppressed. Thus other human modes of thinking could have been used; and a mind like Darwin's, who could have arrived at an accurate understanding of the evolutionary sequence, had to fall short of a correct interpretation because of a misguided habit of thinking rather than because of the results of his investigations.

It also would have been possible to reach an accurate interpretation if Goethe's theory of metamorphosis had been extended correctly. I have always pointed out that Goethe got "stuck" in the development of his theory of metamorphosis. We just have to observe objectively how Goethe viewed the matter. With regard to plants, Goethe observed their development very carefully and arrived at his archetypal plant form (*Urpflanze*). But when it came to the human being and he tried to articulate the metamorphosis of human bones, he felt stymied and simply could go no further. Take, for example, Goethe's brief notation about the morphology of the human skeleton.[†] By examining a broken sheep's skull in Venice, it occurred to him that the skull was a transformed vertebra. But he never went any further than this.

Elsewhere I drew attention to a note I found in Goethe's papers when I was working in the Goethe Archive in Weimar.[†] Goethe suggested that the human brain is a transformation of the ganglia in the spinal cord. Again he took the matter no further. This sentence was written in pencil in one of his notebooks. One can see that Goethe had drawn a line through the latter part of the sentence; he was dissatisfied with what he had written and wanted to investigate further. Scientific research at that time was not sufficiently advanced to be helpful. In our day, research enables us to take a position on this question. Ever since the earliest studies of embryology, there has never been any indication that the form of the human skull could have arisen out of the vertebrae. If you know the current state of embryology, it is clear that we cannot assume that the skull is a transformation of the vertebrae. More recently, Gegenbaur[†] has shown that the nature of the skull and the bones of the face are very different from the observations that were put forward by Goethe at that time.

However, if we know that the present form of the skull leads back to the bones of the body in one's previous earthly incarnation, then we can understand the process of metamorphosis. Thus we are drawn into the presumption of repeated earth lives by means of outward morphology. That is in line with Goethe's teaching about metamorphosis in forms of life. It is impossible, however, that the line of development proposed by Darwin and still accepted by conventional science today will be altered in any way. The misunderstanding of the intellectual fall has corrupted and even ruined contemporary thinking. The situation is even more serious than we are willing to admit.

We must have a clear idea about the way human consciousness has changed over time in order to see the things I have been speaking about in the proper light. We may, for example, say that something is beautiful. Now ask a philosopher what beauty is—certainly a philosopher should know something about beauty—and you will discover that the philosopher comes back with the most unbelievable abstractions. Beauty is a word that we use almost instinctively to describe what we feel. But today no one has any idea what the Greeks in ancient times imagined when they spoke about beauty. We no longer understand that when an ancient Greek spoke about the *cosmos*, the word meant something very concrete. For us, *cosmos*, or "World-All," refers to a great jumble of meanings. We would just as soon not even talk about this today. For the ancient Greeks, the word cosmos encompassed beauty, elegance, grace, artistry. As soon as they spoke about the entire cosmos, they inevitably referred to its beauty. The cosmos meant not only the World-All, it implied Universal Beauty in its natural lawfulness. All of that was implied in the use of the word cosmos.

And when the ancient Greeks stood before a beautiful work of art, when they wished to portray the human being in a work of art, how did they go about it? The ancient Greeks wished to make it beautiful. If you take the definitions of Plato,[†] you get a sense for what the ancient Greeks tried to do when they portrayed the human being in a work of art. Expressing this in words, an ancient Greek would say, "On earth the human being is not the same as an ideal human being would be. Humanity originated in heaven, and I try to portray the human being so that we can see these heavenly origins." The ancient Greek characterized the human being in a beautiful form, as if coming directly from heavenly origins, whereas the actual outer form of a human being would naturally appear quite differently. Human beings do not actually appear as if they had just fallen from heaven; their forms carry everywhere the sign of Cain's fall from grace. That is the ancient Greek image. We are not able to follow this example in our time, for we have forgotten the connection between the human being and pre-earthly existence; that is, heavenly existence. We can say, however, that what the ancient Greeks called beauty was the revelation of the human being's significance in the heavenly realm.

Thus the idea of beauty became concrete. With us, however, beauty is only an abstraction. There has been an interesting debate between two modern philosophers of aesthetics: Friedrich Theodor Vischer,[†] a very intelligent man, who wrote a very important book on aesthetics in the context of our time, and the formalist Robert Zimmermann,[†] who wrote another work on aesthetics. Vischer defined beauty as the revelation of the Idea or ideal in material form. Zimmermann defined beauty as the consistency or the harmony of the parts in relation to the whole form. Thus for Vischer the substance was the most important aspect, and for Zimmermann the form took precedence over substance.

When someone says that beauty is an idea that manifests itself in a material form, what does that tell you about an idea? First of all you have to know what an idea is. Using the corpses of thoughts that people think are ideas today, this definition leads nowhere. But it meant something when an ancient Greek defined a beautiful human being by saying that a beautiful human being is one whose human form embodies the idealized form of one of the gods. A definition like this gives you something concrete that you can try to understand.

It is important that we become aware that human consciousness and the constitution of the soul have changed over the course of time. In the modern era people believe that the ancient Greeks thought in the same way that we do now. Histories of Greek philosophy written in the nineteenth and twentieth centuries make this very clear. For example, the history of Greek philosophy written by Eduard Zeller[†] is considered to be an outstanding scholarly work of the mid-nineteenth century, and it is also highly respected in the twentieth century. Zeller's history of Greek philosophy gives us the impression that Plato never taught at the Platonic Academy; rather, he had a chair at the Berlin University in the nineteenth century, just as Zeller himself did. As soon as we grasp thoughts concretely, we see how impossible it would have been for Plato to teach in a nineteenth-century university such as the one in Berlin. Nevertheless, what Zeller carried over from Plato's work is translated into concepts of the nineteenth century, and this approach has no feeling for the necessity that we must go back and recapture the soul constitution of a different era if we really want to understand Plato.

When we develop a consciousness for the way in which the soul constitution changes over time, then we shall not find it absurd to discover that, with respect to our thinking today about nature and the human being, we have succumbed completely to an intellectual fall. And we must remember something that humanity rarely takes into consideration today, or indeed something people may think is a distorted idea. In today's theoretically oriented knowledge—a way of thinking that is accepted even in the remotest villages—something lives that can be redeemed only through Christ. We have to understand Christianity if we are to begin to grasp this.

Now, if we expect that a modern scientist should understand that his thinking must be redeemed by Christ, then the scientist would shake his head and say, "The deed of Christ may be responsible for many things that have occurred in the world, but to expect me to say that Christ can redeem natural science from an intellectual fall is not something that I can allow." But even when theologians write natural-scientific books, as has often occurred in the nineteenth and twentieth centuries (one has written about ants, another about the brain, and so forth), these books also need to be written out of an understanding of a true Christology. The scientific books by theologians, incidentally, are often excellent, even better than those written by natural scientists, because the theologians are able to write in a more accessible way. Nevertheless, today we need—especially in intellectual disciplines—a rising beyond, an overcoming, of the prevailing widespread intellectual fall.

Thus we see that intellectualism has been contaminated through a misunderstood consciousness of an intellectual fall, but not because a fall has actually occurred; rather, out of a misunderstood consciousness of an intellectual fall. For a misunderstood consciousness of the fall necessitates placing Christ as a higher Being in the middle point of the earth's development, and from there finding our way beyond the influence of the intellectual fall. We also must discover a deeper understanding of human development in spiritual realms.

When we look at medieval Scholasticism in the way it is usually done today, even going back as far back as Augustine,† we cannot expect to gain much from this. It is likely to be unproductive, because we do not see anything beyond the observation that modern natural-scientific consciousness has developed further over time. But that view ignores a higher overarching reality and perspective.

I once gave a presentation in this hall about medieval Scholasticism so that you could see all of the connections. In 1920 I gave a short cycle of lectures about Thomas Aquinas[†] and spoke about the broader connections to his life. But it is painful to note that within our anthroposophic movement the implications of the lectures are not understood. The natural sciences today, brilliant as they are, are not receiving what they need to carry on further. And if forming the connection to Scholasticism is not being pursued, then our [anthroposophic] research institutes,[†] which have come into being through great sacrifices, will remain ineffective. The institutes themselves will have to utilize these insights in order to move forward and not fall prey to fruitless polemics over atomism.

The natural sciences have come so far in establishing facts that they are striving to abandon the sterile modes of thinking that we see everywhere in natural-scientific literature. We know enough about human anatomy and physiology, for example, that if we chose the right method of thinking it would be possible to grasp the metamorphosis of the form of the head arising out of the form of the body in an earlier incarnation. But when we adhere to the material aspect alone, we cannot understand the body's relationship to an earlier life. People will only ask in a clever way, "Well then, we shall have to hold onto physical bones, so that they can be transformed bit by bit in the grave." But the fact of the matter is that the material form is an outward form, and that the formative forces are the ones that undergo metamorphosis.

On the one hand, thinking has been shackled because pre-existence has been shrouded in darkness. On the other hand, knowledge about life after death can be achieved only through a knowledge that goes beyond sense experience. If a human being rejects the possibility of suprasensory knowledge, then life after death remains an article of faith the credibility of which is dependent upon authority. A real understanding of thinking processes leads to pre-earthly life, if human beings are not prohibited to think in this way. Post-existent life, however, can be known only through higher knowledge that is not bound to sense existence. For this you may use the methods that I have described in *How to Know Higher Worlds*.[†] But this knowledge is rejected in the context of contemporary consciousness.

And thus two factors are working together: the continuing influence of the older prohibition to acknowledge the pre-existent life of the human being and today's deep aversion to higher, suprasensory knowledge. When we bring these two together, then anything to do with a suprasensory realm is assigned to the unknowable; that is, to the realm of belief. That means that the non-material can be only a matter of belief for Christendom and not a matter of knowledge. This situation will never permit any science that wishes to be credible as science, to have anything to do with the Being of Christ. And this is precisely the state of affairs that exists today.

But I said at the beginning of today's observations that with regard to human consciousness, which today is filled with intellectualism, humanity has succumbed to an intellectual fall, and unless we rise beyond this condition, the purpose of the earth cannot be fulfilled. The current state of scientific investigation will not allow the earth to fulfill its destiny. But the integrity of the human being in the depths of the soul remains unbroken. When, out of the depths of our souls, we develop higher knowledge with regard to the Christ impulse, then we also shall rise beyond the fall that affects intellectualism today, which (if I may express it in this way) has succumbed to the sin of decadent intellectualism.

First of all it is necessary to understand that intellectual empirical research must be able to grasp what can be known through the spirituality of the cosmos. Science must be imbued with spirit. But this spirituality cannot reach the human being if research is limited to what exists in space or within the boundaries of sequential time.

If we study the form of the human head with regard to the structure of bones, merely in comparison with the structure of other bones such as cylindrical bones, vertebrae, or ribs, we will not accomplish anything. We shall have to go beyond space and time in our concepts, just as we have done with regard to spiritual science, so that we can grasp what happens as a human being moves from one earth existence to another. But we must also be clear that when we look at a human skull it is possible to consider it a transformation of vertebrae. However, what exists today in the human spinal column never transforms itself into a skull in the sphere of earth existence; it must first disintegrate and be transformed into the spiritual in order for vertebrae to become skull bones in an individual's subsequent earth life.

When an instinctively intuitive mind like Goethe's comes along, he recognizes that the form of the skull is the transformed vertebrae. But in order to describe how a perception like this becomes a fact, you need spiritual science. Goethe's theory of metamorphosis becomes significant only in the context of spiritual science. That is the reason why Goethe within his lifetime remained dissatisfied with several of his observations. Likewise, only within the context of anthroposophic spiritual science is it possible to find the right relationship between intellectual fall and rising beyond the intellectual fall. Thus anthroposophic knowledge is not just observation; it has the capacity to bring living substance into the course of human development.

11

REALISM AND NOMINALISM: THE DIVINE ESSENCE IN NATURE AND THE HUMAN BEING

Dornach, January 27, 1923

T HE medieval intellectual life out of which the modern life of the mind originated (at least as far as Europe is concerned) is found in what is known as Scholasticism. At its height Scholasticism contained two well-differentiated streams, *Realism* and *Nominalism*.

If you think about the meaning of the word *realism* in our time, it will not help you to understand the meaning of the term in the context of medieval Scholasticism. Today everything that is outwardly sense-perceptible and can be experienced through its physicality is said to be real; and everything that is not material is considered an illusion. Exactly the opposite was true of medieval Realism. According to medieval Realism, ideas about objects and processes were related to prototypes and ideals, which were real above all else; whereas the Nominalist school thought that language allows us to assign names to things, but words do not stand for something real.

Let us see if we can clarify the difference between the Realist and Nominalist. I have on other occasions turned to the explanation of an old friend, Vincenz Knauer,[†] to clarify the perspective of Realism. Whoever accepts only the reality of what comes through our outer senses (that is, what may be found in matter), will not understand what happens if a wolf is held captive over a long period of time and eats only the flesh of a lamb. Knowing that the material substance of a wolf is completely exchanged for new matter in the course of time, it would seem logical that a wolf that eats only meat from lambs would eventually consist entirely of the substance derived from lambs. Thus the lamb-eating wolf would itself turn into a lamb. But that is not what happens; the wolf remains a wolf. It is not the nature of matter that determines whether an animal is a lamb or a wolf; rather, it is the essential form or inherent constitution of an animal that determines whether an animal is a lamb or a wolf. Therefore, as human beings, we distinguish between the lamb and the wolf by assigning one concept (or idea or form) to the lamb and a different one to the wolf.

When you say that concepts or ideas are nothing, and that only matter distinguishes a lamb from a wolf, then whatever has been part of the lamb and is transferred to the wolf determines if the matter is lamb or wolf. If concepts are meaningless, then in a material sense the wolf must turn into a lamb if it always eats the flesh of a lamb. This is the way in which Vincenz Knauer demonstrates what was meant by the point of view of a Realist steeped in medieval Scholasticism. It is the form that identifies the real, not the way in which matter is organized. And the form is a concept or an idea. This was the perspective of the medieval Realists, who said the concept or idea constitutes what is real. And so they called themselves Realists.

The Nominalists were adamant opponents to the Realists. They asserted that there is nothing other than outward sense-perceptible reality. Concepts and ideas for the Nominalists were nothing more than *names* by which the things which possess material existence are distinguished. Today, however, if we take the Nominalists and compare them to the Realists such as Thomas Aquinas or some other Scholastics, characterizing their views in abstract terms, the differences regarded as so profound at the time are scarcely negligible. Realism and Nominalism seem merely to represent two different points of view.

This is because in the present day we are not inwardly moved and warmed by what is expressed in these spiritual streams. But actually there is something very important here. Take the Realists who say that universals expressed in ideas, concepts, or forms are realities within which the sense-perceptible is ordered. For the Scholastics these universals captured in ideas and concepts were already abstractions, except that they said that these abstractions were *real*. However, their abstractions were remnants of an earlier, more concrete and substantial experience of knowing. In earlier eras human beings did not merely associate the concept of wolf with a material wolf; they actually experienced the presence of the group soul of the wolf in the spiritual world. The group soul was a real being. This actual being was experienced and perceived in a much earlier time; but what once had been experienced in the soul had evaporated into an abstract concept by the time of Scholasticism. Nevertheless, the Realists among the Scholastics still retained something of the earlier living perception, and knew that a concept was not just a "nothing"; the concept still contained an element of the real.

This reality was a remnant, a residue of real beings. In the late medieval period one still had an inkling of these real beings, just as the Ideas of Plato in ancient times were full of life; and indeed they were much livelier than the medieval experience of Ideas of the Scholastics. Ancient Persian archangels,[†] known as the Amshaspands, were also remnants of an earlier era when they, too, were living beings active throughout the universe. Plato's Ideas and Persian archangels were real beings. For Plato these angelic beings had already become somewhat veiled; and by the time of medieval Scholastics, these beings had been reduced to abstractions. That was the last stage of the spiritual clairvoyance that had been carried over from ancient times. Even though the medieval Realists among the Scholastics no longer had access to an older spiritual perception, the living ideas, the concepts, had been handed down over centuries and preserved the universal reality that still lived in the stones, plants, animals, and the physicality of human beings. These ideas, concepts, and universals were still regarded as something spiritual, even if they were perceived in the form of an elusive, watery spiritual aspect. The Nominalists were already closer to modern intellectualism, for they were no longer capable of seeing ideas or concepts as being connected to anything real. For them concepts and ideas were just names that brought order into humanity's understanding of material existence.

The medieval Realism that we find in Thomas Aquinas was not carried over into the worldview of the modern era, for concepts and ideas today have no relationship to what is considered real. If you ask someone today if concepts and ideas stand for something real, you could expect to receive an answer only if you reformulated the question. For example, you could ask a human being who had been educated in a modern way, "would you be satisfied if you existed only as a concept or an idea after you died?" This would make a person feel very unreal after death. In our day this question would seem to imply something

completely unreal about the human being after death. That was not so
for the Realists among the medieval Scholastics. Concepts and ideas
were so real for them that they could still believe in the existence of the
World-All; they could have imagined that after having died they would
still continue to exist in the form of a concept or an idea. Medieval
Realism, as we have already noted, did not continue into modern times.
The modern worldview is thoroughly Nominalist. And people today who
no longer trouble themselves about the inner meaning of concepts and
ideas are the ones who are most steeped in Nominalism.

This, too, has a profound significance. The victory of Nominalism as
the conventional wisdom in modern civilization means that humanity
has lost its capacity to grasp the spiritual aspect inherent within the material world. The family name Smith, for example, now has nothing to do
with the person named Smith who stands before us, because the connection has been utterly lost between the individual called Smith today and
the ancestors who knew why they once had received the name Smith.
Similarly, if the universal principle of wolf or lamb is abandoned and wolf
and lamb are simply names, then the relationship of the animal to its core
reality or its universality is lost as well. In modern civilization, the loss of
connection to the spirit may be traced to the transition from Realism to
Nominalism. The difference between the two streams of Scholasticism,
the difference between Realism and Nominalism, has lost its meaning
because Realism has lost its connection to the spiritual. If I can find the
universal Idea that grasps a deeper reality of the stone, the plant, the
animal, or human physicality, then I can raise the question whether these
thoughts *live* in stones, or plants, or whether these thoughts once arose
from the divine wisdom that created stones or plants. If I consider ideas
and concepts only as if they were names that human beings assigned to
stones and plants, then I sever the connection between stones and plants
with the divine Being; and I myself am no longer able to say that I enter
a relationship to a divine Being.

If I were a Realist in the sense of medieval Scholasticism, I would say
that I immerse myself in the world of stones, in the world of plants, in
the world of the animals. I form within myself thoughts about quartz
crystal, the color vermillion (sulfide of mercury), malachite. I create
thoughts within myself about lilies and tulips. I generate thoughts about

the wolf, the hyena, and the lion. These thoughts are based upon what I perceive with my senses. When these thoughts are also imbued with thoughts about the divine origins of the stones, plants, and animals, then I can also contemplate divinity; that is, I create a connection with the divine through my thinking.

If I were to stand as a lost, forlorn human being on the earth and hear a faint echo of the lion's roar resounding in the word "lion" (for I myself have given the lion this name), then my knowledge lacks a connection between the name I gave the lion and the divine spiritual-creator of earthly beings. The modern human being has lost the capacity to discover the spiritual in nature, and even the last trace of this connection which we could have found in scholastic Realism has been lost.

When we go back to the times when, through the insight of higher knowledge, humanity recognized the true nature of these things, we see that the ancient mystery schools saw in all things a creative and creating principle which is known as the Father-God principle. Moving from sense perception to suprasensory knowledge, human beings felt as if they encountered the divine Father-God principle. The universals expressed in the Ideas and concepts of scholastic Realism were the last examples of humanity's search for the Father-God principle in the natural realm.

Only after scholastic Realism lost ground was it possible to speak about atheism in European civilization. As long as human beings still could discover real, living thoughts within the sense-perceptible world, they could not speak about atheism. To argue that atheists were present among the ancient Greeks is not justified, because the first real atheists appear in modern times. In ancient Greece, however, we do discover the first flashes of an elementary human emotion that became the basis for atheism at a later point in human development. But real theoretical atheism could emerge only after the collapse of scholastic Realism.

Even though the Mystery of Golgotha occurred thirteen or fourteen centuries before the height of scholastic Realism, the Realists still lived strongly under the influence of the divine Father-God principle. The Mystery of Golgotha could be fully understood only within the context of a much earlier time. But those who understood the Mystery of Golgotha in relation to ancient mystery wisdom steeped in the Father-God principle, would see Christ only as the Son of the Father.

Please consider carefully the development of the following ideas. A friend has told you about a man whose name is Miller, and yet all you were told about this man was that this personality named Miller is the son of the old Miller. The only thing you know about the young Miller is that fact that he is the son of the old Miller. Let us say that you want to know more about the son from your friend who knows the son. But your friend just keeps telling you about the characteristics of the old Miller. Finally your friend concludes by saying once again that the young Miller is the son of the older Miller. Something like this occurred during the time of the Mystery of Golgotha. The world of nature owed its existence to the Creator-Father-God, and Christ was identified as the Son of the Father-God. To a great degree, even the Realists among the Scholastics characterized the Christ simply as the Son of the Father. That is of utmost importance.

Then came a reaction to seeing Christ as part of the stream connecting the Mystery of Golgotha to the Father-God principle. The counterstream known as Protestantism emerged during the transition from the medieval to the modern period. One of the most important aspects of Protestantism was its emphasis upon bringing Christ in his own right to the awareness of the believer. The older theology in which Christ was seen primarily as the Son of the Father-God was replaced by an interest in the Gospels, the accounts of the deeds of Christ and the words spoken by Christ as an independent being. In the teachings of John Wycliffe,[†] at the heart of German Protestantism in the sixteenth century, and in the new directions forged by Johann Amos Comenius[†] lay the task of presenting Christ as an independent, autonomous Being.

But the time had passed when human beings still perceived the spirit in nature and the spiritual origins of things. Nominalism had taken hold of modern mentality and suppressed people's feeling for the spirit; and so human beings no longer looked for the divine-spiritual in Christ. In the new theology the divine-spiritual was increasingly absent. Christ, as I have often pointed out, even for the theologians, became the humble Man of Nazareth.

If we look at the book *What is Christianity?* by Adolf von Harnack,[†] we discover a modern theologian returning to an older theological position and identifying Christ once again with the Father-God principle. Everywhere in this book, it is possible to substitute "Father-God" for any mention of "Christ"; there is almost no difference between the two in this work.

As long as the Father-God wisdom encompassed Christ as the Son of God, to a certain extent one could still approach the spiritual reality of Christ. But if one wanted to grasp Christ himself in his individuality as a divine-spiritual Being, then one had already lost this spiritual perception and could not approach Christ. And as a specific example, it is very interesting to note that Christian Geyer,[†] the senior Lutheran pastor in Nuremberg, once gave a lecture in Basel in which he openly took the position that modern Lutheran theologians do not have a Christ, only the universal God. Geyer said this because he understood that wherever there was talk about Christ, it was in fact only an expression of the Father-God principle. This is related to the fact that the human being who could still perceive the spirit in nature could actually discover only the Father-God principle in nature. Since the collapse of scholastic Realism, even seeing the Father-God in nature was no longer possible. As soon as one can no longer find the spiritual in the Father-God principle, atheistic perspectives appear.

But if we wish to go beyond seeing Christ merely as the Son of God, if we wish to grasp this Son in his own Being, then we must see him not only as a human being who was born like all other human beings. We must ourselves experience him in an inner way, even when initially this inward deepening appears as a dimly perceived awakening. It will be necessary to proceed through the following stages of consciousness. You must say to yourself that if you simply remain the human being you were by nature at birth; if you continue to see with your eyes just as you saw the day you were born; if you continue to only perceive with your senses what nature reveals to you; if you continue to be led by your intellect as you try to penetrate beneath the outer face of nature, then you will never attain your full humanity. You will not be able to feel your full humanity or to discover all of the capacities available to you as a human being. To do that, you must awaken within yourself the capacities that lie deep within you. You must not be satisfied with the legacy you received at birth. You must in full consciousness bring forth what exists as nascent capacities within the depths of your being.

Today if we only attempt to educate the unconcealed gifts of the human being, we will not enable the child to take hold of its full humanity. In order to tap all of the capacities living in the human being, we must encourage and teach each human being to search the depths of his or her being, and to draw forth out of one's innermost being the inner light that, once it has been lit, will accompany us throughout earthly life.

How did this come about? It came about because Christ went through the Mystery of Golgotha, he is united with the life of the earth, and also lives within the depths of the human being. When individually each one of us takes on the task of inner self-awakening, we also can experience the living Christ. Christ is not found through the ordinary consciousness with which we were born, or which we have developed in the course of our lives; Christ has to be brought up from the depths of the human soul. The consciousness of Christ first occurs as an event in the life of soul. Thus you really can say (as I have often expressed it) that the human being who does not find the Father-God was in some way born into deficient circumstances, and is not entirely healthy. To be an atheist means that a person is in some way physically ill. Not to find Christ, however, is a question of destiny not of ill health; for finding Christ is an experience, not a reflection of one's physical constitution. We find the Father-God principle because we are able to see Him everywhere in nature. An individual finds Christ through an experience of inner resurrection, an experience of rebirth. Christ becomes part of the experience of rebirth as an independent Being, not simply as the Son of the Father. Thus we are able to understand that if as human beings in the modern era we were to cling only to the Father-God, we would not be able to enter into our full humanity. This is reason that the Father sent His Son—it is through the Son that the work of the Father on earth can be fulfilled. Can you understand now, why in order to fulfill the purposes of the Father-God, Christ had to be an independent Being?

In the present age it is only through spiritual science that we are able to understand the process leading to inner awakening in a practical, experiential, and living way. Spiritual science supports the experiences drawn out of soul depths as conscious knowledge, which sheds light upon the encounter with Christ. To summarize this, I wish to remind you that during the course of scholastic Realism the possibility of expanding further the principle of knowing the Father-God was exhausted. In every form of Realism the spirit is recognized as something real. Realism within the context of anthroposophy shows that the Son at last can be recognized as an independent Being. This enables us to find the divine-spiritual in an independent way as we encounter the Christ.

The Father-God principle played the greatest role imaginable over a long period of time. Medieval theology, which grew out of ancient mystery wisdom, was interested only in the Father-God principle. What questions resulted from this? Did the Father and the Son both exist throughout eternity, or was the Son born in the course of time?[†] There was even interest in the genealogy of the Father. Everywhere in the history of dogma, great emphasis was placed upon the genealogy of Christ. When the Spirit was added to the Father and the Son, once again the question was raised whether the Spirit existed with the Father and the Son, or if the Spirit arose out of the Father or the Son, and so forth. Theologians constantly explored the genealogy of the three divine persons, for the continuing interest in the divine lineage was rooted in the Father-God principle.

When the strife between scholastic Realism and Nominalism was at its height, the old concepts about the lineage of the Son from the Father and the lineage of the Spirit through the Father and the Son were no longer understood. You see, three divine beings were identified; and yet these three divine persons were supposed to form a single God. The Realists drew the three divine persons into one Idea; for them the composite Idea was Real. A single God was a reality in their understanding. The Nominalists could not accept the possibility of a single God made up of three persons. They recognized the Father, Son, and Spirit; but to combine them into a unity was simply creating a word or name that denied the integrity of the Three Persons. During the time of the controversy between the Realists and Nominalists over the Godhead, it was not possible to come to an agreement about the divine Trinity. A living formulation of the threefold Divinity could no longer be sustained.

After Nominalism triumphed over Realism, no one knew how to reconcile the individual persons of the Godhead. People went back to whichever tradition they were inclined to accept, but they could not think the matter through with clarity. The Lutheran confession placed Christ in the foreground; but because Lutherans were under the influence of Nominalism, they could not grasp the divine spiritual individuality of Christ. One simply did not know how to understand the concept of the three divine persons. The old dogma of the threefold nature of the divine was left dangling.

These things were of great importance to human beings during the time when spiritual feelings were inwardly experienced and contributed to the happiness or misfortune of human souls. But these things have been pushed into the background by the philistinism of modern times. What does it matter today if a modern person is pulled into the theological controversy about the relationship among the Father-God, Son, and Spirit? People now can hardly imagine why this question was ever a burning issue for human souls. The modern person has become a philistine; that is, an individual who has no true feeling experience of an awakening spirituality. This person lives entirely within the sphere of habit. Without the presence of the spirit it is impossible to experience the fullness of one's humanity. The philistine prefers to live without the spirit; to wake up without the spirit, to eat breakfast without the spirit, to go to the office without the spirit, to eat mid-day without the spirit, to play billiards without the spirit, and so forth. The narrow-minded individual wants to do everything without the spirit. Nevertheless, throughout one's life the spirit unconsciously accompanies every human being. In the case of the philistine, however, the presence of the spirit is of no interest.

In this regard, it may seem as if anthroposophy ought to uphold the ideal of the Universal Divine. Anthroposophy, however, does not do this, for an anthroposophist recognizes the divine-spiritual in the Father-God; and separately from this, also recognizes the divine-spiritual in the Son of God. If we compare the earlier approach to knowing the Father-God with the anthroposophic approach, we notice that, above all, the knowledge of the Father-God posed the following question about Christ: Who is his father? If we can show who the Father is, then we shall have knowledge of the Father. If we know who the Father is, then we can presume that through the Father we also shall gain knowledge of Christ. Of course we must remember that anthroposophy is rooted in modern life. As we have extended our knowledge of nature, so, too, we have amplified our knowledge of the Father-God. But if we wish to develop a knowledge of Christ, this knowledge arises solely out of his person. To accomplish this we must study history, trace the descent in the unfolding of history, discover the Mystery of Golgotha at its deepest point, and then follow the subsequent ascent in human development. By studying nature, anthroposophy allows the Father-God principle to be resurrected anew. By studying history, anthroposophy discovers Christ. These are the two different paths by which we come to know both the Father and the Son. It is as if you travel to City A and meet there an older man; and then go to City B and become acquainted with a younger man. Thus I learn about the older man and the younger man, each as separate persons. Each of the two interests me. Afterward it occurs to me that the two have a certain similarity. As I consider their similarity, I soon realize that the younger one is the son of the older man. The same thing occurs in anthroposophy. You encounter Christ, you discover the Father; afterward you learn about the relationship between the two; whereas the ancient wisdom about the Father-God flowed out from the Father, and you arrived at an understanding of the relationship between the Father and the Son out of its common origins.

You can see that anthroposophy forges a new path, and you have to be ready to transform your thinking and feeling if you wish to enter into anthroposophy. It is not helpful to anthroposophy if anthroposophists consider the anthroposophic worldview as if it were more or less like a materialist perspective, or as more or less in accord with older, traditional forms of knowledge. Then they espouse an approach such as anthroposophy because that position is more pleasing to them than one of the other worldviews. That is not the point at issue. You must not move back and forth from one perspective to another; that is, from a materialist, monistic point of view to an anthroposophic perspective, and say to yourself that now the anthroposophic position speaks to you more fully that the other viewpoints. Rather you have to acknowledge that the capacity that allows you to understand the

monistic-materialist model is not capable of enabling you to understand anthroposophic insights.

The theosophists have believed that the perspective of a materialistic-
monistic image enables them to perceive the spiritual. Holding this
unusual perspective allows them to describe the monistic-materialistic
worldview: everything is matter; the human being also consists entirely
of matter; the substance of nerves, blood, and so forth is matter. The
theosophists (I am referring to the members of the Theosophical
Society) say that no, that is a materialistic perspective; spirit also exists.
Then they begin to describe the human being according to the spirit.
The physical body is solid. The etheric body is somewhat thinner,
rather like a thin fog. Both of these are materialistic representations.
The astral body is even thinner, but it is still a material substance. Then
a ladder reaches a still thinner matter that is called spirit. This is also
materialism; it is just that the matter becomes thinner and thinner.
Materialism is at least honest and calls what is material, matter. But
the theosophists present what is material and call it spirit. You have to
acknowledge that it is necessary to transform your thinking, to learn to
imagine the spiritual in a way other than the manner in which you form
an imagination of the material.

The Theosophical Society in one way looks at history in an especially interesting way. Materialists speak about atoms. Atoms can be
described in very different ways. Materialists who take into account the
material qualities of these bodies have created a number of different
images of atoms. Among them there is a theory of the atom in which
atoms are portrayed as making a swinging motion back and forth, as if
they were made of very thin matter that moves in spiral forms. When
you read what Leadbeater[†] says about atoms, you will recognize this
portrayal. Recently in an article printed in an English newspaper,[†] the
question was raised whether Leadbetter had actually seen this phenomenon, or whether he was speaking out of occult observation; that is,
whether he had read the book describing this and then translated it
spiritually.

We have to take these things seriously. We ourselves have to examine
whether we still cling to materialism and merely assign spiritual names
to matter. A transformation of thinking and feeling is required if we

wish to achieve a spiritual worldview. When we attain that, we can gain a perspective derived from a practice through which we may strive, through our own efforts, to rise beyond the intellectual fall instead of succumbing to it ourselves.

12

HERMANN GRIMM AND FRIEDRICH NIETZSCHE IN RELATION TO THE NEW LIFE OF THE SPIRIT

MORAL AND ANTI-MORAL IMPULSES AS SEEDS OF A FUTURE ORDER OF NATURE

Dornach, January 28, 1923

Among the personalities who have experienced the new life of the spirit and have developed in our era a feeling for the way we can draw these impulses, these insights right into the fabric of our lives, two individuals come to mind: Herman Grimm[†] and Friedrich Nietzsche.[†] Both Grimm and Nietzsche lived strongly within the spiritual and intellectual life of the present time. They both tried to discover how human beings can experience within their souls what happens today in the spirit.

We can see that Herman Grimm tried to describe human beings or a specific personality out of a clear understanding and sensitivity to our modern era. With Nietzsche it is more a matter of learning how he himself inwardly felt the inner and outer forces active in the late nineteenth century, and knew personally what it meant to live in the late nineteenth century. As we watch Herman Grimm portraying humanity in general or an individual in particular, it is clear that he always had a picture in his imagination. His words had a pictorial quality, his descriptions evoked vivid images. And yet Grimm's profiles often made it seem as if those he was writing about carried a great weight on their back. Even in Grimm's book about Michelangelo and his work, you have the impression that Michelangelo labored under a great burden. The artistic giant literally had to carry an enormous weight on his back everywhere he went. Grimm himself experienced and spoke about the nature of this burden[†]: "We modern human beings," he said, "labor constantly under *the weight of history.*"

Indeed we modern men and women do stagger under the weight of history. Even if we sat at our desks at school and were too lazy to care about studying history, we would still have felt burdened by the study of history. From the time we entered elementary school as six-year-old children, we already felt the weight of what we were expected to learn about history. We still are not free, for we carry history with us today as if it were a heavy sack thrown over one shoulder.

Turning to Friedrich Nietzsche, we come to a personality who shook almost hysterically because of what he perceived as the constraints of modern intellectual life. If you looked at him closely in his daily life, it wouldn't matter if he were on one of his travels in Italy or taking a summer stroll around the Swiss village of Sils Maria,[†] he would shudder. He habitually shuddered and shook himself until his upper body bent forward. And if we looked carefully, we would see that he wanted to shake off history, to get rid of a kind of historical knapsack that, in fact, we all carry on our shoulders.

Nietzsche clearly felt the weight of history, for at a comparatively early age he wrote an essay entitled "On the Use and Abuse of History for Life."[†] He pleaded with his contemporaries to push history out of the forefront: You will lose your lives if you drag history with you wherever you go. You do not know how to live in the present. You ask at every opportunity what people in olden times would have done in this or that circumstance. But you do not bring anything creative to the fore out of your own thinking, feeling, and willing, in order to live as men and women of the present day.

I have brought these two individuals to your attention to show you how modernity affects the human being now. Herman Grimm always described human beings as if they were laboring under a great weight, and Nietzsche himself lived as if he were constantly trying to shake off a burden that he had to carry on his back. We must take these individuals into account if we want to capture the effect of intellectual and spiritual life during the last third of the nineteenth century and beginning of the twentieth. When you go more deeply into the matter, you will see the human being, exhausted and gasping for air, under the press of historical knowledge. It is as if the modern human being were a dog who is overheated, lets its tongue hang out, and pants for air. Likewise, people living in the modern era are burdened down by history; they gasp and whimper under its weight.

If we wish to understand humanity during ancient times, we, too, have to look into the past with the same vision as the ancients possessed. It would be extremely difficult for us to grasp their experiences unless we brought up the same pictures that human beings saw long ago. In order to do that we distinguish between what the ancients experienced in their day and what we no longer experience in our day. Now I would like to make some preliminary observations that will help us to let the knapsack of history fall to the ground.

Observing nature in ancient times inspired the creation of myths, for the ancients were able to draw myths out of the creative powers of their souls. For them, nature's phenomena appeared before the human soul as a living perception of the essential processes in the world. The modern human being can no longer create myths out of scientific observations. Indeed we no longer create any myths. When a modern person tries to create a myth, it is so literary and contrived that it seems forced and wooden. We have lost the capacity to transform what lives in the natural world into myths. At best, modern human beings can try to interpret ancient myths. Unable to create myths, we turn our attention to human history. That change occurred not so very long ago. We have lost the power to create myths, and yet we also find it difficult to establish a right relationship to history. That is the reason why, in the nineteenth century, historicist professors of law have argued that we cannot create the law; rather, we must study the history of lawmaking. The historicist school of law[†] (and this is something most remarkable) is an evidence, an admission, of the complete lack of creativity among human beings of the present age. The historicist professors of law say that they cannot create a framework for what is "right" in human relations; and therefore they must study the history of laws and promulgate only the laws they have learned from history. That was the situation that arose at the beginning of the nineteenth century. Particularly in Central European law schools the prevalent viewpoint declared that the modern human was not yet capable of living in the present, and therefore should live only as a human being in touch with history.

Nietzsche, who studied in schools or universities that venerated historical precedence, wanted to shake off this approach, and even wrote an essay, "On the Use and Abuse of History for Life."

Looking back at his student years and at everything that had been brought to him about ancient times, Nietzsche commented, "No one can breathe in this atmosphere. There is dust everywhere. It prevents you from ever breathing freely. Away with this kind of history! Let us live in the present!"

In the late nineteenth century, the historicist approach to knowledge generated anxiety. This anxiety, associated figuratively with the gnashing of one's teeth, arose whenever humanity tried to observe and understand nature. I am referring now to the emergence of anthropomorphism, that is, the insertion of a kind of invisible human hand into scientific explanations or models. In ancient times humanity was able to experience what was observed in nature, because human beings knew that nature was created by the divine. Nature itself was divine. Likewise, human beings took their inner substance that was connected to the divine and brought it together with the substance connected with nature; they came face to face with truth. Modern people, however, shudder whenever they suspect that anthropomorphism has crept into the study of nature or of humanity. It sends shivers up and down the spine. Modernity brings with it a fear of anthropomorphism.

We still experience anxiety in the face of anthropomorphism, and yet we do not even notice that we ourselves tolerate anthropomorphisms. In physics we talk about the elasticity of two spheres and refer to an external impulse (it could even be a nudge set in motion with your own hand) that is transferred to the elasticity in the sphere. We do not even notice the human intervention in this example. We only take note when the human impulse seems to have a global effect. The fear of anthropomorphism developed in response to the excessive historicism in modern civilization. And we still live under the influence of this anxiety today.

Our anxiety about historicism and anthropomorphism breaks every connection between humanity and the outside world. Above all, the connection between the human being and a living experience of the Christ Being has been severed. The experience of Christ has to be a living one, not simply a knowledge rooted in the historical record. This is not just a matter of avoiding the seemingly historical, or undermining the myth-generating capacity of historical interpretation; rather it is a matter of actually reaching behind what is hidden and grasping its essential reality.

When today we want to speak about human striving, we typically do not speak out of our own immediate experience; we interpret *Parzival*, or some other early work or tradition. We interpret, clarify, or explain. But our explanations do not illuminate; we obscure rather than enlighten through our so-called clarifications.

This unfortunate situation comes about because we lack the courage to truly grasp the world with our souls. On the one hand, we have established a way of observing nature that extends from the hazy origins of the universe through increasingly complex stages leading to the death of what lives in our world. Morality has no living place in our world; it is only an abstraction. I have often mentioned this state of affairs. On the other hand, we have no capacity to see that the foundation we lay today through our moral impulses becomes the basis for moral consequences in the future.[†] The consequences of moral actions today become reality in the future. As I mentioned yesterday, this capacity has been undermined by the collapse of scholastic Realism.

Thus our moral impulses have become merely thoughts about intentions; and we, as part of a higher order within the structure of nature, do not know what to do about this. At the very most we look at the condition toward which the earth ought to be transformed. To be honest, we have to say that morality is nothing more than a cemetery where moral ideals that we have thought about are buried. We have no real idea of how a new planet can grow out of our decadent, decaying earth; nor do we understand that the new earth will develop out of the impulses humanity is developing today. Today we lack the courage to *think*, to *envision* that moral impulses are the seeds for the world of the future. But the courage to connect a new world order with a reality that allows us to prepare for a new physical planet that will replace our dying earth is sorely needed.

Now we shall look at the other side of the natural order. Across from the moral order stands the natural order, which has brought about our awe-inspiring modern natural science. The thrust of the natural sciences now affects every aspect of human culture. Farmers today know more about modern science than they know about a spiritual worldview. Under what circumstances have the newer natural sciences developed? We can make this clear by using the example of electricity, a discovery that was quickly followed by its practical application. At the turn of the eighteenth to the nineteenth centuries, a physicist[†] was dissecting the leg of a frog. The frog's leg came in contact with the metal window frame, and the leg twitched. That is how the physicist discovered electricity. That happened less than 150 years ago. And now electricity is a central ingredient of modern civilization. But it is not just a matter of producing changes in daily life. The very substance of scientific explanations also changed very rapidly. When people born in the third quarter of the nineteenth century were going to school and studying physics, no one thought of describing atoms as anything other than tiny, inelastic balls that bumped up against one another. Physicists even calculated the force necessary to produce the impact between atoms. It had not yet occurred to anyone that an atom would be described as an electron, as if it were an entity that consists entirely of electricity. But the latter is what is taught in schools today.

The extent to which human thinking has become saturated with electricity is a fairly recent development. Now we speak about atoms as if they were tiny suns surrounded by orbiting electrons. When we look around us at the forces within the universe, we presume that electricity is everywhere. This permeates our entire culture, including our manner of thinking. If we did not ride trains so frequently, we might not have associated atoms so quickly with electricity.

If we were to look at the ideas that humanity had before the Age of Electricity, we could see that at one time an observer of nature still had the freedom to recognize the spiritual aspect of nature, at least to the point of thinking about it abstractly. A tiny remnant of scholastic Realism still remained to facilitate this perspective. But electricity is so pervasive in the lives of modern human beings that it gets on our nerves. Our sensitivity to electricity made it impossible to maintain a connection to the spiritual.

The effects of this go even further. The true light that floods the space of our universe is increasingly compromised in its purity, and even suffers the degradation of being seen as something similar to artificially generated light. When we begin to speak openly about these things, anyone who is completely committed to the value of the electrical culture thinks that we are out of our senses. But that is so because a person who thinks a criticism of electricity is nonsense is someone weighed down by excessive historicism, and who cannot find a connection to the immediate present.

With electricity we enter a sphere that presents something different to the imaginative observation than what we receive from other aspects of nature. As long as you deal only with light and sound (that is, optics and acoustics), then you do not need to make a moral judgment about what is manifest in a stone, plant, animal, light in its form as color, or the world of sound as tone; for you still may perceive a slight echo of the reality behind these ideas and concepts. Electricity, however, drives away this echo. If, on the one hand, we cannot discover the reality of moral impulses, then, on the other hand, we also shall fail to observe and perceive the moral essence within nature itself.

If you ascribe a real power and effect to a moral impulse, so that these impulses inherently have both potential and power, just as the seed already contains the germ of a fully grown plant, you may be called a half of a fool. If you were to go still further and attribute moral impulses to natural processes, then you will be called a complete fool. If you have felt an electrical current in its spiritual nature surging through your nervous system, you would know that electricity is not just a force of nature; electricity is also something moral. Whenever we enter the realm of electricity, we are giving ourselves over to something moral. If you put your finger into a closed circuit of electricity, you immediately feel that you have expanded the realm of the inner core of the human being, out of which there arises what is moral. The electricity that resides within the human being is also the area out of which your moral impulses originate. Whoever experiences the totality of electricity, at the same time experiences the moral within nature. Without meaning to do so, modern physicists have created a certain kind of hocus-pocus. They have theorized that the atom has an electrical nature and have forgotten, because of the general consciousness of our time, that when they present the atom as electrical in nature, they have ascribed a moral impulse, and therewith a moral nature, to it. But now I have just said something that is not so. By making the atom into an electron, you are not attributing to it a moral aspect, but rather an *immoral* essence. Within electricity all kinds of moral impulses of nature are swimming; but actually they are immoral, instinctively evil impulses that must be overcome with the help of the higher worlds.

The greatest contrast to electricity is natural light. Looking at electrically generated light we see a mixture of good and evil. We have lost a real perception of evil in the natural order. We do not notice that by electrifying the ideation of atoms, they then become conveyors of evil. I described in my recent natural-scientific course[†] that by attributing electricity to the constitution of the atom it causes atoms to become purveyors of death. Physicists continue to put forward an atomic theory and assign it everywhere to matter. As soon as the atomic form of matter is identified with electricity, it also identifies nature with evil. In that case atoms composed of electrons are tiny, evil *daemons*.

It has been argued that the modern characterization of nature is on its way to being bound to evil. At the end of the medieval era those who had been frightened by Agrippa of Nettesheim[†] and Tritemius of Sponheim,[†] and those who later sensed that the evil poodle in Goethe's *Faust* was being permitted to run around loose, tried awkwardly to express this fear. Their ideas may have been incorrect, but their fear was well founded. For when physicists declare, as they do today unthinkingly, that nature is made up of electrons, then they are actually saying that nature is composed of little *daemons* of evil. To the extent that we accept this explanation of nature, then we must also accept that evil is being ascribed to the creators of the universe. If we wish to be human beings of the present age and not be satisfied to go along with the explanations of the past, and if we base our knowledge on reality, then we will see that electricity in nature is also morality. If we observe our surroundings today, we see pictures of a moral reality, one that is wrapped in evil.

If anthroposophy were either fanatical or ascetic, a great storm would be brought to bear against the culture of electricity. Of course that would be absurd, for the only people who could talk this way have a worldview that does not take reality into account. They might say, "Oh, that is the work of Ahriman! Away with it!" But you can only do that in the abstract. Those who would organize a sectarian gathering and thunder about protecting themselves from Ahriman are the same ones who leave the meeting and step right into an electric tram. So the entire storm about Ahriman, which sounds like such a virtuous position to take, is nonsense. You cannot avoid the fact that you have to learn to live with Ahriman. But you must find the right way to live with him; for you cannot allow yourself to be overpowered by him.

If you turn to the final scene of my first mystery drama,† *The Portal of Initiation*, you can see the effect of unconsciousness in this matter. Read this scene again and you will understand the difference between being in Ahriman's presence unconsciously and confronting him in full consciousness. Ahriman and Lucifer have their greatest power over human beings when we are unconscious of being in their presence; for then we can be manipulated by these beings without even being aware of it. This is pointed out in the last scene of *The Portal of Initiation*. Thus the power of the ahrimanic aspect of electricity over human beings in our culture can hold sway only so long as we are unconscious and unaware of the significance of the electrification of the atom, and blindly assume that electricity is harmless. Thus we would remain unprotected from the fact that nature bound up with electricity produces a nature made up of tiny *daemons* connected to evil. It is frightening to witness the extent to which today's scientific research is *daemon*-idolatry, a worship or veneration of *daemons*. We must become aware of this, for by awakening our inner consciousness we also become aware that we are living in the time of the consciousness soul.

Why do we not recognize that we live in the age of the consciousness soul? On the one hand, we are weighed down by an inner paralysis and a preference for the explanations and ideas generated in the past; and on the other hand, we are unwilling to work with new ideas and to immerse ourselves in understandings that open the way to a healthy future.

And if we were to feel as Nietzsche did, we would be flooded with criticism; and yet, like Nietzsche, we still would be stuck in old forms. Nor would we be able to show the new way that would bring us forward. Nietzsche himself was not able to point out the direction in which future development ought to go. Just look at the brilliant essay that Nietzsche wrote in his early maturity, "On the Use and Abuse of

History for Life." In flaming rhetoric he urged his readers to throw off the weight of history and to become human beings living fully with the present, for humanity needs to replace the primacy of the past with the living present. Then what did Nietzsche do? Nietzsche took Darwinism and amplified it; out of animal species arose the human being, and so the human being would continue to evolve over time into a "super human being." But this Super-Man remained an abstraction, a scarecrow without any substance. You could say almost anything about the physicality of the Super-Man, but it is impossible to form a real imagination of him. Certainly we can refer to scientists today as math whizzes—as Nietzsche might well have done[†]—for scientists rarely do more than substantiate their research through mathematical calculations. And scientists such as Goethe, who do not use calculations, are thrown out of the temple of natural science by the scientists themselves.

The critical issue, however, is found elsewhere. *Courage* is the key:

- to recognize the reality that stands behind moral deeds;
- to see the moral idealism in nature in its proper perspective;
- to understand that moral impulses are the seeds for a natural order that may be attained in the future;
- to acknowledge that nature's order today, with its electricity, is a moral order as well as an anti-moral order connected to evil.

We must have courage to see moral qualities in nature in the right way.

In addition to courage, a true understanding of the human being is absolutely necessary. If an individual recognized an immoral impulse that would damage his or her physical body and tried to understand this impulse from the perspective of today's physiology and biology, it would be foolish to expect helpful insights from conventional science. We could learn about the function of the circulatory and nervous systems, but there would be no mention of morality. Likewise, scientists talk about electricity and even recognize the presence of electricity within the human being, but they have nothing to say about the fact that the electricity within the human being can absorb immoral impulses. Today we talk about the absorption of oxygen and many other examples of absorption in a material sense. But you never hear that the electricity within the human being absorbs the immoral impulses within us, and that this phenomenon is a natural law like other natural laws. Nor is it ever mentioned that the light that we take into our bodies from the outer world conserves the absorption of good, moral impulses. We need to bring spiritual knowledge into the science of physiology.

We shall be able to achieve this only when we free ourselves from the ideas and theories espoused in the past that irritate and suffocate us, and make us trudge along as if we were carrying a heavy burden of knowledge no longer useful. We have to remember that with the collapse of scholastic Realism, our ideas and concepts are just words that no longer guide us to an experience of the reality behind the ideas. We do not live into our words anymore; otherwise, by following the sound of words, they would convey to us something living. Recall how often I have said that the spirit that holds sway in speech is a wise spirit, much wiser than a single human being can ever be. You can discover this at every turn if you develop a feeling for the wonder that inspires and lives within the formulation of words. Think about the example I mentioned a short time ago. It is one that holds true in other languages, too. Take one of the verbs for remembering or recalling. The infinitive form, to recall or to remember, is *besinnen*; the reflexive form, "I myself recall" is *ich besinne mich*; the present perfect, "I have recalled" is *ich habe mich besonnen*.[1]

Typically a teacher drags the weight of the historical ideation of grammar into the classroom, not bothering to toss it away and begin afresh. Rather the teacher lamely points out to the students the simplest grammatical terminology: "When you say 'I myself remember,' it describes an action in the present. 'I have recalled' is called the perfect tense of the verb and refers to something that happened in the past."

But when I use the perfect participle *besonnen*, I should feel the root word, "sun," and think "I have placed myself in the light of the sun."

---

1. Translator's note: The German word for the infinitive *besinnen* and present tense *ich besinne mich* contain the word *Sinne*, which refers to human senses and sense perception; the past participle *besonnen* encompasses the word for the sun, *Sonne*. Thus when a person recalls something, he or she is drawing something up from memory and placing it once again in its sense reality; that is, quite literally one is re-membering, bringing elements from memory back into the world of the senses and material reality.

When I use the present tense of the German reflexive verb, *Ich besinne mich*, I put myself in the service of the sunlight within me: the "o" contracts and becomes an "I." That is to say that when the sun lives within me, it becomes material. When I give myself over to the sun, I discover that I no longer have contact with the senses, for they are already within the sun. By means of my senses I move out into the world. I become a part of the cosmos to the extent that I receive the past within myself. We need to directly experience speech and language. We must feel what it means when an "i" becomes an "o." It is significant when as human beings we recreate this change in the world as we speak, when we allow an "i" to be transformed into an "o."

These things indicate how important it is for us to return to the fundamental bases of our humanity, in order to understand the profound longings that became manifest in the lives of distinguished human beings like Herman Grimm and Nietzsche in the nineteenth century. When we understand the longings of human beings in our day, and recognize that the art of eurythmy also arose out of human longings, then we shall be able to create an art of movement that arises out of fundamental bases of our time. That is why it is so important that anthroposophists accurately grasp the fundamental bases of the human being so that they can also create an art like eurythmy[†] in our age. This depends upon our capacity as anthroposophists to feel what truly constitutes a renewal of civilization today.

It is no longer important whether we carry history around with us, but it is of utmost importance that we are human beings deeply rooted in the present. That is the consciousness that must arise in the souls of anthroposophists. Otherwise, what it means to be an anthroposophist will again and again be misunderstood. Time and again efforts are made that show a false idea of what could be done in the world today: "Couldn't we bring just a little bit of eurythmy into this or that venue so that people will get an idea of what eurythmy is?" But to introduce a taste of eurythmy or anthroposophy here or there can never be our goal. In all honesty we must place in the world exactly what anthroposophy really wishes to be. Otherwise we shall not move forward. If we are constantly taking into account what seemed valuable in former epochs, we shall never accomplish the things that I have spoken about;

nor shall we discover how these things must be achieved if humanity itself is to avoid death.

Yesterday I asked you to imagine a complete transformation of thinking [umdenken] and a complete transformation of empathetic understanding [umempfinden]. That is, I encouraged you to turn your thinking and knowing inside out and to fundamentally renew the way you think and understand with the forces of your heart. We have to do more than observe from the outside in order to come to a different way of imagining or picturing the cosmos. We have to muster our courage, so that when we speak about electricity we can use moral and anti-moral concepts in our discussions. Human beings in the modern era shudder at thoughts like these. We find it unpleasant to realize that when we enter an electric tram we have to sit in Ahriman's seat. Many of us would rather ignore this and prefer to organize sectarian gatherings where people can talk about how to protect themselves from Ahriman's influence. But in fact the most important task we have is to know that, from now on, the development of earth existence calls for the integration of natural forces into cultural life. That means that the active influence of Ahriman must be taken into account as a reality. We have to be fully conscious of this in order to put ourselves in the right relationship to it.

It matters if you develop a knowledge of the tasks that belong to a true anthroposophist. Anthroposophy is not a kind of replacement for the confessions of faith in the past. There are many well-educated individuals who have concluded that anthroposophy has become boring, but anthroposophy is neither boring nor attached to one or another religious confession or worldview from the past. It is not important whether you have an affinity to one or another worldview. Turn your full attention to anthroposophy. As anthroposophists we are committed to anthroposophy in its present stage of development. As anthroposophists who understand the consciousness of our time, we must feel an objective devotion within our hearts to the divine heart of the universe. Clearly that may be attained by pursuing the paths I have described in these lectures.

APPENDIX I

Historical Background to the course of lectures compiled in Lebendiges Naturerkennen, intellektueller Sündenfall und spirituelle Sündenerhebung, *GA 220 (literal translation: Living Knowledge of Nature, Intellectual Fall, Rising beyond the Fall, the Future of Humanity and the Earth).*

Prepared by Caroline Wispler, editor of the 1982 German edition of GA 220.

The lectures included in this volume, CW 220, were given in Dornach on January 5, 6, 7, 12, 13, 14, 19, 20, 21, 26, 27, 28, 1923 in the Carpentry Shop (*Schreinerei*), a provisional wooden building that was used for technical, artistic, and spiritual-scientific purposes during the decade-long construction of the Goetheanum. The cultural center known as the Goetheanum was built by a large number of artists and craftsmen from many (seventeen) nations according to the plans and under the direction of Rudolf Steiner. The building, constructed principally of wood in the form of two intersecting domes, was destroyed by fire on New Year's Eve 1922–1923 shortly after the evening lecture given by Rudolf Steiner. There was no interruption of the activities planned for the first week of January 1923, and the performance of the Oberufer Three Kings drama took place as scheduled on New Year's Day in the Carpentry Shop. In addition to the participants in the Christmas Conference (December 23-31, 1922), individuals attending a gathering of natural-scientific researchers (*Vereinigung der Naturforscher*) and members of the Branch of the Anthroposophical Society at the Goetheanum were invited to be present.

The lectures on the theme of "The Spiritual Communion of Humanity," given during the Christmas Conference 1922, were open to all members of the Anthroposophical Society. See Rudolf Steiner, *Man and the World of Stars. The Spiritual Communion of Mankind* (CW 219) New York: Anthroposophic Press, 1962. *Das Verhältnis der Sternenwelt zum Menschen und des Menschen zur Sternenwelt. Die geistige Communion der Menschheit* (GA 219), 12 lectures, Dornach, November 26–December 31, 1922. The science course held during the last week of December 1922 and the first week of January 1923 was open to natural-scientific researchers, university students, interested persons, and members of the Anthroposophical Society.

See Rudolf Steiner, *The Origins of Natural Science* (CW 326) New York: Anthroposophic Press, 1985. *Der Entstehungsmoment der Naturwissenschaft in der Weltgeschichte und ihre seitherige Entwickelung* (GA 326), 9 lectures, Dornach, December 24, 1922–January 6, 1923. Dornach: Rudolf Steiner Verlag, 1977.

For audience composition at lecture cycles given during December 1922 and January 1923, see: Rudolf Steiner, *Der Entstehungsmoment...*, GA 326, PB 632,

p. 154.; Christoph Lindenberg, *Rudolf Steiner: Eine Chronik*; Rudolf Steiner, *The Origins of Natural Science*, CW 326, Introduction by Own Barfield, p. vii.

For the background to the burning of the Goetheanum, see Marie Steiner, ed., *Rudolf Steiner und die Zivilisationsaufgaben der Anthroposophie. Ein Rueckblick auf das Jahr 1923*. Dornach: Philosophisch-Anthroposophischer Verlag, 1943.

Rudolf Steiner, *Das Schicksalsjahr 1923 in der Geschichte der Anthroposophischen Gesellschaft vom Goetheanumbrand zur Weihnachtstagung* (GA 259. Dornach: Rudolf Steiner Verlag, 1991.

Emil Leinhas, "Silvester 1922-1923 Goetheanumbrand," in *Aus der Arbeit mit Rudolf Steiner*. Basel: Zbinden & Co., 1950.

APPENDIX II

Archival sources and German and English Editions
of GA/CW 220

The lectures were recorded by Helene Finckh. Her copy was the basis for the early editions of various lectures published under the guidance of Marie Steiner. The first edition of the twelve lectures included in GA 220 was prepared by Wolfram Groddeck. The 1982 edition was prepared by Caroline Wispler. Problematic passages were compared with the original stenographic copy during the preparation of the 1982 edition.

Editions of GA 220 in German:

Rudolf Steiner, *Lebendiges Naturerkennen, Intellecktueller Sündenfall und spirituelle Sündenerhebung*, ed., Wolfram Groddeck, GA 220, 12 lectures, Dornach, January 5, 6, 7, 12, 13, 14, 19, 20, 21, 26, 27, 28, 1923. Dornach: Rudolf Steiner Verlag, 1966.

Rudolf Steiner, *Lebendiges Naturerkennen, Intellecktueller Sündenfall und spirituelle Sündenerhebung*, ed., Caroline Wispler, GA 220, 12 lectures, Dornach, January 5, 6, 7, 12, 13, 14, 19, 20, 21, 26, 27, 28, 1923. Dornach: Rudolf Steiner Verlag, 1982.

Editions of individual lectures or partial collections of lectures from GA 220 in German:

Lectures 1, 2, 3. "Die Not nach dem Christus. Die Aufgabe der akademischen Jugend. Die Herz-Erkenntnis des Menschen," Dornach, January 5, 6, 7, 1923. Dornach: Philosophisch-Anthroposophischer Verlag, 1942.

Lecture 2. "Die Erkenntnis-Aufgabe der akademischen Jugend," Dornach, January 6, 1923, in *Die Erkenntnis-Aufgabe der Jugend*. Dornach: Rudolf Steiner Nachlassverwaltung, 1957, 155pp.

_____ . GA 217a. Dornach: Rudolf Steiner Verlag, 1981, 246 pp.

Lectures 4, 5, 6, "Das Suchen nach der Welt im Menschen, nach dem Menschen in der Welt," Dornach, January 12, 13, 14, 1923. Dornach: Philosophisch-Anthroposophischer Verlag, 1943.

Lectures 7, 8, 9, 10, 11, 12, *Lebendiges Naturerkennen. Intellektueller Sündenfall und spirituelle Sündenerhebung*, Dornach, January 19, 20, 21, 26, 27, 28, 1923. Dornach: Philosophisch-Anthroposophischer Veralg, 1943, 77 pp.

Lecture 7, "Wahrheit, Schönheit, Güte," Dornach, January 19, 1923, in *Kunst im Lichte der Mysterienweisheit*, Dornach, 1928.

_____ . Dresden: Emil Weises Buchhandlung, Karl Eymann, 1940.

_____ . Freiburg i. Br.: Novalis, 1947, 1954, 1957, 1980.

_____ . Dornach: Rudolf Steiner Nachlassverwaltung, 1957, 1968.

_____ . Dornach: Rudolf Steiner Verlag, 1980, 1993.

Editions of individual lectures or partial collections of lectures from CW 220 in English translation:

Lecture 1, "Man's New Need for the Christ," Dornach, January 5, 1923, trans. unknown. Typescript Z41 in a London collection.

Lecture 2, "The Task of Academic Youth," Dornach, January 6, 1923, trans. R. H. Bruce. Typescript.

Lecture 3, "Man and Cosmos," Dornach, January 7, 1923, trans. unknown, *Anthroposophic News Sheet*, Vol. XVI, Nrs. 1 and 2, January 11, 1948, 16 pp.

"The Widening of Man's Perception," Dornach, January 7, 1923, trans. unknown, *Biodynamics*, March/April, 2002.

Lecture 4, "Giordano Bruno, Jacob Boehme, and Francis Bacon." Dornach, January 12, 1923, trans. unknown, *Anthroposophy: A Quarterly Review of Spiritual Science*, Vol. V, 1930, pp. 389-405.

Lecture 5, "Salt, Mercury, Sulphur," Dornach, January 13, 1923, tr. unk., *Anthroposophy: A Quarterly Review for Spiritual Science*, Vol. VI, Nr. 1, Easter 1931, pp. 1-17.

_____ . H. Collison, ed., New York: The Anthroposophic Press, n.d.

Lecture 6, "Waking and Sleeping of Man, Formerly and Today," Dornach, January 14, 1923, trans. unknown, *Anthroposophic News Sheet*, Vol. II, Nrs. 6, 7, 9, February 11, 18, March 4, 1934.

Lecture 7, "Truth, Beauty, Goodness," Dornach, January 19, 1923, trans. unknown. London: Anthroposophical Publishing Co., 1927.

_____ . London: Rudolf Steiner Publishing, 1923, 1927.

_____ . New York: Anthroposophic Press, 1927.

_____ . London: Rudolf Steiner Press, 1986.

_____ . Spring Valley, NY: St. George Publications, 1986.

Lecture 7 is included in:

Rudolf Steiner, *Art in the Light of Mystery Wisdom.* Introduction by Marie Steiner. Trans. S. M. K. Gandall, Henry B. Monges. London: Anthroposophic Press, 1935.

Rudolf Steiner, *Art in the Light of Mystery Wisdom.* Trans. Johanna Collis. London: Rudolf Steiner Press, 1970.

Lecture 8, "A Living Knowledge of Nature," Dornach, January 20, 1923, trans. unknown, Supplement to *Anthroposophical Movement*, London, Vol. IX, Nr. 14, 1932.

"Man and the Nature Spirits: Consequences of an Anthroposophical World View," Dornach, January 20, 1923, tr. Gerald F. Karnow, Spring Valley, NY: Mercury Press, 1983.

Lecture 9, "The Intellectual Fall of Man," Dornach, January 21, 1923, trans. unknown, *Anthroposophic News Sheet*, Dornach, Vol. II, 1934.

"Fall and Redemption," Dornach, January 21, 1923, trans. unknown., Spring Valley, NY: Mercury Press, 1995.

Lecture 10, "Man's Fall and Redemption, Dornach, January 26, 1923, trans. unknown, *Anthroposophic News Sheet*, Dornach, Vol. II, Nrs. 20, 22, Whitsun 1934.

Lecture 11,"Realism and Nominalism," Dornach, January 27, 1923, trans. unknown, *Anthroposophic News Sheet*, Dornach, Supplement 3, 1934.

Lecture 12, "Concerning Electricity," An Extract, Dornach, January 28, 1923, trans. unknown, *Anthroposophic News Sheet*, Dornach, Vol. VIII, Nrs. 23, 24, 1940

Lectures 7, 8, 9, *Fall and Redemption*, trans., Gerald F. Karnow, Spring Valley, NY: Mercury Press, 1995.

_____ . "Truth, Beauty and Goodness," Dornach, January 19, 1923.

_____ . "Man and the Nature Spirits: Consequences of an Anthroposophical World View," Dornach, January 20, 1923.

_____ . "Fall and Redemption," Dornach, January 21, 1923.

Compiled by Jann W. Gates

EDITORIAL AND REFERENCE NOTES

Notes are listed according to page and quotation of relevant text.

Lecture 1

Page 1, "the Goetheanum was destroyed by fire"
Regarding the destruction of the Goetheanum by fire on the night of December 31, 1922 to January 1, 1923, see Rudolf Steiner, *Wege zu einem neuen Baustil,* Dornach: Philosophisch-Anthroposophish Verlag, 1926; also published under the same title as (GA 286), Stuttgart: Freies Geistesleben, 1957; and as (GA 286), Dornach: Rudolf Steiner Verlag, 1982. Also see:

Rudolf Steiner, *Der Baugedanke des Goetheanum,* Dornach: Philosophisch-Anthroposophisch Verlag, 1932; also published under the same title as (GA 290), Stuttgart: Freies Geistesleben, 1958.

_____, *Das Goetheanum als Gesamtkunstwerk. Rudolf Steiner, Der Baugedanke des Goetheanum. Einleitende Vortrag mit Erklärungen zu den Lichtbildern des Goetheanum-Baus gehalten in Bern am 29. Juni 1921.* Dornach: Am Goetheanum, 1986.

Christoph Lindenberg, *Rudolf Steiner: Eine Chronik.* Stuttgart: Freies Geistesleben, pp. 502–503.

Available in English translation:

Steiner, *Ways to a New Style in Architecture, Five lectures given during the building of the First Goetheanum, June–July,* 1914. London/New York: Anthroposophical Publishing Co., 1927.

_____, *Architecture as a Synthesis of the Arts* (CW 286), ed. and introduction by Christian Thal-Jantzen. New York: Rudolf Steiner Press, 1999.

Page 1, "I presented lectures"
Steiner, *Man and the World of Stars: The Spiritual Communion of Mankind* (CW 219). 12 lectures, Dornach, November 26–December 31, 1922. New York: Anthroposophic Press, 1982.
_____, *Das Verhältnis der Sternen Welt zum Menschen und des Menschen zur Sternenwelt,* (GA 219). Dornach: Rudolf Steiner Verlag, 1994.

Page 1, "the phenomena of the changing seasons"
See especially the lecture in Dornach on December 29, 1922, "From Man's Living Together with the Course of Cosmic Existence Arises the Cosmic Cult" (CW 219, see above).

Page 1, "The course I gave last year about philosophy, cosmology, and religion"
Steiner, *Philosophy, Cosmology and Religion*, (CW 215), New York: Anthroposophic Press, 1984.
_____, *Die Philosophie, Kosmologie und Religion in der Anthroposophie* (GA 215). Dornach: Rudolf Steiner Verlag, 1980.

Page 3, "Julian the Apostate"
331–363 C.E., Roman Emperor 361–363.

Page 3, "I have spoken about this on another occasion"
See Rudolf Steiner's lectures of April 19 and 24, 1917, in Berlin.
Steiner, *Building Stones for an Understanding of the Mystery of Golgotha*, (CW 175). London: Rudolf Steiner Press, 1972.
_____, *Baustine zu einer Erkenntnis des Mysteriums von Golgatha* (GA 175). Dornach: Rudolf Steiner Verlag, 1994.

Page 4, "as it seemed to be for various Roman writers"
Tacitus, Annales XV, 44,2; Sueton, Vita Caesarum. Claudius 25; Plinius the Younger, Epistolae X, 96; Flavius Josephus, Jüdische Altertümer XVIII, 63–64 and XX, 9.1.

Page 4, *An Outline of Esoteric Science*
(CW 13). Written in 1910, Great Barrington, MA: SteinerBooks, 1997. Also published as *An Outline of Occult Science*. New York: Anthroposophic Press, 1972.
See Chapter 4, "Cosmic Evolution and the Human Being."

Page 5, "in my recent lectures about the origins of modern natural science"
Steiner, *The Origins of Natural Science* (CW 326). New York: Anthroposophic Press, 1985.
_____, *Der Entstehungsmoment der Naturwissenschaft in der Weltgeschichte und ihre seitherige Entwickelung* (GA 326). Dornach, Rudolf Steiner Verlag, 1977.

Page 7, "Emperor Constantine's testimony"
Constantine I, 274–337 C.E., Roman Emperor 313–337. Constantine I issued the Edict of Milan in 313 C.E., which granted religious toleration to all religions including Christianity. Theodosius I issued the Edict of Thessalonica in 380 C.E. and thus gave imperial sanction to Christianity.

Page 7, "The historian Zosimus explained"
Zosimus, 490s–510s C.E., Byzantine historian, wrote a history of the Roman emperors.

Page 8, "Copernicus"
Nicholas Copernicus, 1473–1543, *De revolutionibus orbium coelestium, Libri VI*, Nuremberg: 1543.
Nicholas Copernicus, *Complete Works, Volume II: On the Revolutions.* Johns Hopkins University Press, 1992.
_____, "Commentariolus," in Three Copernican Treatises. Dover, 2004.

Page 11, "Copernicus articulated three laws."
This third 'law' was formulated in the following way: In the course of 26,000 years, the earth axis traces a cone with the ecliptic pole as its axis. Compare Rudolf Steiner's lecture in Stuttgart on January 2, 1921, in *Das Verhältnis der verschiedenen naturwissenschaftlichen Gebiete zur Astronomie* (Astronomy Course) (GA 323). Dornach: Rudolf Steiner Verlag, 1997.

Page 11, "I spoke about astronomy in the natural science course in Stuttgart"
See Rudolf Steiner's lecture in Stuttgart on January 2, 1921, in *Das Verhältnis der verschiedenen naturwissenschaftlichen Gebiete zur Astronomie* (Astronomy Course) (GA 323). Dornach: Rudolf Steiner Verlag, 1997.

Page 12, "Kepler"
Johannes Kepler, 1571–1630, *Astronomia nova*, 1609. *Harmonices mundi*, 1619.

Page 12, "Newton"
Isaac Newton, 1642–1727, *Philosophiae naturalis principia mathematica*, 1687.

Page 12, "Leibniz"
Gottfried Wilhelm Leibniz, 1646–1716, *Essai de Theodicée, (Theodicy: Essays on the Goodness of God, the Freedom of Man, and the Origins of Evil.)* 1710. *Monaden, (Monadology)*, 1714.

Page 12, "Galilei"
Galileo Galilei, 1564–1642, discovered the Law of Gravity, famous for his research in astronomy.

Page 14, "I have yet many things to say to you, but you cannot bear them now"
John 16: 12.

Page 14, "And I am with you always...."
Matthew 28: 20.

Lecture 2

Page 15, "Let us take note that a recent course ..."
Rudolf Steiner, *The Origins of Natural Science* (CW 326), New York: Anthroposophic Press, 1985.
_____, *Der Entstehungsmoment der Naturwissenschaft in der Weltgeschichte und ihre seitherige Entwickelung* (GA 326). Dornach, Rudolf Steiner Verlag, 1977.

Lecture 3

Page 25, "We know by means of anthroposophic observation"
Regarding the development Rudolf Steiner's twelve senses of the human being, see:

Rudolf Steiner, *A Psychology of Body, Soul and Spirit* (CW 115). Berlin, 12 lectures, October 1909, November 1910, December 1911. Great Barrington, MA: SteinerBooks, 1999.

_____, *The Riddle of Humanity: The Spiritual Background of Human History* (CW 170). Dornach, 15 lectures, July–September 1916. n.p.: Rudolf Steiner Press, 1990.

_____, *The Riddles of the Soul* (CW 21) Written 1917. Great Barrington, MA: SteinerBooks, 2012.

_____, *The Foundations of Human Experience* (CW 293). 14 lectures, August–September 1919. Great Barrington, MA: SteinerBooks, 1996.

_____, *Man as a Being of Sense and Perception* (CW 206, incomplete). Dornach, 3 lectures, July 22–24, 1921. n.p.: Steiner Book Centre, 1981.

_____, *Anthroposophie, Psychosophie, Pneumatosophie* (GA 115). Berlin, 12 Lectures, 1909, 1910, 1911, Dornach: Rudolf Steiner Verlag, 2001.

_____, *Das Rätsel des Menschen* (GA 170). Dornach, 15 lectures, July–September 1916. Dornach: Rudolf Steiner Verlag, 1992.

_____, *Von Seelenrätseln* (GA 21). Written 1917. Dornach: Rudolf Steiner Verlag, 1983. See the chapter entitled "Über die wirklichen Grundlagen der intentionalen Beziehung."

_____, *Allgemeine Menschenkunde als Grundlage der Pädagogik (1)* (GA 293). Stuttgart, 14 lectures, August–September, 1919. Dornach: Rudolf Steiner Verlag, 1992.

_____, *Menschenwerden, Weltenseele und Weltengeist*, Part II (GA 206). Dornach, 11 lectures, July–August 1921. Dornach: Rudolf Steiner Verlag, 1991.

Page 29, "the liver receives a certain picture of all that is tin"
Compare this with Rudolf Steiner's lecture in Prague, March 28, 1911.
Rudolf Steiner, *An Occult Physiology* (CW 128) Prague, 8 lectures, March 20–28, 1911. London: Rudolf Steiner Press, 2005.

_____, *Eine okkulte Physiologie* (GA 128) Dornach: Rudolf Steiner Verlag, 1991.

See also:
G. Husemann, *Erdengebärde und Menschengestalt: Das Zinn in Erde und Mensch.* Stuttgart: Freies Geistesleben, 1962.

Page 37, "the intuitions Goethe described"
Johann W. von Goethe, *Wilhelm Meisters Wanderjahren*, published in 1821.

Lecture 4

Page 39, "Giordano Bruno"

1548–1600. Italian philosopher, was forced to leave the Dominican order in 1576, brought before the Inquisition and held in prison for seven years, and burned at the Campo di Fiore, Rome. A memorial was erected at that place in Bruno's honor in 1889.

Page 39, "Jacob Boehme"

1575–1624. Protestant mystic. *Aurora oder Morgenröte im Aufgang*, 1610. *Beschreibung der drei Pincipia göttlichen Wesens*, 1619. *Mysterium Magnum*, 1623.

Page 39, "Francis Bacon"

1561–1626. Lord Chancellor and Baron of Verulam. *Novum organum scientiarum, 1620, a critique of Aristotle's Organum. De dignitate et augmentis scientiarum*, 1623.

Page 41, "the philosopher Fichte"

Johann Gottlieb, 1762–1814. German philosopher.

Page 41, "A culmination on Sunday:"

See Lecture Five in this volume.

Page 42, "the position taken by the prominent scholar DuBois-Reymond"

Emil du Bois-Reymond, 1818–1896. German physician, "father of experimental electrophysiology," professor of physiology (1858–1896) at the Friedrich-Wilhelms Universität, Berlin. As University Rector in 1882, Du Bois-Reymond gave a speech entitled "Goethe und Kein Ende," Emil Du Bois-Reymond, *Reden*. Leipzig: Verlag von Veit, 1886. Also reprinted recently by BiblioLife, 2009.

Du Bois-Reymond criticized Goethe's scientific methodology and then added his personal advice to Goethe's Faust. "It would have been better if Faust had not chosen a life at court, nor handed out paper money, and certainly not been granted his ascent to mothers in the fourth dimension. Rather he should have married Gretchen, legitimized the birth of Gretchen's child, and used his capacities to invent electric machines and air pumps."

Page 43, "Merlin"

Merlin, wise man and wizard in Celtic legends; defender of King Arthur. *Merlin and the Grail: Joseph of Arimathea, Merlin, Perceval. The Trilogy of Arthurian Prose Romances attributed to Robert de Boron.* UK: Boydell Brewer Ltd., 2008.

Page 43, "Karl Lebrecht Immermann"

Karl Immermann, 1796–1840, *Merlin*. Mainz: Strassen, 1984. First published in 1832.

Page 44, "I have already pointed out..."
See Rudolf Steiner's lecture in Dornach, July 29, 1922 in:

Rudolf Steiner, *The Mystery of the Trinity and the Mission of the Spirit* (CW 214). Dornach, Oxford, London, 8 lectures July–August, 1922. New York: Anthroposophic Press, 1991.

_____, *Das Geheimnis der Trinität*, (GA 214). Dornach, 11 Lectures, July 23–August 9, 1922.

Page 44, "Trithemius von Sponheim"
(Johannes Heidenberg), 1462–1516. Humanist, cryptographer, occultist. Abbot of the Sponheim Benedictine Cloister (1483–1506), later abbot of the St. James Abbey, Würzburg.

Page 44, "Agrippa von Nettesheim"
1486–1535. Theologian, occultist, astrologer, philosopher.

Cornelius Agrippa von Nettesheim, *De occulta philosophia*, 1510–1531. *De incertitudine et vanita scientiarum*, 1527, 1530.

_____, *The Three Books of Occult Philosophy*. Trans. James Freake. St. Paul, MN: Llewellyn, 1993.

_____, *Of the Vanitie and Vncertainie of Artes and Sciences*, ed. Catherine M. Dunn. Northridge, CA: California State University Foundation, 1974.

Page 44, "Georgius Sabellicus"
Georgius Sabellicus Faustus, c. 1480–1535. Historical archetype of the magician Faust in folk tradition. Reputedly an astrologer and magician; was mentioned by Trithemius in a letter of April 20, 1507.

Page 44, "Paracelsus"
Philippus Aureolus Theophrastus Bombastus von Hohenheim, 1493–1541, physician, botanist, philosopher, occultist, astrologer, alchemist.

Paracelsus, *Paragranum*, 1529/30. Astonomia magna, 1537/1538.

_____, *The Hermetic and Alchemical Writings of Paracelsus*, 2 volumes. London, 1894; revised edition, 2002.

K. Sudhoff, ed. Critical edition of Paracelus' Works. Vol. I–XIV. Munich-Berlin. 1922–33. Second edition, Wiesbaden, 1955ff. New Paracelsus edition, on-line, 2008.

Page 47, "Condillac"
Etienne Bonnot de Condillac, 1715–1780. French philosopher, empiricist psychologist of the workings of the human mind, founder of "sensationism."

Page 47, "La Mettrie"
Julien Offray de La Mettrie, 1709–1751. French physician, materialist philosopher. *L'homme machine*, 1748.

Lecture 5

Page 53, "just as I presented here a short time ago in the course on philosophy..."

Rudolf Steiner, *Philosophy, Cosmology, and Religion* (CW 215). New York: Anthroposophic Press, 1984.

_____, *Die Philosophie, Kosmologie und Religion in der Anthroposophie* (GA 215). Dornach: Rudolf Steiner Verlag, 1980.

Page 63, "we have performed the Oberfuer plays several times"

Helene Jacquet, ed., *Christmas Plays from Oberufer*. London: Rudolf Steiner Press, 2007.

Weihnachtspiele aus altem Volkstum: Die Oberuferer Spiele, ed. Karl Julius Schröer, essay by Rudolf Steiner. Dornach, Rudolf Steiner Verlag, 1990.

The Oberufer Christmas plays were folk plays widely performed in the sixteenth through the eighteenth centuries, but it is difficult to establish the time when these plays first appeared.

Page 63, "in the much earlier Germanic lay of the *Heliand*"

Heliand. An Old Saxon epic poem retelling parts of the Gospels and several Genesis traditions, written in the ninth century C.E., two substantial manuscripts and several fragments. The title means "savior."

Tonya Kim Dewey, *An Annotated English Translation of the Old Saxon Heliand: A ninth-century Biblical Paraphrase in the Germanic Epic Style*. U.S.: Elwin Mellen Press, 2011.

The text referred to by Rudolf Steiner may be found in the *Heliand*, Part V, Verses 563 ff. See also Rudolf Steiner's lecture from April 2, 1915, *Wege der geistigen Erkenntnis und der Erneuerung künstlerischer Weltanschauung* (GA 161). Dornach, 13 lectures, January–May, 1915. Dornach, Rudolf Steiner Verlag, 1999.

Page 64, "we find mention of Balaam"

Book of Numbers, Chapters 22–24.

Page 65, "pre-earthly existence was dogmatically veiled in darkness"

The earliest ecclesiastical condemnation of the teaching of human pre-existence, one that is still cited today, is found in the documents of Justinian, 483–565 C.E., Emperor of the Byzantine or Eastern Roman Empire, 527–565.

Liber adversus Origenem, 543 C.E. contains nine "Canons against Origen," teachings attributed to Origen that were declared to be "anathema." The first anathema stated that "Whoever says or thinks that human souls pre-existed, that is, that they previously had been spirits and had holy powers, but that saturated with the vision of God, they had turned to evil, and in this way the divine love in them had died out and they therefore were called souls (*psychas*) and were condemned to punishment in bodies, shall be anathema." The authenticity of the document was confirmed by Cassiodorus, the historian to the Pope Vigilius (540-555). See the footnote regarding Justinian's canons against Origen in Heinrich Denzinger and Clemens Gannwart, *Enchiridion Symbolorum.* Freiburg: Herder Verlag, 1928.

See also:
Steiner's lecture in Dornach, April 8, 1921, given during the second anthroposophical *Hochschulkurs* and published in *Die befruchtenden Wirkung der Anthroposophie auf die Fachwissenschaften* (GA 76). Dornach: Rudolf Steiner Verlag, 1977.

_____, Lecture in Berlin on September 18, 1920. *Spiritual Science as the Foundation for Social Forms* (CW 199). New York: Anthroposophic Press, 1986.

_____, *Geisteswissenschaft als Erkenntnis der Grundimpulse sozialer Gestaltung* (GA 199), 15 lectures, Dornach, August–September 1920, 2 lectures, Berlin, September 17–18, 1920. Dornach: Rudolf Steiner Verlag, 1985.

Page 65, "an intervention came to suppress the knowledge of pre-earthly human existence"
The Fifth Lateran Council 1512–1517 declared that the soul from the moment of union with its body in its individuality is created by God from nothing and is personally immortal.

Ludwig Ott, *Grundriss der Katholischen Dogmatik.* Freiburg: Herder Verlag, 1970, pp., 118, 121.

Lecture 6

Page 67, "I explicitly pointed out that the consolidation of the Anthroposophical Society is an absolute necessity"
Rudolf Steiner is referring to his lecture of December 30, 1922 published in *Man and the World of Stars; The Spiritual Communion of Mankind* (CW 219). Dornach, 12 lectures, November 26–December 31, 1922. New York: Anthroposophic Press, 1963.

_____, *Das Verhältnis der Sternenwelt zum Menschen und des Menschen zur Sternenwelt; Die geistige Kommunion der Menschheit,* (GA 219). Dornach, 12 lectures, November–December 1922. Dornach: Rudolf Steiner Verlag, 1994.

Page 69, "what was recorded in a letter ... "
In 388 C.E. the Sophist teacher of rhetoric, Libanius (c. 314–c.394) appealed to Theodosius, the Roman Emperor 379–395 C.E., to refrain from destroying the cultural heritage of the Hellenistic temples.

See Ernst von Lasaulx, *Der Untergang des Hellenismus und die Einziehung seiner Tempelgüter during die christlichen Kaiser* (1854). Stuttgart, Freies Geistesleben, 1965.

Page 69, "When the Athenian school of philosophy was closed in 529 C.E."
See Ernst von Lasaulx, *Der Untergang des Hellenismus und die Einziehung seiner*

Tempelgüter during die christlichen Kaiser (1854). Stuttgart, Freies Geistesleben, 1965.

Page 69, "But even Saint Benedict"
Benedict of Nursia c. 480–547 C.E., founder of a monastic community at Monte Cassino in southern Italy. Formulated the Rule of Benedict observed by autonomous abbeys that later became known as Benedictine cloisters.

Page 70, "It is simply incorrect to say that 'nature or world history can never make a developmental leap.'"
First by Fournier, *Variétés historiques et littéraires*, 1613, 9, 247: "Natura non fecit saltum" (Nature does not take leaps). In a similar formulation by Carl von Linné, 1707–1778, *Philosophia Botanica*, 1751, Nr. 77.

See also Gottfried Wilhelm Leibniz 1646–1716, *Nouveaux essais sur l'entendement humain*, 1765, IV, 16. Leibniz, *Essays on Human Understanding*. UK: Cambridge University Press, 1996.

Page 70, "For example, when the Theosophical Society was founded"
The Theosophical Society was founded by H.P. Blavatsky and H.S. Olcott in 1875 in New York City. Shortly thereafter the center of the society was relocated to Madras, India.

Page 71, "the essentially human quality was expressed as 'the thinker'."
See Rudolf Steiner's lecture in Stuttgart on January 3, 1920, in Rudolf Steiner, *The Genius of Language* (CW 299), 6 lectures, Stuttgart, December 1919–January 1920. Great Barrington, MA: SteinerBooks, 1995.
_____, *Geisteswissenschaftlicheh Sprachbetrachtungen* (GA 299). Dornach: Rudolf Steiner Verlag, 1981.

Page 73, "the shepherd named Huckle tries to awaken his fellow shepherd Buckle."
Gallus and Stichl (Huckle and Buckle in the English translation) were two of the shepherds in the Oberufer Christmas play of the Nativity.
Christmas Plays from Oberufer. London: Rudolf Steiner Press, 2007.
Weihnachtspiele aus altem Volkstum: Die Oberuferer Spiele, ed. Karl Julius Schröer, essay by Rudolf Steiner. Dornach, Rudolf Steiner Verlag, 1990.

Page 74, "Du Bois-Reymond said."
As University Rector in 1872, Du Bois-Reymond gave a highly publicized speech iterating the limits of the human capacity to understand nature, "Über die Grenzen des Naturerkennens" (On the Limits of our Understanding of Nature).

Page 74, "my book *The Philosophy of Freedom*"
Rudolf Steiner, *The Philosophy of Freedom* (CW 4). Written 1894, revised 1918. London: Rudolf Steiner Press, 2011.

Also published as: *The Philosophy of Spiritual Activity.* Great Barrington, MA: SteinerBooks, 2007.

Intuitive Thinking as a Spiritual Path. Great Barrington, MA: SteinerBooks, 1995.
_____, *Die Philosophie der Freiheit.* (GA 4), Dornach, Rudolf Steiner Verlag, 1995.

Page 75, "When in fact Dr. Galle"
Johann Gottfried Galle, 1812–1910, astronomer, Berlin Observatory 1835–1851, afterward professor of astronomy and director of the Astronomical Observatory in Breslau, made a visual sighting of the planet Neptune in 1846. The French astronomer Urbain Le Verrier, 1811–1877, had sent Galle his calculations for the location of a planet that could exert gravitational pull sufficient to cause irregularities in the orbit of Uranus.

Page 76, "Or recall how Mendeleev"
Dimitri Ivanovich Mendeleev, 1834–1907, Russian chemist who classified elements according to similar chemical properties and published a periodic table of the elements in his *Principles of Chemistry*, 1868–1870.

Page 76, "humanity must be able to experience what the philosopher Johann Gottlieb Fichte expressed"
Johann Gottlieb Fichte, 1762–1814, German philosopher. See Book II of his *Die Bestimmung des Menschen* (1800). In English: *The Vocation of Man,* trans. William Smith. Chicago, Open Court, 1906.
  There is nothing enduring, either out of me, or in me, but only a ceaseless change. I know of no being, not even of my own. There is no being. I myself absolutely know not, and am not. Pictures are:—they are the only things which exist, and they know of themselves after the fashion of pictures:—pictures which float past without their being anything past which they float; which, by means of like pictures, are connected with each other:—pictures without anything that is pictured in them, without significance and without aim. I myself am one of these pictures;—nay, I am not even this, but merely a confused picture of the pictures. All reality is transformed into a strange dream, without a life which is dreamed of, and without a mind which dreams it;—into a dream which is woven together in a dream of itself. (p. 89)

Page 76, "the error we find in the philosophy of Schopenhauer"
Arthur Schopenhauer, 1788–1860, German philosopher. See Rudolf Steiner's *The Riddles of Philosophy* (CW 18), Part I, Chapter VIII, "Reactionary World Conceptions." Great Barrington, MA: SteinerBooks, 2009.

Page 76, "It is interesting to consider what Eduard von Hartmann said"
Edward von Hartmann, 1842–1906, German philosopher and significant acquaintance of Rudolf Steiner. See Rudolf Steiner's *Autobiography* (CW 28), Chapter 23. Great Barrington, MA: SteinerBooks, 2005; and his *The Riddles of Philosophy*

(CW 18), Part II, Chapter VI, "Modern Idealistic World Conceptions." Great Barrington, MA: SteinerBooks, 2009.

Page 77, "Hartmann pushes the thing-in-itself to the limit"
See Edward von Hartmann's chapter "Gundlegung des transzendentalen Realismus," in the second edition of *Das Ding an sich und seine Beschaffenheit.* Berlin, 1875.

Page 77, "I characterized at the end of the Christmas course of lectures"
See Rudolf Steiner's lecture in Dornach, January 6, 1923 in:

Rudolf Steiner, *The Origins of Natural Science* (CW 326). New York: Anthroposophic Press, 1985.
_____, *Der Entstehungsmoment der Naturwissenschaft in der Weltgeschichte und ihre seitherige Entwickelung* (GA 326). Dornach, Rudolf Steiner Verlag, 1977.

Lecture 7

Page 80, "The human being worked out the spiritual prototype, the spiritual form of the physical body in union with higher spiritual beings."
See Rudolf Steiner's lecture from November 26, 1922, in Rudolf Steiner, *Man and the World of Stars: The Spiritual Communion of Mankind* (CW 219). 12 lectures, Dornach, November 26–December 31, 1922, trans. D. S. Osmond. New York: Anthroposophic Press, 1963.
_____, *Das Verhältnis der Sternen Welt zum Menschen und des Menschen zur Sternenwelt* (GA 219). Dornach: Rudolf Steiner Verlag, 1994.

Page 83, "In recent lectures I have described how we acquire the etheric or life body"
See Rudolf Steiner's lecture from November 26, 1922, (CW 219), cited above.

Page 87, "in the sense that I described several decades ago in my book *The Philosophy of Freedom*"
Rudolf Steiner, *The Philosophy of Freedom* (CW 4). Written 1894, revised 1918. London: Rudolf Steiner Press, 2011. For example:

Only when I follow my love for my objective is it I myself who act. I act, at this level of morality, not because I acknowledge a lord over me, or an external authority, or a so-called inner voice; I acknowledge no external principle for my action, because I have found in myself the ground for my action, namely, my love of the action. I do not work out mentally whether my action is good or bad; I carry it out because I love it. My action will be "good" if my intuition, steeped in love, finds its right place within the intuitively experienceable world continuum; it will be "bad" if this is not the case.

—from Chapter 9, "The Idea of Freedom."

Lecture 8

Page 99, "There was once an occasion in a college of law"
An experiment such as the one described by Rudolf Steiner was carried out by the Strafrechtlehrer Franz von Liszt, 1859–1919.

Lecture 9

Page 106, "On several occasions I have tried to characterize what religions mean by the Fall of Humanity."
See, for example, Rudolf Steiner's lecture in Karlsruhe on October 7, 1911, in:

From Jesus to Christ (CW 131). 11 lectures, Karlsruhe, October 4–14, 1911. London: Rudolf Steiner Press, 2005.

_____, *Von Jesus zu Christus* (GA 131). Dornach: Rudolf Steiner Verlag, 1988.

_____, Berlin lecture on December 7, 1921, in *Nordische und mitteleuropäische Geistimpulse: Das Fest der Erscheinung Christi* (GA 209). 11 lectures, Oslo, Berlin, Basel, November–December 1921. Dornach: Rudolf Steiner Verlag, 1982.

_____, Dornach lecture on May 7, 1922, in *Menschliches Seelenleben und Geistesstreben im Zusammenhange mit Welt- und Erdenentwichelung* (GA 212). 9 lectures, Dornach, April 29–June 17, 1922. Dornach: Rudolf Steiner Verlag, 1998.

_____, Dornach lecture, September 23, 1922, in *Supersensible Influences in the History of Mankind with Special Reference to Cult in Ancient Egypt* (CW 216). 6 lectures, Dornach, September 22–October 1, 1922. London: Rudolf Steiner Press, 1956.

_____, *Die Grundimpulse des weltgeschichlichen Werdens der Menschheit* (GA 216). 8 lectures, Dornach, September 16–October 1, 1922. Dornach: Rudolf Steiner Verlag, 1988.

Page 108, "Emil du Bois Reymond, for example, claimed that there were limits ... "
As University Rector in 1872, Du Bois-Reymond, gave a highly publicized speech iterating the limits of the human capacity to understand nature, "Über die Grenzen des Naturerkennens" (On the Limits of our Understanding of Nature).

Page 109, "When you examine his writings to see if he might have pursued this direction [Goethe's]"
J.W. Goethe, *Naturwissenschaftliche Schriften*, Vol. I, *Bildung und Umbildung organischer Naturen*, ed., Rudolf Steiner, (1884). Dornach: Rudolf Steiner Verlag, 1975.

Page 110, "we expect to apply Goethe's theory of metamorphosis"
See Rudolf Steiner's lecture in Stuttgart, September 1, 1919, in *The Foundations of Human Experience* (CW 293). 14 lectures, Stuttgart, August–September, 1919.

Great Barrington, MA: SteinerBooks, 1996. (Also published as *The Study of Man.* London: Rudolf Steiner Press.)
_____, *Allgemeine Menschenkunde als Gundlage der Pädagogik* (GA 293). Dornach: Rudolf Steiner Verlag, 1992.

Page 110, "I am referring to my book, *The Philosophy of Freedom*"
Rudolf Steiner, *The Philosophy of Freedom* (CW 4). Written 1894, revised 1918. London: Rudolf Steiner Press, 2011. (Also published as: *The Philosophy of Spiritual Activity.* Great Barrington: SteinerBooks, 2007. *Intuitive Thinking as a Spiritual Path.* Great Barrington, MA: SteinerBooks, 1995.)
_____, *Die Philosophie der Freiheit.* (GA 4). Dornach, Rudolf Steiner Verlag, 1995.
_____, *Truth and Knowledge* (CW 3). Written 1892. Great Barrington, MA: SteinerBooks, 2007. Rudolf Steiner, *Wahrheit und Wissenschft* (GA 3). Dornach: Rudolf Steiner Verlag, 1980.
_____, *Goethe's Theory of Knowledge* (CW 2). Written 1886. Great Barrington, MA: SteinerBooks, 2008. Rudolf Steiner, *Grundlinien einer Erkenntnistheorie der Goetheschen Weltanschauung, mit besonderer Rücksicht auf Schiller* (GA 2). Dornach: Rudolf Steiner Verlag, 2003.

Page 111, "I said some years ago during a lecture in Mannheim…"
A review of Rudolf Steiner's lectures in Mannheim in the years 1911, 1912, and 1913 did not uncover existing written texts. However, see Rudolf Steiner's lectures in Karlsruhe in *From Jesus to Christ* (CW 131). 11 lectures, Karlsruhe, October 4–14, 1911. London: Rudolf Steiner Press, 2005.
_____, *Von Jesus zu Christus* (GA 131). Dornach: Rudolf Steiner Verlag, 1988.

Page 112, "in the lecture I mentioned earlier"
See the reference above about lectures given in Mannheim and Karlsruhe.

Page 114, "If you really wish to understand animals"
Compare this with Rudolf Steiner's lectures in Dornach from October 19 to November 11, 1923, in *Harmony of the Creative Word* (GA 230). Forest Row, U.K.: Rudolf Steiner Press, 2002.
_____, *Der Mensch als Zusammenklang des schaffenden, bildenden und gestaltenden Weltenwortes* (GA 230). 12 lectures, Dornach, October 19–November 11, 1923. Dornach: Rudolf Steiner Verlag, 1993.

Page 115, "just like the sleepy shepherd in the nativity play"
Gallus is speaking to Stichl (Huckle and Buckle in the English translation); the two characters were shepherds in the Oberufer Christmas play of the Nativity.

Helene Jacquet, ed., *Christmas Plays from Oberufer.* London: Rudolf Steiner Press, 2007.

Karl Julius Schröer, ed. *Weihnachtsspiele aus altem Volkstum: Die Oberuferer Spiele,* with essay by Rudolf Steiner. Dornach, Rudolf Steiner Verlag, 1990.

Page 118, "There are insects that are vegetarian when they are fully grown."
See Wilhelm von Buttlar, *Instinkt und Verstand der Tiere*, Berlin/Leipzig, n.d., pp. 48–50. Rudolf Steiner may well have consulted this book, which was found in his personal library. He used the example of the *Schlupfwespe* in a lecture for the workers on the construction of the Goetheanum in Dornach on January 5, 1923.

Rudolf Steiner, *From Comets to Cocaine: Answers to Questions* (CW 348). 18 lectures in Dornach, October 1922–February 1923. London: Rudolf Steiner Press, 2000.
_____, *Über Gesundheit und Krankheit. Grundlagen einer geisteswissenschaftlichen Sinneslehre* (GA 348). Dornach: Rudolf Steiner Verlag, 1997.

Page 120, "is the movement for religious renewal"
The Christian Community was founded in the autumn of 1922 in cooperation with Dr. Friedrich Rittelmeyer. See Rudolf Steiner, *Awakening to Community* (CW 257). 10 lectures, Dornach and Stuttgart, January 23–March 4, 1923. New York: Anthroposophic Press, SteinerBooks, 1974.
_____, *Anthroposophische Gemeinschaftsbildung*, (GA 257). Dornach: Rudolf Steiner Verlag, 1989.

Lecture 10

Page 123, "The thoughts that modern human beings have about nature are actually corpses of thoughts."
Steiner, "How to Achieve Existence in the World of Ideas." Dornach, 4 lectures in December 1914, in *Inner Reading and Inner Hearing, How to Achieve Existence in the World of Ideas* (CW 156). 11 lectures, Dornach and Basel, October 3–December 27, 1914. Great Barrington, MA: SteinerBooks, 2008.
_____, *Okkultes Lesen und okkultes Hören* (GA 156). Dornach: Rudolf Steiner Verlag, 2003.

Page 125, "The pre-existence of the human being was declared a heresy."
See notes to Lecture Five above.

Page 125, "Think back to 1413 c.e."
The fourth post-Atlantean (Greco-Latin) cultural epoch ended about 1413, and the fifth era of the consciousness soul began. See Chapter 4, "Cosmic Evolution and the Human Being," in Rudolf Steiner, *An Outline of Esoteric Science* (CW 13). Written 1910. Great Barrington, MA: SteinerBooks, 1997.
_____, *Die Geheimwissenschaft im Umriss* (GA 13). Dornach: Rudolf Steiner Verlag, 1989.

Page 125, "the Darwinism that appeared in 1858"
Charles Darwin, 1809–1882, argued that all forms of life are to a certain degree related to one another, and over a very extended period of time have developed from simple organisms into increasingly complicated species. His most famous

work entitled *The Origin of Species by Means of Natural Selection* was first published in 1859.

Page 127, "they would *reverse* the direction of the line of animal and human development"

The American Transcendentalist Bronson Alcott maintained and defended a more vaguely detailed version of this contrary direction of evolution (his doctrine of "Genesis") throughout his life, often to the consternation of his contemporaries. See Odell Shepard, *Pedlar's Progress: The Life of Bronson Alcott.* Boston: Little, Brown and Co., 1938. (pp. 452–462).

Page 128, "Goethe's brief notation about the morphology of the human skeleton"

Steiner, ed., *Goethes Naturwissenschaftliche Schriften,* 5 Volumes. Dornach, Rudolf Steiner Verlag, 1975. See Vol. I, p. 316. The episode at the Lido in Venice described in Goethe's Annals from 1790 is mentioned in the footnotes.

See also Goethe's article, "Bedeutende Fördernis durch ein einziges gestreiches Word," in *Naturwissenschaftliche Schriften,* Vol. II, p. 34.

Rudolf Steiner, *Nature's Open Secret: Introductions to Goethe's Scientific Writings* (1883) (CW 1). Great Barrington, MA: SteinerBooks, 2000.

Page 128, "when I was working in the Goethe Archive in Weimar"

In 1890 Rudolf Steiner left Vienna in order to take a position at the Goethe-Schiller Archive in Weimar, Germany. He was given the immediate task of working on Goethe's morphology and continued his editorial work on Goethe's scientific writings.

See Chapters XIV–XXI in Rudolf Steiner, *Autobiography* (CW 28). Great Barrington, MA: Steiner Books, 2005.

————, *Mein Lebensgang.* Dornach: Rudolf Steiner Verlag, 2000.

Page 128, "Gegenbaur"

Carl Gegenbaur, 1826–1903. Professor of anatomy and zoology at Jena (1855–1873) and Heidelberg (1873–1903). His research in comparative anatomy was used to support Darwin's theory of evolution. Carl Gegenbaur, *Grundriss der vergleichenden Anatomie,* Leipzig, 1874, 2nd edition, 1878.

————, *Elements of Comparative Anatomy,* trans. W.F. Jeffrey Bell, 1878. See Gegenbaur's discussion of the skull.

Page 129, "If you take the definitions of Plato"

See in Plato's *Symposium,* Socrates' exposition of love through the teachings of Diotima.

Page 130, "Friedrich Theodor Vischer"

1807–1887. Professor of aesthetics at Tübingen, Zürich, Stuttgart. *Ästhetik oder Wissenscaft des Schönen,* 4 vol. Stuttgart, 1847–1858.

Page 130, "Robert Zimmermann"
1824–1898. Professor of philosophy, University of Vienna. *Geschichte der Aesthetik als Philosophischer Wissenschaft*, 2 vol. Vienna, 1858–1865.

Page 130, "Eduard Zeller"
1814–1908. Philosopher, theologian. Professor of philosophy at universities in Heidelberg and Berlin 1862–1895.

Eduard Zeller, *Die Philosophie der Griechen in ihrer geschictlichen Entwicklung*. Second edition in 5 volumes, Leipzig, 1855–1868.

_____, *Grundriss der Geschichte der Griechischen Philosophie*, 1883; 5th edition, 1898.

_____, *Outline of the History of Greek Philosophy*, trans. Sarah Frances Alleyne and Evelyn Abbott. London: Longmans Green, 1901.

Page 131, "Augustine"
Aurelius Augustinus, Augustine of Hippo, 354–430. Church father whose thinking, writings, and subsequent influence have been equally important for the development of philosophy and theology.

Page 132, "I gave a short cycle of lectures about Thomas Aquinas"
Steiner, *The Redemption in Thinking: A Study of the Philosophy of Thomas Aquinas* (CW 74). 3 lectures, Dornach, May 22–24, 1920. Great Barrington, MA: SteinerBooks, 1993.

_____, *Die Philosophie des Thomas von Aquino*, (GA 74). Dornach, Rudolf Steiner Verlag, 1993.

Page 132, "then our [anthroposophic] research institutes"
Beginning in 1912 anthroposophic impulses for chemistry, biology, and pharmaceutical science were carried out in research laboratories in Arlesheim, Switzerland, and Stuttgart and Schwäbisch-Gmund in Germany.

See the historical overview in the listing of anthroposophical institutions in *Die Konstitution der Allgemeinen Antroposophischen Gesellschaft*, (GA 260a). Dornach: Rudolf Steiner Verlag, 1987.

For the Klinisch-Therapeutisches Institut in Arlesheim, consult page 715. For Weleda A.G., consult page 723.

Page 132, "*How to Know Higher Worlds*"
Steiner, *How to Know Higher Worlds: A Modern Path of Initiation* (CW 10). Written 1904. Great Barrington, MA: SteinerBooks, 1994.

_____, *Wie erlangt man Erkenntnisse der höheren Welten?* (1904) (GA 10). Dornach: Rudolf Steiner Verlag, 1993.

Lecture 11

Page 135, "Vincenz Knauer"
1828–1894. Theologian, Benedictine order, *Privatdozent* in philosophy at the universities in Innsbruck and Vienna.

Vincenz Knauer, *Die Hauptprobleme der Philosophie in ihrer Entwicklung und Theilweisen Lösung von Thales bis Robert Hemerling,* 21 lectures given at the Vienna University, Vienna/Leipzig, 1892.

Rudolf Steiner often referred to Knauer's description/definition of realism.

Steiner, Stuttgart lecture on August 17, 1908, "Philosophie and Anthroposophie" in *Philosophie und Anthroposophie* (GA 35). Dornach: Rudolf Steiner Verlag, 1984, p. 90 ff. Also see *Von Seelenrätseln,* (1917) (GA 21). Dornach: Rudolf Steiner Verlag, 1983, p. 139 ff.
_____, *Riddles of the Soul* (1917) (CW 21). Great Barrington, MA: SteinerBooks, 2012.

Page 137, "Ancient Persian archangels"
The twelve Persian archangelic beings modified the activity of the cosmic divine being of light, Ahura Mazdao, and the latter's opposing force, Ahriman, as they moved through the Zodiac.

Compare this with Rudolf Steiner's lecture entitled, "Zarathustra," in Berlin on January 19, 1911, in Rudolf Steiner, *Turning Points in Spiritual History* (CW 60). 6 lectures, Berlin, October 1910–March 1911, Great Barrington, MA: SteinerBooks, 2007.
_____, *Antworten der Geisteswissenschaft auf die Grossen Fragen des Daseins,* (GA 60), 15 lectures, Berlin, October 20, 1910–March 16, 1911. Dornach, Rudolf Steiner Verlag, 1983.

Page 140, "John Wycliffe"
c. 1320–1384, English precursor to the sixteenth century Protestant Reformation, translated the Bible into English.

Page 140, "Johann Amos Comenius"
1592–1670, was known as the "father of modern education," teacher, educational reformer, pastor and later bishop of the Moravian Brethren. His efforts to renew pedagogy, curriculum, and educational organization also encompassed the entire scope of spiritual life.

Page 140, "Adolf von Harnack"
1851–1930.
Von Harnack, *Das Wesen des Christentums,* 16 lectures, University of Berlin, open to all students and faculty, winter semester 1899/1900, Leipzig, 1901.

_____, *What is Christianity?* London: Williams and Norgate, 1901. Also republished in New York: Harper, 1957.

Page 141, "Christian Geyer"
1862–1929. Was the senior pastor at the main Lutheran church in Nuremberg, a close friend and colleague of Friedrich Rittelmeyer, 1872–1938, founder in 1922 of The Christian Community, Movement for Religious Renewal.

Page 143, "Did the Father and the Son both exist throughout eternity ... ?"
At the Council of Nicaea, 325 C.E. and the Council of Constantinople, 381 C.E., the equality of the Father, Son, and Holy Spirit was proclaimed as dogma of the church. The Roman Catholic Church later added to this dogma that the Holy Spirit proceeded equally from the Father and the Son, a position that in 1054 led to the schism between the Roman and Eastern Orthodox churches.

Page 146, "Leadbeater"
Charles W. Leadbeater, 1847–1934. Was one of the leaders of the Theosophical Society.

Page 146, "Recently in an article printed in an English newspaper"
It was not possible to identify the newspaper mentioned by Rudolf Steiner.

Lecture 12

Page 148, "Herman Grimm"
1828–1901. Art historian, professor at the Friedrich Wilhelm University, Berlin. *Leben Michelangelos*, 2 vol., Berlin, 1860–1863. *Life of Michel Angelo*, 2 vol., Boston, 1906.

Page 148, "Friedrich Nietzsche"
1844–1900. German philologist, philosopher, and poet.

Page 148, "Grimm himself ... spoke about the nature of this burden."
For example, see Herman Grimm, *Homer's Iliad*, 2 vol., Berlin, 1895, p. 3:
"It seems to me as if humanity feels oppressed by the weight of history, that human beings themselves have condemned themselves to carry with them this great burden."

Page 149, "Sils Maria"
Sils Maria, Switzerland, is a village within view of two lakes and surrounding mountains where Nietzsche spent the summer months during 1881 and from 1883 to 1888. He worked productively in this peaceful setting.

Page 149, "an essay entitled "On the Use and Abuse of History for Life"
"On the Use and Abuse of History for Life" (1874), in *Friedrich Nietzsche, Unfashionable Observations I–IV*, vol. 2 of the Complete Works. Palo Alto, CA:

Stanford University Press, 1995.

_____,"Von Nutzen und Nachteil der Historie für das Leben," in *Unzeitgemässe Betrachtungen* (1873–1876).

Page 150, "the historicist school of law"

Friedrich Carl von Savigny, 1779–1861. Founder of the historical or historicist school of law. Legal positivism emerged out of the historicist legal tradition of the early nineteenth century, which required a judge to remain true to historical legal precedent even when the judge personally regarded the precedent as unjust. The philosophical presumption for the historicist position holds that the laws reflect the social mores of the society that generated them, and that the historical law should take precedence over philosophically based jurisprudence.

Page 152, "the foundation we lay today through our moral impulses ..."

See Rudolf Steiner's lecture in Dornach, on March 28, 1920, in *Heilfaktoren für den sozialen Organismus* (GA 198). 17 lectures, Dornach and Bern, March 20–July 9, 1920. Dornach: Rudolf Steiner Verlag, 1984.

Page 153, "At the turn of the eighteenth to the nineteenth centuries, a physicist"

Luigi Galvani, 1737–1798. Was an Italian physician, anatomist, physicist, and scientific researcher. In 1789 Galvani discovered a new aspect of electricity during an experiment in which an electrical impulse stimulated movement in a dead frog's leg. This field of research was later called electrophysiology.

Page 155, "I described in my recent natural-scientific course"

Steiner, *The Origins of Natural Science* (CW 326). New York: Anthroposophic Press, 1985.

_____, *Der Entstehungsmoment der Naturwissenschaft in der Weltgeschichte und ihre seitherige Entwickelung* (GA 326). Dornach, Rudolf Steiner Verlag, 1977.

Page 155, "Agrippa of Nettesheim"

Cornelius Agrippa von Nettesheim, 1486–1535. Theologian, occultist, astrologer, philosopher. See note to p. 44, above.

Page 155, "Tritemius of Sponheim"

Trithemius von Sponheim (Johannes Heidenberg), 1462–1516, was a humanist, cryptographer, and occultist. See note to p. 44, above.

Page 156, "my first mystery drama"

Steiner, "The Portal of Initiation," in *Four Mystery Dramas* (CW 14). Written 1910–1913. Great Barrington, MA: SteinerBooks, 2014.

_____, "Dir Pforte der Einweihung," in *Vier Mysteriendramen* (GA 14). Dornach: Rudolf Steiner Verlag, 1998.

Page 157, "Certainly we can refer to scientists today as math whizzes ..."

Compare this to Friedrich Nietzsche, *Die fröhliche Wissenschaft*, 1882, segment on "science" as prejudice.

_____, *The Gay Science*. Mineola, NY: Dover, 2006.

Page 159, "so that they can also create an art like eurythmy"
Steiner, *Eurythmy as Visible Music* (CW 278). Dornach, 8 lectures, February 19–17, 1924. London: Rudolf Steiner Press, 1977.

_____, *Eurythmy as Visible Speech* (CW 279). Dornach, 15 lectures, June–July, 1924; August 4, 1922; Penmaenmawr, August 26, 1923. London: Rudolf Steiner Press, 1984.

_____ , *Eurythmy: Its Birth and Development* (CW 277a). Basel, September 16–24, 1912; Dornach, August 18–September 11, 1915. UK: Anastasi Ltd., 2002.

_____, *Eurythmie als sichtbarer Gesang* (GA 278). Dornach: Rudolf Steiner Verlag, 2001.

_____, *Eurythmie als sichtbare Sprache* (GA 279). Dornach: Rudolf Steiner Verlag, 1990.

_____, *Die Entstehung und Entwickelung der Eurythmie* (GA 277a). Dornach: Rudolf Steiner Verlag, 1998.

RUDOLF STEINER'S COLLECTED WORKS

The German Edition of Rudolf Steiner's Collected Works (the Gesamtausgabe [GA] published by Rudolf Steiner Verlag, Dornach, Switzerland) presently runs to over 354 titles, organized either by type of work (written or spoken), chronology, audience (public or other), or subject (education, art, etc.). For ease of comparison, the Collected Works in English [CW] follows the German organization exactly. A complete listing of the CWs follows with literal translations of the German titles. Other than in the case of the books published in his lifetime, titles were rarely given by Rudolf Steiner himself, and were often provided by the editors of the German editions. The titles in English are not necessarily the same as the German; and, indeed, over the past seventy-five years have frequently been different, with the same book sometimes appearing under different titles.

For ease of identification and to avoid confusion, we suggest that readers looking for a title should do so by CW number. Because the work of creating the Collected Works of Rudolf Steiner is an ongoing process, with new titles being published every year, we have not indicated in this listing which books are presently available. To find out what titles in the Collected Works are currently in print, please check our website at www.steinerbooks.org, or write to SteinerBooks 610 Main Street, Great Barrington, MA 01230

Written Work

CW 1	Goethe: Natural-Scientific Writings, Introduction, with Footnotes and Explanations in the text by Rudolf Steiner
CW 2	Outlines of an Epistemology of the Goethean World View, with Special Consideration of Schiller
CW 3	Truth and Science
CW 4	The Philosophy of Freedom
CW 4a	Documents to "The Philosophy of Freedom"
CW 5	Friedrich Nietzsche, A Fighter against His Own Time
CW 6	Goethe's Worldview
CW 6a	Now in CW 30
CW 7	Mysticism at the Dawn of Modern Spiritual Life and Its Relationship with Modern Worldviews
CW 8	Christianity as Mystical Fact and the Mysteries of Antiquity
CW 9	Theosophy: An Introduction into Supersensible World Knowledge and Human Purpose
CW 10	How Does One Attain Knowledge of Higher Worlds?
CW 11	From the Akasha-Chronicle
CW 12	Levels of Higher Knowledge
CW 13	Occult Science in Outline
CW 14	Four Mystery Dramas
CW 15	The Spiritual Guidance of the Individual and Humanity

Public Lectures

CW 275   Art in the Light of Mystery-Wisdom

CW 276   The Artistic in Its Mission in the World. The Genius of Language. The World of Self-Revealing Radiant Appearances – Anthroposophy and Art. Anthroposophy and Poetry

CW 277   Eurythmy. The Revelation of the Speaking Soul

CW 277a   The Origin and Development of Eurythmy

CW 278   Eurythmy as Visible Song

CW 279   Eurythmy as Visible Speech

CW 280   The Method and Nature of Speech Formation

CW 281   The Art of Recitation and Declamation

CW 282   Speech Formation and Dramatic Art

CW 283   The Nature of Things Musical and the Experience of Tone in the Human Being

CW 284/285   Images of Occult Seals and Pillars. The Munich Congress of Whitsun 1907 and Its Consequences

CW 286   Paths to a New Style of Architecture. "And the Building Becomes Human"

CW 287   The Building at Dornach as a Symbol of Historical Becoming and an Artistic Transformation Impulse

CW 288   Style-Forms in the Living Organic

CW 289   The Building-Idea of the Goetheanum: Lectures with Slides from the Years 1920-1921

CW 290   The Building-Idea of the Goetheanum: Lectures with Slides from the Years 1920-1921

CW 291   The Nature of Colors

CW 291a   Knowledge of Colors. Supplementary Volume to "The Nature of Colors"

CW 292   Art History as Image of Inner Spiritual Impulses

CW 293   General Knowledge of the Human Being as the Foundation of Pedagogy

CW 294   The Art of Education, Methodology and Didactics

CW 295   The Art of Education: Seminar Discussions and Lectures on Lesson Planning

CW 296   The Question of Education as a Social Question

CW 297   The Idea and Practice of the Waldorf School

CW 297a   Education for Life: Self-Education and the Practice of Pedagogy

CW 298   Rudolf Steiner in the Waldorf School

CW 299   Spiritual-Scientific Observations on Speech

CW 300a   Conferences with the Teachers of the Free Waldorf School in Stuttgart, 1919 to 1924, in 3 Volumes, Vol. 1

CW 300b   Conferences with the Teachers of the Free Waldorf School in Stuttgart, 1919 to 1924, in 3 Volumes, Vol. 2

CW 300c   Conferences with the Teachers of the Free Waldorf School in Stuttgart, 1919 to 1924, in 3 Volumes, Vol. 3
CW 301   The Renewal of Pedagogical-Didactical Art through Spiritual Science
CW 302   Knowledge of the Human Being and the Forming of Class Lessons
CW 302a   Education and Teaching from a Knowledge of the Human Being
CW 303   The Healthy Development of the Human Being
CW 304   Methods of Education and Teaching Based on Anthroposophy
CW 304a   Anthroposophical Knowledge of the Human Being and Pedagogy
CW 305   The Soul-Spiritual Foundational Forces of the Art of Education. Spiritual Values in Education and Social Life
CW 306   Pedagogical Praxis from the Viewpoint of a Spiritual-Scientific Knowledge of the Human Being. The Education of the Child and Young Human Beings
CW 307   The Spiritual Life of the Present and Education
CW 308   The Method of Teaching and the Life-Requirements for Teaching
CW 309   Anthroposophical Pedagogy and Its Prerequisites
CW 310   The Pedagogical Value of a Knowledge of the Human Being and the Cultural Value of Pedagogy
CW 311   The Art of Education from an Understanding of the Being of Humanity
CW 312   Spiritual Science and Medicine
CW 313   Spiritual-Scientific Viewpoints on Therapy
CW 314   Physiology and Therapy Based on Spiritual Science
CW 315   Curative Eurythmy
CW 316   Meditative Observations and Instructions for a Deepening of the Art of Healing
CW 317   The Curative Education Course
CW 318   The Working Together of Doctors and Pastors
CW 319   Anthroposophical Knowledge of the Human Being and Medicine
CW 320   Spiritual-Scientific Impulses for the Development of Physics 1: The First Natural-Scientific Course: Light, Color, Tone, Mass, Electricity, Magnetism
CW 321   Spiritual-Scientific Impulses for the Development of Physics 2: The Second Natural-Scientific Course: Warmth at the Border of Positive and Negative Materiality
CW 322   The Borders of the Knowledge of Nature
CW 323   The Relationship of the various Natural-Scientific Fields to Astronomy
CW 324   Nature Observation, Mathematics, and Scientific Experimentation and Results from the Viewpoint of Anthroposophy
CW 324a   The Fourth Dimension in Mathematics and Reality
CW 325   Natural Science and the World-Historical Development of Humanity since Ancient Times

SIGNIFICANT EVENTS
IN THE LIFE OF RUDOLF STEINER

1829: June 23: birth of Johann Steiner (1829-1910)—Rudolf Steiner's father—in Geras, Lower Austria.

1834: May 8: birth of Franciska Blie (1834-1918)—Rudolf Steiner's mother—in Horn, Lower Austria. "My father and mother were both children of the glorious Lower Austrian forest district north of the Danube."

1860: May 16: marriage of Johann Steiner and Franciska Blie.

1861: February 25: birth of *Rudolf Joseph Lorenz Steiner* in Kraljevec, Croatia, near the border with Hungary, where Johann Steiner works as a telegrapher for the South Austria Railroad. Rudolf Steiner is baptized two days later, February 27, the date usually given as his birthday.

1862: Summer: the family moves to Mödling, Lower Austria.

1863: The family moves to Pottschach, Lower Austria, near the Styrian border, where Johann Steiner becomes stationmaster. "The view stretched to the mountains...majestic peaks in the distance and the sweet charm of nature in the immediate surroundings."

1864: November 15: birth of Rudolf Steiner's sister, Leopoldine (d. November 1, 1927). She will become a seamstress and live with her parents for the rest of her life.

1866: July 28: birth of Rudolf Steiner's deaf-mute brother, Gustav (d. May 1, 1941).

1867: Rudolf Steiner enters the village school. Following a disagreement between his father and the schoolmaster, whose wife falsely accused the boy of causing a commotion, Rudolf Steiner is taken out of school and taught at home.

1868: A critical experience. Unknown to the family, an aunt dies in a distant town. Sitting in the station waiting room, Rudolf Steiner sees her "form," which speaks to him, asking for help. "Beginning with this experience, a new soul life began in the boy, one in which not only the outer trees and mountains spoke to him, but also the worlds that lay behind them. From this moment on, the boy began to live with the spirits of nature...."

1869: The family moves to the peaceful, rural village of Neudörfl, near Wiener-Neustadt in present-day Austria. Rudolf Steiner attends the village school. Because of the "unorthodoxy" of his writing and spelling, he has to do "extra lessons."

1870: Through a book lent to him by his tutor, he discovers geometry: "To grasp something purely in the spirit brought me inner happiness. I know that I first learned happiness through geometry." The same tutor allows him to draw, while other students still struggle with their reading and writing. "An artistic element" thus enters his education.

1871: Though his parents are not religious, Rudolf Steiner becomes a "church child," a favorite of the priest, who was "an exceptional character." "Up to the age of ten or eleven, among those I came to know, he was far and away the most significant." Among other things, he introduces Steiner to Copernican, heliocentric cosmology. As an altar boy, Rudolf Steiner serves at Masses, funerals, and Corpus Christi processions. At year's end, after an incident in which he escapes a thrashing, his father forbids him to go to church.

1872: Rudolf Steiner transfers to grammar school in Wiener-Neustadt, a five-mile walk from home, which must be done in all weathers.

1873-75: Through his teachers and on his own, Rudolf Steiner has many wonderful experiences with science and mathematics. Outside school, he teaches himself analytic geometry, trigonometry, differential equations, and calculus.

1876: Rudolf Steiner begins tutoring other students. He learns bookbinding from his father. He also teaches himself stenography.

1877: Rudolf Steiner discovers Kant's *Critique of Pure Reason*, which he reads and rereads. He also discovers and reads von Rotteck's *World History*.

1878: He studies extensively in contemporary psychology and philosophy.

1879: Rudolf Steiner graduates from high school with honors. His father is transferred to Inzersdorf, near Vienna. He uses his first visit to Vienna "to purchase a great number of philosophy books"—Kant, Fichte, Schelling, and Hegel, as well as numerous histories of philosophy. His aim: to find a path from the "I" to nature.

October 1879-1883: Rudolf Steiner attends the Technical College in Vienna—to study mathematics, chemistry, physics, mineralogy, botany, zoology, biology, geology, and mechanics—with a scholarship. He also attends lectures in history and literature, while avidly reading philosophy on his own. His two favorite professors are Karl Julius Schröer (German language and literature) and Edmund Reitlinger (physics). He also audits lectures by Robert Zimmerman on aesthetics and Franz Brentano on philosophy. During this year he begins his friendship with Moritz Zitter (1861-1921), who will help support him financially when he is in Berlin.

1880: Rudolf Steiner attends lectures on Schiller and Goethe by Karl Julius Schröer, who becomes his mentor. Also "through a remarkable combination of circumstances," he meets Felix Koguzki, a "herb gatherer" and healer, who could "see deeply into the secrets of nature." Rudolf Steiner will meet and study with this "emissary of the Master" throughout his time in Vienna.

1881: January: "... I didn't sleep a wink. I was busy with philosophical problems until about 12:30 a.m. Then, finally, I threw myself down on my couch. All my striving during the previous year had been to research whether the following statement by Schelling was true or not: *Within everyone dwells a secret, marvelous capacity to draw back from the stream of time—out of the self clothed in all that comes to us from outside—into our innermost being and there, in the immutable form of the Eternal, to look into ourselves.* I believe, and I am still quite certain of it, that I discovered this capacity in myself; I had long had an inkling of it. Now the whole of idealist philosophy stood before me in modified form. What's a sleepless night compared to that!"

Rudolf Steiner begins communicating with leading thinkers of the day, who send him books in return, which he reads eagerly.

July: "I am not one of those who dives into the day like an animal in human form. I pursue a quite specific goal, an idealistic aim—knowledge of the truth! This cannot be done offhandedly. It requires the greatest striving in the world, free of all egotism, and equally of all resignation."

August: Steiner puts down on paper for the first time thoughts for a "Philosophy of Freedom." "The striving for the absolute: this human yearning is freedom." He also seeks to outline a "peasant philosophy," describing what the worldview of a "peasant"—one who lives close to the earth and the old ways—really is.

1881-1882: Felix Koguzki, the herb gatherer, reveals himself to be the envoy of another, higher initiatory personality, who instructs Rudolf Steiner to penetrate Fichte's philosophy and to master modern scientific thinking as a preparation for right entry into the spirit. This "Master" also teaches him the double (evolutionary and involutionary) nature of time.

1882: Through the offices of Karl Julius Schröer, Rudolf Steiner is asked by Joseph Kurschner to edit Goethe's scientific works for the *Deutschen National-Literatur* edition. He writes "A Possible Critique of Atomistic Concepts" and sends it to Friedrich Theodore Vischer.

1883: Rudolf Steiner completes his college studies and begins work on the Goethe project.

1884: First volume of Goethe's *Scientific Writings* (CW 1) appears (March). He lectures on Goethe and Lessing, and Goethe's approach to science. In July, he enters the household of Ladislaus and Pauline Specht as tutor to the four Specht boys. He will live there until 1890. At this time, he meets Josef Breuer (1842-1925), the coauthor with Sigmund Freud of *Studies in Hysteria*, who is the Specht family doctor.

1885: While continuing to edit Goethe's writings, Rudolf Steiner reads deeply in contemporary philosophy (Edouard von Hartmann, Johannes Volkelt, and Richard Wahle, among others).

1886: May: Rudolf Steiner sends Kurschner the manuscript of *Outlines of Goethe's Theory of Knowledge* (CW 2), which appears in October, and which he sends out widely. He also meets the poet Marie Eugenie Delle Grazie and writes "Nature and Our Ideals" for her. He attends her salon, where he meets many priests, theologians, and philosophers, who will become his friends. Meanwhile, the director of the Goethe Archive in Weimar requests his collaboration with the *Sophien* edition of Goethe's works, particularly the writings on color.

1887: At the beginning of the year, Rudolf Steiner is very sick. As the year progresses and his health improves, he becomes increasingly "a man of letters," lecturing, writing essays, and taking part in Austrian cultural life. In August-September, the second volume of Goethe's *Scientific Writings* appears.

1888: January-July: Rudolf Steiner assumes editorship of the "German Weekly" (*Deutsche Wochenschrift*). He begins lecturing more intensively, giving, for example, a lecture titled "Goethe as Father of a New Aesthetics." He meets and becomes soul friends with Friedrich Eckstein (1861-1939), a vegetarian, philosopher of symbolism, alchemist, and musician, who will introduce him to various spiritual currents (including Theosophy) and with whom he will meditate and interpret esoteric and alchemical texts.

1889: Rudolf Steiner first reads Nietzsche (*Beyond Good and Evil*). He encounters Theosophy again and learns of Madame Blavatsky in the Theosophical circle around Marie Lang (1858-1934). Here he also meets well-known figures of Austrian life, as well as esoteric figures like the occultist Franz Hartman and Karl Leinigen-Billigen (translator of C.G. Harrison's *The Transcendental Universe*.) During this period, Steiner first reads A.P. Sinnett's *Esoteric Buddhism* and Mabel Collins's *Light on the Path*. He also begins traveling, visiting Budapest, Weimar, and Berlin (where he meets philosopher Edouard von Hartmann).

1890: Rudolf Steiner finishes volume 3 of Goethe's scientific writings. He begins his doctoral dissertation, which will become *Truth and Science* (CW 3). He also meets the poet and feminist Rosa Mayreder (1858-1938), with whom he can exchange his most intimate thoughts. In September, Rudolf Steiner moves to Weimar to work in the Goethe-Schiller Archive.

1891: Volume 3 of the Kurschner edition of Goethe appears. Meanwhile, Rudolf Steiner edits Goethe's studies in mineralogy and scientific writings for the *Sophien* edition. He meets Ludwig Laistner of the Cotta Publishing Company, who asks for a book on the basic question of metaphysics. From this will result, ultimately, *The Philosophy of Freedom* (CW 4), which will be published not by Cotta but by Emil Felber. In October, Rudolf Steiner takes the oral exam for a doctorate in philosophy, mathematics, and mechanics at Rostock University, receiving his doctorate on the twenty-sixth. In November, he gives his first lecture on Goethe's "Fairy Tale" in Vienna.

1892: Rudolf Steiner continues work at the Goethe-Schiller Archive and on his *Philosophy of Freedom*. *Truth and Science*, his doctoral dissertation, is published. Steiner undertakes to write introductions to books on Schopenhauer and Jean Paul for Cotta. At year's end, he finds lodging with Anna Eunike, née Schulz (1853-1911), a widow with four daughters and a son. He also develops a friendship with Otto Erich Hartleben (1864-1905) with whom he shares literary interests.

1893: Rudolf Steiner begins his habit of producing many reviews and articles. In March, he gives a lecture titled "Hypnotism, with Reference to Spiritism." In September, volume 4 of the Kurschner edition is completed. In November, *The Philosophy of Freedom* appears. This year, too, he meets John Henry Mackay (1864-1933), the anarchist, and Max Stirner, a scholar and biographer.

1894: Rudolf Steiner meets Elisabeth Förster Nietzsche, the philosopher's sister, and begins to read Nietzsche in earnest, beginning with the as yet unpublished *Antichrist*. He also meets Ernst Haeckel (1834-1919). In the fall, he begins to write *Nietzsche, A Fighter against His Time* (CW 5).

1895: May, *Nietzsche, A Fighter against His Time* appears.

1896: January 22: Rudolf Steiner sees Friedrich Nietzsche for the first and only time. Moves between the Nietzsche and the Goethe-Schiller Archives, where he completes his work before year's end. He falls out with Elisabeth Förster Nietzsche, thus ending his association with the Nietzsche Archive.

1897: Rudolf Steiner finishes the manuscript of *Goethe's Worldview* (CW 6). He moves to Berlin with Anna Eunike and begins editorship of the *Magazin für Literatur*. From now on, Steiner will write countless reviews, literary and philosophical articles, and so on. He begins lecturing at the "Free Literary Society." In September, he attends the Zionist Congress in Basel. He sides with Dreyfus in the Dreyfus affair.

1898: Rudolf Steiner is very active as an editor in the political, artistic, and theatrical life of Berlin. He becomes friendly with John Henry Mackay and poet Ludwig Jacobowski (1868-1900). He joins Jacobowski's circle of writers, artists, and scientists—"The Coming Ones" (*Die Kommenden*)—and contributes lectures to the group until 1903. He also lectures at the "League for College Pedagogy." He writes an article for Goethe's sesquicentennial, "Goethe's Secret Revelation," on the "Fairy Tale of the Green Snake and the Beautiful Lily."

1898-99: "This was a trying time for my soul as I looked at Christianity.... I was able to progress only by contemplating, by means of spiritual perception, the evolution of Christianity .... Conscious knowledge of real Christianity began to dawn in me around the turn of the century. This seed continued to develop. My soul trial occurred shortly before the beginning of the twentieth century. It was decisive for my soul's development that I stood spiritually before the Mystery of Golgotha in a deep and solemn celebration of knowledge."

1899: Rudolf Steiner begins teaching and giving lectures and lecture cycles at the Workers' College, founded by Wilhelm Liebknecht (1826-1900). He will continue to do so until 1904. Writes: *Literature and Spiritual Life in the Nineteenth Century; Individualism in Philosophy; Haeckel and His Opponents; Poetry in the Present;* and begins what will become (fifteen years later) *The Riddles of Philosophy* (CW 18). He also meets many artists and writers, including Käthe Kollwitz, Stefan Zweig, and Rainer Maria Rilke. On October 31, he marries Anna Eunike.

1900: "I thought that the turn of the century must bring humanity a new light. It seemed to me that the separation of human thinking and willing from the spirit had peaked. A turn or reversal of direction in human evolution seemed to me a necessity." Rudolf Steiner finishes *World and Life Views in the Nineteenth Century* (the second part of what will become *The Riddles of Philosophy*) and dedicates it to Ernst Haeckel. It is published in March. He continues lecturing at *Die Kommenden*, whose leadership he assumes after the death of Jacobowski. Also, he gives the Gutenberg Jubilee lecture before 7,000 typesetters and printers. In September, Rudolf Steiner is invited by Count and Countess Brockdorff to lecture in the Theosophical Library. His first lecture is on Nietzsche. His second lecture is titled "Goethe's Secret Revelation." October 6, he begins a lecture cycle on the mystics that will become *Mystics after Modernism* (CW 7). November-December: "Marie von Sivers appears in the audience...." Also in November, Steiner gives his first lecture at the Giordano Bruno Bund (where he will continue to lecture until May, 1905). He speaks on Bruno and modern Rome, focusing on the importance of the philosophy of Thomas Aquinas as monism.

1901: In continual financial straits, Rudolf Steiner's early friends Moritz Zitter and Rosa Mayreder help support him. In October, he begins the lecture cycle *Christianity as Mystical Fact* (CW 8) at the Theosophical Library. In November, he gives his first "Theosophical lecture" on Goethe's "Fairy Tale" in Hamburg at the invitation of Wilhelm Hubbe-Schleiden. He also attends a gathering to celebrate the founding of the Theosophical Society at Count and Countess Brockdorff's. He gives a lecture cycle, "From Buddha to Christ," for the circle of the *Kommenden*. November 17, Marie von Sivers asks Rudolf Steiner if Theosophy needs a Western-Christian spiritual movement (to complement Theosophy's Eastern emphasis). "The question was posed. Now, following spiritual laws, I could begin to give an answer...." In December, Rudolf Steiner writes his first article for a Theosophical publication. At year's end, the Brockdorffs and possibly Wilhelm Hubbe-Schleiden ask Rudolf Steiner to join the Theosophical Society and undertake the leadership of the German section. Rudolf Steiner agrees, on the condition that Marie von Sivers (then in Italy) work with him.

1902: Beginning in January, Rudolf Steiner attends the opening of the Workers' School in Spandau with Rosa Luxemberg (1870-1919). January 17, Rudolf Steiner joins the Theosophical Society. In April, he is asked to become general secretary of the German Section of the Theosophical Society, and works on preparations for its founding. In July, he visits London for a Theosophical congress. He meets Bertram Keightly, G.R.S. Mead, A.P. Sinnett, and Annie Besant, among others. In September, *Christianity as Mystical Fact* appears. In October, Rudolf Steiner gives his first public lecture on Theosophy ("Monism and Theosophy") to about three hundred people at the Giordano Bruno Bund. On October 19-21, the German Section of the Theosophical Society has its first meeting; Rudolf Steiner is the general secretary, and Annie Besant attends. Steiner lectures on practical karma studies. On October 23, Annie Besant inducts Rudolf Steiner into the Esoteric School of the Theosophical Society. On October 25, Steiner begins a weekly series of lectures: "The Field of Theosophy." During this year, Rudolf Steiner also first meets Ita Wegman (1876-1943), who will become his close collaborator in his final years.

1903: Rudolf Steiner holds about 300 lectures and seminars. In May, the first issue of the periodical *Luzifer* appears. In June, Rudolf Steiner visits London for the first meeting of the Federation of the European Sections of the Theosophical Society, where he meets Colonel Olcott. He begins to write *Theosophy* (CW 9).

1904: Rudolf Steiner continues lecturing at the Workers' College and elsewhere (about 90 lectures), while lecturing intensively all over Germany among Theosophists (about a 140 lectures). In February, he meets Carl Unger (1878-1929), who will become a member of the board of the Anthroposophical Society (1913). In March, he meets Michael Bauer (1871-1929), a Christian mystic, who will also be on the board. In May, *Theosophy* appears, with the dedication: "To the spirit of Giordano Bruno." Rudolf Steiner and Marie von Sivers visit London for meetings with Annie Besant. June: Rudolf Steiner and Marie von Sivers attend the meeting of the Federation of European Sections of the Theosophical Society in Amsterdam. In July, Steiner begins the articles in *Luzifer-Gnosis* that will become *How to Know Higher Worlds* (CW 10) and *Cosmic Memory* (CW 11). In September, Annie Besant visits Germany. In December, Steiner lectures on Freemasonry. He mentions the High Grade Masonry derived from John Yarker and represented by Theodore Reuss and Karl Kellner as a blank slate "into which a good image could be placed."

1905: This year, Steiner ends his non-Theosophical lecturing activity. Supported by Marie von Sivers, his Theosophical lecturing—both in public and in the Theosophical Society—increases significantly: "The German Theosophical Movement is of exceptional importance." Steiner recommends reading, among others, Fichte, Jacob Boehme, and Angelus Silesius. He begins to introduce Christian themes into Theosophy. He also begins to work with doctors (Felix Peipers and Ludwig Noll). In July, he is in London for the Federation of European Sections, where he attends a lecture by Annie Besant: "I have seldom seen Mrs. Besant speak in so inward and heartfelt a manner...." "Through Mrs. Besant I have found the way to H.P. Blavatsky." September to October, he gives a course of thirty-one lectures for a small group of esoteric students. In October, the annual meeting of the German Section of the Theosophical Society, which still remains very small, takes place. Rudolf Steiner reports membership has risen from 121 to 377 members. In November, seeking to establish esoteric "continuity," Rudolf Steiner and Marie von Sivers participate in a "Memphis-Misraim" Masonic ceremony. They pay forty-five marks for membership. "Yesterday, you saw how little remains of former esoteric institutions." "We are dealing only with a 'framework'... for the present, nothing lies behind it. The occult powers have completely withdrawn."

1906: Expansion of Theosophical work. Rudolf Steiner gives about 245 lectures, only 44 of which take place in Berlin. Cycles are given in Paris, Leipzig,

Stuttgart, and Munich. Esoteric work also intensifies. Rudolf Steiner begins writing *An Outline of Esoteric Science* (CW 13). In January, Rudolf Steiner receives permission (a patent) from the Great Orient of the Scottish A & A Thirty-Three Degree Rite of the Order of the Ancient Freemasons of the Memphis-Misraim Rite to direct a chapter under the name "Mystica Aeterna." This will become the "Cognitive-Ritual Section" (also called "Misraim Service") of the Esoteric School. (See: *Freemasonry and Ritual Work: The Misraim Service* (CW 265). During this time, Steiner also meets Albert Schweitzer. In May, he is in Paris, where he visits Edouard Schuré. Many Russians attend his lectures (including Konstantin Balmont, Dimitri Mereszkovski, Zinaida Hippius, and Maximilian Woloshin). He attends the General Meeting of the European Federation of the Theosophical Society, at which Col. Olcott is present for the last time. He spends the year's end in Venice and Rome, where he writes and works on his translation of H.P. Blavatsky's *Key to Theosophy*.

1907: Further expansion of the German Theosophical Movement according to the Rosicrucian directive to "introduce spirit into the world"—in education, in social questions, in art, and in science. In February, Col. Olcott dies in Adyar. Before he dies, Olcott indicates that "the Masters" wish Annie Besant to succeed him: much politicking ensues. Rudolf Steiner supports Besant's candidacy. April-May: preparations for the Congress of the Federation of European Sections of the Theosophical Society—the great, watershed Whitsun "Munich Congress," attended by Annie Besant and others. Steiner decides to separate Eastern and Western (Christian-Rosicrucian) esoteric schools. He takes his esoteric school out of the Theosophical Society (Besant and Rudolf Steiner are "in harmony" on this). Steiner makes his first lecture tours to Austria and Hungary. That summer, he is in Italy. In September, he visits Edouard Schuré, who will write the introduction to the French edition of *Christianity as Mystical Fact* in Barr, Alsace. Rudolf Steiner writes the autobiographical statement known as the "Barr Document." In *Luzifer–Gnosis*, "The Education of the Child" appears.

1908: The movement grows (membership: 1,150). Lecturing expands. Steiner makes his first extended lecture tour to Holland and Scandinavia, as well as visits to Naples and Sicily. Themes: St. John's Gospel, the Apocalypse, Egypt, science, philosophy, and logic. *Luzifer-Gnosis* ceases publication. In Berlin, Marie von Sivers (with Johanna Mücke (1864-1949) forms the *Philosophisch-Theosophisch* (after 1915 *Philosophisch-Anthroposophisch*) *Verlag* to publish Steiner's work. Steiner gives lecture cycles titled *The Gospel of St. John* (CW 103) and *The Apocalypse* (104).

1909: *An Outline of Esoteric Science* appears. Lecturing and travel continues. Rudolf Steiner's spiritual research expands to include the polarity of Lucifer and Ahriman; the work of great individualities in history; the Maitreya Buddha and the Bodhisattvas; spiritual economy (CW 109); the work of the spiritual hierarchies in heaven and on earth (CW 110). He also deepens and intensifies his research into the Gospels, giving lectures on the Gospel of St. Luke (CW 114) with the first mention of two Jesus children. Meets and becomes friends with Christian Morgenstern (1871-1914). In April, he lays the foundation stone for the Malsch model—the building that will lead to the first Goetheanum. In May, the International Congress of the Federation of European Sections of the Theosophical Society takes place in Budapest. Rudolf Steiner receives the Subba Row medal for *How to Know Higher Worlds*. During this time, Charles W. Leadbeater discovers Jiddu Krishnamurti (1895-1986) and proclaims him the future "world teacher," the bearer of the Maitreya Buddha and the "reappearing Christ." In October, Steiner delivers seminal lectures on "anthroposophy," which he will try, unsuccessfully, to rework over the next years into the unfinished work, *Anthroposophy (A Fragment)* (CW 45).

1910: New themes: *The Reappearance of Christ in the Etheric* (CW 118); *The Fifth Gospel; The Mission of Folk Souls* (CW 121); *Occult History* (CW 126); the evolving development of etheric cognitive capacities. Rudolf Steiner continues his Gospel research with *The Gospel of St. Matthew* (CW 123). In January, his father dies. In April, he takes a month-long trip to Italy, including Rome, Monte Cassino, and Sicily. He also visits Scandinavia again. July-August, he writes the first mystery drama, *The Portal of Initiation* (CW 14). In November, he gives "psychosophy" lectures. In December, he submits "On the Psychological Foundations and Epistemological Framework of Theosophy" to the International Philosophical Congress in Bologna.

1911: The crisis in the Theosophical Society deepens. In January, "The Order of the Rising Sun," which will soon become "The Order of the Star in the East," is founded for the coming world teacher, Krishnamurti. At the same time, Marie von Sivers, Rudolf Steiner's coworker, falls ill. Fewer lectures are given, but important new ground is broken. In Prague, in March, Steiner meets Franz Kafka (1883-1924) and Hugo Bergmann (1883-1975). In April, he delivers his paper to the Philosophical Congress. He writes the second mystery drama, *The Soul's Probation* (CW 14). Also, while Marie von Sivers is convalescing, Rudolf Steiner begins work on *Calendar 1912/1913*, which will contain the "Calendar of the Soul" meditations. On March 19, Anna (Eunike) Steiner dies. In September, Rudolf Steiner visits Einsiedeln, birthplace of Paracelsus. In December, Friedrich Rittelmeyer, future founder of the Christian Community, meets Rudolf Steiner. The *Johannes-Bauverein*, the "building committee," which would lead to the first Goetheanum (first planned for Munich), is also founded, and a preliminary committee for the founding of an independent association is created that, in the following year, will become the Anthroposophical Society. Important lecture cycles include *Occult Physiology* (CW 128); *Wonders of the World* (CW 129); *From Jesus to Christ* (CW 131). Other themes: esoteric Christianity;

Christian Rosenkreutz; the spiritual guidance of humanity; the sense world and the world of the spirit.

1912: Despite the ongoing, now increasing crisis in the Theosophical Society, much is accomplished: *Calendar 1912/1913* is published; eurythmy is created; both the third mystery drama, *The Guardian of the Threshold* (CW 14) and *A Way of Self-Knowledge* (CW 16) are written. New (or renewed) themes included life between death and rebirth and karma and reincarnation. Other lecture cycles: *Spiritual Beings in the Heavenly Bodies and in the Kingdoms of Nature* (CW 136); *The Human Being in the Light of Occultism, Theosophy, and Philosophy* (CW 137); *The Gospel of St. Mark* (CW 139); and *The Bhagavad Gita and the Epistles of Paul* (CW 142). On May 8, Rudolf Steiner celebrates White Lotus Day, H.P. Blavatsky's death day, which he had faithfully observed for the past decade, for the last time. In August, Rudolf Steiner suggests the "independent association" be called the "Anthroposophical Society." In September, the first eurythmy course takes place. In October, Rudolf Steiner declines recognition of a Theosophical Society lodge dedicated to the Star of the East and decides to expel all Theosophical Society members belonging to the order. Also, with Marie von Sivers, he first visits Dornach, near Basel, Switzerland, and they stand on the hill where the Goetheanum will be built. In November, a Theosophical Society lodge is opened by direct mandate from Adyar (Annie Besant). In December, a meeting of the German section occurs at which it is decided that belonging to the Order of the Star of the East is incompatible with membership in the Theosophical Society. December 28: informal founding of the Anthroposophical Society in Berlin.

1913: Expulsion of the German section from the Theosophical Society. February 2-3: Foundation meeting of the Anthroposophical Society. Board members include: Marie von Sivers, Michael Bauer, and Carl Unger. September 20: Laying of the foundation stone for the *Johannes Bau* (Goetheanum) in Dornach. Building begins immediately. The third mystery drama, *The Soul's Awakening* (CW 14), is completed. Also: *The Threshold of the Spiritual World* (CW 147). Lecture cycles include: *The Bhagavad Gita and the Epistles of Paul* and *The Esoteric Meaning of the Bhagavad Gita* (CW 146), which the Russian philosopher Nikolai Berdyaev attends; *The Mysteries of the East and of Christianity* (CW 144); *The Effects of Esoteric Development* (CW 145); and *The Fifth Gospel* (CW 148). In May, Rudolf Steiner is in London and Paris, where anthroposophical work continues.

1914: Building continues on the *Johannes Bau* (Goetheanum) in Dornach, with artists and coworkers from seventeen nations. The general assembly of the Anthroposophical Society takes place. In May, Rudolf Steiner visits Paris, as well as Chartres Cathedral. June 28: assassination in Sarajevo ("Now the catastrophe has happened!"). August 1: War is declared. Rudolf Steiner returns to Germany from Dornach—he will travel back and forth. He writes the last chapter of *The Riddles of Philosophy*. Lecture cycles include: *Human and Cosmic Thought* (CW 151); *Inner Being of Humanity between Death and a New Birth* (CW 153); *Occult Reading and Occult Hearing* (CW 156). December 24: marriage of Rudolf Steiner and Marie von Sivers.

1915: Building continues. Life after death becomes a major theme, also art. Writes: *Thoughts during a Time of War* (CW 24). Lectures include: *The Secret of Death* (CW 159); *The Uniting of Humanity through the Christ Impulse* (CW 165).

1916: Rudolf Steiner begins work with Edith Maryon (1872-1924) on the sculpture "The Representative of Humanity" ("The Group"—Christ, Lucifer, and Ahriman). He also works with the alchemist Alexander von Bernus on the quarterly *Das Reich*. He writes *The Riddle of Humanity* (CW 20). Lectures include: *Necessity and Freedom in World History and Human Action* (CW 166); *Past and Present in the Human Spirit* (CW 167); *The Karma of Vocation* (CW 172); *The Karma of Untruthfulness* (CW 173).

1917: Russian Revolution. The U.S. enters the war. Building continues. Rudolf Steiner delineates the idea of the "threefold nature of the human being" (in a public lecture March 15) and the "threefold nature of the social organism" (hammered out in May-June with the help of Otto von Lerchenfeld and Ludwig Polzer-Hoditz in the form of two documents titled *Memoranda*, which were distributed in high places). August-September: Rudolf Steiner writes *The Riddles of the Soul* (CW 20). Also: commentary on "The Chemical Wedding of Christian Rosenkreutz" for Alexander Bernus (*Das Reich*). Lectures include: *The Karma of Materialism* (CW 176); *The Spiritual Background of the Outer World: The Fall of the Spirits of Darkness* (CW 177).

1918: March 18: peace treaty of Brest-Litovsk—"Now everything will truly enter chaos! What is needed is cultural renewal." June: Rudolf Steiner visits Karlstein (Grail) Castle outside Prague. Lecture cycle: *From Symptom to Reality in Modern History* (CW 185). In mid-November, Emil Molt, of the Waldorf-Astoria Cigarette Company, has the idea of founding a school for his workers' children.

1919: Focus on the threefold social organism: tireless travel, countless lectures, meetings, and publications. At the same time, a new public stage of Anthroposophy emerges as cultural renewal begins. The coming years will see initiatives in pedagogy, medicine, pharmacology, and agriculture. January 27: threefold meeting: " We must first of all, with the money we have, found free schools that can bring people what they need." February: first public eurythmy performance in Zurich. Also: "Appeal to the German People" (CW 24), circulated March 6 as a newspaper insert. In April, *Towards Social Renewal* (CW 23) appears—"perhaps the most widely read of all books on politics appearing since the war." Rudolf Steiner is asked to undertake the "direction and leadership" of the school founded by the Waldorf-Astoria Company. Rudolf Steiner begins to talk about the "renewal" of education. May 30: a building is selected and purchased for the future Waldorf School. August-September, Rudolf Steiner gives a lecture course for Waldorf teachers, *The Foundations of Human Experience (Study of Man)* (CW 293). September 7: Opening of the first Waldorf School. December (into January): first science course, the *Light Course* (CW 320).

1920: The Waldorf School flourishes. New threefold initiatives. Founding of limited companies *Der Kommende Tag* and *Futurum A.G.* to infuse spiritual values into the economic realm. Rudolf Steiner also focuses on the sciences. Lectures: *Introducing Anthroposophical Medicine* (CW 312); *The Warmth Course* (CW 321); *The Boundaries of Natural Science* (CW 322); *The Redemption of Thinking* (CW 74). February: Johannes Werner Klein—later a cofounder of the Christian Community—asks Rudolf Steiner about the possibility of a "religious renewal," a "Johannine church." In March, Rudolf Steiner gives the first course for doctors and medical students. In April, a divinity student asks Rudolf Steiner a second time about the possibility of religious renewal. September 27-October 16: anthroposophical "university course." December: lectures titled *The Search for the New Isis* (CW 202).

1921: Rudolf Steiner continues his intensive work on cultural renewal, including the uphill battle for the threefold social order. "University" arts, scientific, theological, and medical courses include: *The Astronomy Course* (CW 323); *Observation, Mathematics, and Scientific Experiment* (CW 324); the *Second Medical Course* (CW 313); *Color.* In June and September-October, Rudolf Steiner also gives the first two "priests' courses" (CW 342 and 343). The "youth movement" gains momentum. Magazines are founded: *Die Drei* (January), and—under the editorship of Albert Steffen (1884-1963)—the weekly, *Das Goetheanum* (August). In February-March, Rudolf Steiner takes his first trip outside Germany since the war (Holland). On April 7, Steiner receives a letter regarding "religious renewal," and May 22-23, he agrees to address the question in a practical way. In June, the Klinical-Therapeutic Institute opens in Arlesheim under the direction of Dr. Ita Wegman. In August, the Chemical-Pharmaceutical Laboratory opens in Arlesheim (Oskar Schmiedel and Ita Wegman are directors). The Clinical Therapeutic Institute is inaugurated in Stuttgart (Dr. Ludwig Noll is director); also the Research Laboratory in Dornach (Ehrenfried Pfeiffer and Gunther Wachsmuth are directors). In November-December, Rudolf Steiner visits Norway.

1922: The first half of the year involves very active public lecturing (thousands attend); in the second half, Rudolf Steiner begins to withdraw and turn toward the Society—"The Society is asleep." It is "too weak" to do what is asked of it. The businesses—*Der Kommende Tag* and *Futura A.G.*—fail. In January, with the help of an agent, Steiner undertakes a twelve-city German lecture tour, accompanied by eurythmy performances. In two weeks he speaks to more than 2,000 people. In April, he gives a "university course" in The Hague. He also visits England. In June, he is in Vienna for the East-West Congress. In August-September, he is back in England for the Oxford Conference on Education. Returning to Dornach, he gives the lectures *Philosophy, Cosmology, and Religion* (CW 215), and gives the third priests' course (CW 344). On September 16, The Christian Community is founded. In October-November, Steiner is in Holland and England. He also speaks to the youth: *The Youth Course* (CW 217). In December, Steiner gives lectures titled *The Origins of Natural Science* (CW 326), and *Humanity and the World of Stars: The Spiritual Communion of Humanity* (CW 219). December 31: Fire at the Goetheanum, which is destroyed.

1923: Despite the fire, Rudolf Steiner continues his work unabated. A very hard year. Internal dispersion, dissension, and apathy abound. There is conflict—between old and new visions—within the society. A wake-up call is needed, and Rudolf Steiner responds with renewed lecturing vitality. His focus: the spiritual context of human life; initiation science; the course of the year; and community building. As a foundation for an artistic school, he creates a series of pastel sketches. Lecture cycles: *The Anthroposophical Movement; Initiation Science* (CW 227) (in England at the Penmaenmawr Summer School); *The Four Seasons and the Archangels* (CW 229); *Harmony of the Creative Word* (CW 230); *The Supersensible Human* (CW 231), given in Holland for the founding of the Dutch society. On November 10, in response to the failed Hitler-Ludendorf putsch in Munich, Steiner closes his Berlin residence and moves the *Philosophisch-Anthroposophisch Verlag* (Press) to Dornach. On December 9, Steiner begins the serialization of his *Autobiography: The Course of My Life* (CW 28) in *Das Goetheanum*. It will continue to appear weekly, without a break, until his death. Late December-early January: Rudolf Steiner refounds the Anthroposophical Society (about 12,000 members internationally) and takes over its leadership. The new board members are: Marie Steiner, Ita Wegman, Albert Steffen, Elizabeth Vreede, and Guenther Wachsmuth. (See *The Christmas Meeting for the Founding of the General Anthroposophical Society* (CW 260). Accompanying lectures: *Mystery Knowledge and Mystery Centers* (CW 232); *World History in the Light of Anthroposophy* (CW 233). December 25: the Foundation Stone is laid (in the hearts of members) in the form of the "Foundation Stone Meditation."

1924: January 1: having founded the Anthroposophical Society and taken over its leadership, Rudolf Steiner has the task of "reforming" it. The process begins with a weekly newssheet ("What's Happening in the Anthroposophical Society") in which Rudolf Steiner's "Letters to Members" and "Anthroposophical Leading Thoughts" appear (CW 26). The next step is the creation of a new esoteric class, the "first class" of the "University of Spiritual Science" (which was to have been followed, had Rudolf Steiner lived longer, by two more advanced classes). Then comes a new language for Anthroposophy—practical, phenomenological, and direct; and Rudolf Steiner creates the model for the second Goetheanum. He begins the series of extensive "karma" lectures (CW 235-40); and finally, responding to needs, he creates two new initiatives: biodynamic agriculture and curative education. After the middle of the year, rumors begin to circulate regarding Steiner's health. Lectures: January-February, *Anthroposophy* (CW 234); February: *Tone Eurythmy* (CW 278); June: *The Agriculture Course* (CW 327); June-July: Speech [?] Eurythmy (CW 279); *Curative Education* (CW 317); August: (England, "Second International Summer School"), *Initiation Consciousness: True and False Paths in Spiritual Investigation* (CW 243); September: *Pastoral Medicine* (CW 318). On September 26, for the first time, Rudolf Steiner cancels a lecture. On September 28, he gives his last lecture. On September 29, he withdraws to his studio in the carpenter's shop; now he is definitively ill. Cared for by Ita Wegman, he continues working, however, and writing the weekly installments of his *Autobiography* and *Letters to the Members/ Leading Thoughts* (CW 26).

1925: Rudolf Steiner, while continuing to work, continues to weaken. He finishes *Extending Practical Medicine* (CW 27) with Ita Wegman. On March 30, around ten in the morning, Rudolf Steiner dies.

INDEX

Aeschylus, 68
Age of Electricity, 153
Agrippa von Nettesheim, 44, 155
Ahriman, 155-156, 160
ahrimanic, 156
Amshaspands, 137
  as ancient Persian archangels, 137
animal kingdom, 34-35, 44, 62, 96,
  110, 114, 118, 126-127, 135-136,
  139. *See also* birds, *and also* fish
animals, understanding of, 110, 114
anthropomorphism, 151
anthroposophic/anthroposophy, 9, 15-
  17, 20-23, 27, 36-38, 41, 43, 48, 52,
  56-57, 62, 66-67, 73-80, 93-94, 96-
  103, 106, 110, 112, 114, 116-117,
  119-121, 132-134, 143-146, 155,
  159-160
  as a "cosmic life-legacy," 23
  as a "cosmic life-potency and force," 23
anthroposophical movement, 16-18, 21,
  23, 37, 98, 105, 120, 132
Anthroposophical Society, 17, 21, 23,
  67, 77, 97-98, 101-103, 105-106,
  117, 119-121
Antichrist, 43
antipathies/antipathy, 101, 115
Aquinas, Thomas, 132, 136, 137
arrogance/arrogant, 115-117
art/artistic, 47, 71, 83, 85
Arthurian, 43
ascend/ascent, 112
astral, 60-61
  body, 25, 31-36, 50, 70, 72, 87-88,
  98, 101-102, 146
  forces, 61
astronomer/astronomy, 11, 37
atheism/atheistic, 139, 141-142
Atlantean, 4-5
Augustine (St.), 131
awakening, inner, 77, 105, 141, 143
  inner self-awakening, 142
awareness, 102

Bacon, Francis, 39-42, 45-48, 50-54,
  57, 62-63, 65, 67-68
Balaam, 64
balance, 85
  counter-balance, 30
banality, 41
beautiful/beauty, 80, 83-88, 98, 100-
  101, 129-130
Being of Knowledge, 117
Benedict, St., 69
Benedictine Order, 69
Beor, 64
Bible, 126
birds, 94-96, 100, 102-104, 113-114
blood, 24
  circulation, 68-69
Boehme, Jacob, 39-42, 45-52, 54-55,
  57-59, 62-63, 65, 67-68, 73
breathing, 20, 60, 104-105, 125, 151
  birds, 95
Bruno, Giordano, 39-42, 45-54, 57, 59,
  62-63, 65, 67-68, 73

Cain, 129
causality, 115
celestial bodies, 30-31, 34-37, 113, 115
Christ, 3-10, 12-14, 43, 113-114, 131,
  133, 140-145, 151
  bearer of the I, 10
  Christ-impulse, 133
  Christ-permeated Light, 9
  consciousness of, 142
  Cosmic Word, 58-59
  deeds of, 131, 140
  Higher Being, 113
  historical tradition, 7-8
  humble Man of Nazareth, 140
  illuminator of our knowledge, 9
  language of (cosmic), 113-114
  Light of Humanity, 4
  living Christ, 14, 142
  Logos, 58
  Son of the Father, 140, 142
  Son of the Father-God, 140
  Son of God, 141, 144

217